Bennett H. Young

A HISTORY

OF

JESSAMINE COUNTY,

KENTUCKY,

FROM ITS

EARLIEST SETTLEMENT TO 1898.

By BENNETT H. YOUNG,

PRESIDENT POLYTECHNIC SOCIETY; MEMBER FILSON CLUB; MEMBER CONSTITUTIONAL
CONVENTION, 1890; AUTHOR HISTORY OF THE CONSTITUTIONS OF KEN-
TUCKY, OF "BATTLE OF BLUE LICKS, ETC., ETC.

S. M. DUNCAN, ASSOCIATE AUTHOR.

Southern Historical Press, Inc.
Greenville, South Carolina

TO

My Father, Robert Young,

AND

My Mother, Josephine Young,

I DEDICATE THIS VOLUME.

My father was a resident of Jessamine County for sixty-five years. He was honest, upright, patriotic, public-spirited, and always the friend of the poor and suffering. My mother—God bless her name and memory!—had a heart full of human sympathy and tenderness, and also of the love of Christ, whose teachings she faithfully followed for sixty years, in the midst of the people of Jessamine. Descended from Revolutionary sires, they both ardently loved the freedom of this free land with an unquenchable love, and taught their children, as the noblest aim of life, to serve God and be true to the glorious liberty their ancestors had so courageously fought to win. They sleep in the cemetery at Lexington, Ky., and I trust they have a kindly remembrance with the people among whom they lived and died.

PREFACE.

Jessamine county is one of the few great counties of the state whose history remains unwritten. For a long time after its beginning, it was overshadowed in many ways by Lexington, Danville, Paris, Harrodsburg, and Winchester. The county had no postoffice until 1801. Mails were infrequent and carried by hand. Lexington was the great town south of the Ohio and west of the Alleghenies. When the county was organized, Lexington had a population of nearly 2,000, while Cincinnati had less than 500, and was buying its merchandise in Lexington; which was already the seat of a university; it had churches and schools, and was the great trading point for a large part of Kentucky, and portion of Ohio, Indiana and Tennessee.

Brick houses had begun to be erected, and newspapers had been published for eleven years, and being only twelve miles from Nicholasville, it was inevitable that it should draw to it a very large share of the trade of Jessamine. Lexington was then, and remained for many years thereafter, the political, intellectual, and commercial metropolis of Kentucky, and it necessarily dwarfed the surrounding towns and attracted the best trade from the counties within a radius of fifty miles.

Lexington, too, had the first railroad in the west. The line to Frankfort was finished and operated in December, 1835, and by 1851, trains were run through from Louisville to Lexington. In 1854, a train ran from Covington to Lexington, and from Lexington to Paris in 1853. These railways diverted the trade from the steamboats on the Kentucky river and they made Lexington a great center.

The enterprise and courage of her people received a just and ample reward. Fayette county and Lexington always exhibited great enterprise as well as the highest public spirit, and in commerce as well as education they attained high rank, because they had the sagacity and the enterprise to improve the opportunities which presented themselves.

Jessamine county had no railway until 1857. From that time Nicholasville assumed a new importance. Long the terminus of the Kentucky Central, there came to it both travel and trade, and it began to improve. The loss of slaves and the destruction of values; the result of the war of 1861-65, greatly affected both the town and the county, but after the period necessary for a recuperation from these troubles, the county and town have developed with steady and constant growth, and both are now taking the position to which their natural advantages entitle them.

Jessamine county has never lacked in public spirit. She has liberally responded to all calls for public improvement. She never repudiated any of her obligations. She always paid what she agreed to pay, and her subscription to the Kentucky Central Railroad, to the Cincinnati Southern Railroad, to the improvement of the Kentucky river, and to the Richmond, Nicholasville, Irvine and Beattyville line; is highest evidence of her sagacity and generosity, and placed the county in the best possible position for the development of all its resources.

Looking back one hundred years, the people of Jessamine can feel a glow of honest pride at what a century has accomplished. The smallest, except fifteen, of the one hundred and nineteen counties in the state, with an area of only 158 square miles, it has always maintained a prominent place among the rich and large agricultural counties. For its population it is surpassed in wealth by only a very few counties, and it ranks as one of the great producing counties of Kentucky. Its land, per acre, has always, for taxation, been valued at a very high rate.

In 1846 it was the sixth county in value of lands per acre, and in 1870, notwithstanding the great cities in other counties, it stood ninth; and still maintains that place.

Led by the guiding hand of fate to make my home in the greatest of all Kentucky's counties, Jefferson, I have never lost my love for Jessamine, and its capital city, Nicholasville; and oftentimes there creeps into my heart a longing to spend the evening of life where I first saw the light, and an absence of thirty-seven years, has neither destroyed nor dimmed my love for the people who have always remembered me in my comings to the old home place, with such generous hospitality and unchanging kindness.

No one else offering to write a history of the county, I have undertaken the task. The work has been done hurriedly and while under the pressure of a busy professional life; but it is a labor of love, and if the story of the sacrifices, courage, and patriotism of our forefathers who settled and organized the county, shall be efficient in creating upon the present and future sons and daughters of Jessamine higher love of their ancestors, great devotion to Kentucky, and better apprehension of the cost and value of the freedom of our country, I shall be more than repaid for the labor and cost of producing this volume. It does not contain all that a history of the county should include, but it does for the first time put in permanent form the leading facts connected with the organization of the county and accounts of the men who first cut down the forests, grubbed the cane brakes and drove out the savages who disputed its possession, and it will, at least be a help to those who may hereafter desire to write a more extended history of Jessamine and of its people.

Mr. S. M. Duncan, of Nicholasville, has for more than forty years been gathering notes of the history of the people who have lived in Jessamine. He has done more for the preservation of its history than any one man who ever lived in the county. He has generously given me the use of all his facts. I have by research gotten others and verified his, and I have, as is his just due, placed his name upon the title page of this book as associate author. Although the preparation and publication was assumed by me, I consider it both a privilege and a duty to thus connect Mr. Duncan with the first history of the county.

I beg to acknowledge with gratitude the assistance of Col. R. T. Durrett, Rev. E. O. Guerrant, Samuel D. Young, Miss Henrietta W. Brown, Mrs. Virginia Noland, Robert G. Wright, Miss Jessie Woodson, Mrs. Anna Meade Letcher, Dr. L. B. Todd, J. Willard Mitchell, Dr. Chas. Mann, Miss Josephine Mann, John S. Bronaugh, N. L. Bronaugh, Henry Glass, Melancthon Young, Wm. L. Steele, B. M. Arnett, and Emil Ilhardt, the skillful photographer, who have spared no effort to help me place in durable form the important events in the history of the county.

BENNETT H. YOUNG.

Louisville, Ky., Sept. 16, 1898.

History of Jessamine County.

In 1767 John Finley, a woodsman and hunter, from North Carolina, moved by a spirit of adventure and a love for hunting, entered the country known as the Bluegrass region. He was the first white man, history asserts, that ever penetrated the wilderness and forests of Kentucky sufficiently to see the central part of the state. Who came with him, whither they went and how long the party remained, neither traveler, legend, nor written story tells. It is most likely that they passed through Jessamine county and were the first of their race to look upon its pristine beauty and glory. Two years later, Finley returned with Daniel Boone to that wonderful land he had described to his neighbors and associates in North Carolina, with such eloquence and enthusiasm as to arouse within them an inextinguishable desire to visit a land which then was looked upon as "God's own country." What became of him after this second visit is unknown, but it is a reasonable conclusion that somewhere in the stillness and sublime silence of the great forests to which he had led the white man, the red man took his life and left him as his shroud the leaves of the forest and his monument the mighty trees which stood sentinel for ages over the fertile and genial soil of Kentucky.

Dr. Thomas Walker, from Virginia, had in 1750 explored a portion of Kentucky, but he only skirted the Bluegrass and rode over the mountains of Southeastern Kentucky, and what he saw and reported, created no spirit of exploration and no desire of emigration. Finley was the man who saw the huntsman's paradise, and whose soul was fired for its possession, and into whose mind was burned memories which made life miserable away from the glories of the new land into which he had by accident come.

Some months after his return, while wandering along the Yadkin river in North Carolina, Finley met a kindred spirit, one of the master woodsmen of his age. In the solitude of the wilderness of North Carolina, far out beyond the advance of civilization and settlement, he found a rude cabin, in which dwelt a young man, not much beyond his majority. By his side was a brave woman, who, amid the dangers and hardships of the wild, wild frontier, shared his life and hopes and brightened the solitude and drearyness of his isolated home. By the humble, but hospitable fireside of the young hunter, Finley was welcomed as a guest, and again and again he told the story of his journey toward the north, of the magnificent region where there would be an eternal feast for the hunter, where game was so abundant that the droves of buffalo could be counted like herds of cattle, where deer licked the hand of the intruder, and coons, 'possums, turkeys and pheasants, were so plentiful as to obstruct the path along which men would tread.

Finley had found a heart which would respond in fullest harmony to his words, a harp which answered his touch, and each day gave back not only sweetest note, but varied and sympathetic chords; a man whose brave soul was devoid of all fear and who wanted nothing better for time or eternity than that glorious and distant region of which the new found friend spoke. A compact, offensive and defensive, was then and there signed. Boone had at last heard of a land for which his soul sighed, a land which filled his ideal of a paradise and to see it, to tread its traces and to enjoy its pleasure, he resolved to give up his home, his wife, his children, and if need be to surrender his life. To once see such a land as Finley described, he felt would be compensation for all that earth could bestow.

Sparse settlements along the Holston, 200 miles away, and the forts on the Ohio at Pittsburgh and the few houses strung along the line of the wilderness now were the closest neighbors to Kentucky.

Boone came in 1769, and brought his family in 1775.

The founding of the Transylvania colony by Henderson, in 1775, gave an armed and trained force to meet Indian attack, and Harrodsburg and St. Asaphs, or Logan's Fort, formed the military triangle about which and in which the new settlers made their homes.

The Transylvania land scheme of 1775 did not include Jessamine county. Its lines followed the south or western side of the Kentucky river, and left the eastern boundary always in Virginia.

When by act of the Virginia House of Burgesses, in 1780, Kentucky was divided into three counties, Fayette, Jefferson and Lincoln; Jessamine was comprised within the limits of Fayette, and so remained until, December 17, 1798, when it was separated from the parent county, and became the thirty-sixth county of the state.

The initial lines of pioneer travel did not traverse Jessamine. The Wilderness road, entering the state at Cumberland Gap, divided at Rockcastle river, one branch going to Boonesboro, and the other by Crab Orchard, Danville and Bardstown, to Louisville.

The persistent assaults of the Indians on the settlers in Kentucky in 1782, caused the abandonment of all the forts in the state east of the Kentucky, except five, Lexington, Bryants, McConnells, McClellans (Georgetown) and Boones.

The county of Kentucky was established in 1775, and divided into three counties in 1780; and prior to 1792 six more were added, making, at the inception of its statehood, nine in all.

Added: Bourbon, 1785; Madison, 1785; Mason, 1789; Mercer, 1785; Nelson, 1781; Woodford, 1788.

The first fort and only fort in Jessamine county was established by Levi Todd in 1779. This was one year before Lexington was built. The line of travel between Harrodsburg and the Fayette county stations, passed through the northern and western parts of the county, and on this trace, near Keene, Todd's station was built.

The isolation of the forts and the constant and destructive marauds of the Indians, now officered by Englishmen and provided with improved arms, terrified the settlers east of the Kentucky river. They were nearest to the homes of the Indians from the northwest, who had now become the most dreadful of all the savages who invaded the state, and 1780-81-82, they drove in, the outposts, and with great difficulty the white men were able to maintain their stations at all in and around Lexington. It was then that personal safety compelled Todd to abandon his Jessamine holdings and take such help and protection as the four stations around Lexington offered to the almost hopeless men and women who occupied the limited territory in Fayette, which remained after the terrible fatality of Ruddell's and Martin's stations in June, 1780.

The land law enacted by the Virginia Legislature, in the settling of land made location easy and popular. The wonderful accounts of the fertility, beauty and salubrity of Kentucky turned an immense tide of immigration to the state. In 1782, the population did not exceed 1500; in 1790, it had grown to 61,133 white people; 114 colored free people, and 12,340 slaves; a total of 73,-677, while ten years later, in 1800, it had 179,873 white, 739 free colored, and 40,343 slaves; a total of 220,995, an increase in ten years of 224 1-2 per cent.

Of this extraordinary improvement, Jessamine county received a full share. In 1782, it had not a single settler, and yet in 1800, eighteen years thereafter, it had 5,461 inhabitants. This was the first decade in which a census could be taken. Fayette, from which Jessamine was entirely taken, had, in 1800, 18,410 inhabitants, or one-fourth of the entire population of the state. As a part of Clark was included in this enumeration, and assuming that Jessamine had grown in proportion as other parts of Fayette, the county in 1790 had about 2,000 inhabitants.

A great proportion of Jessamine immigration, came from Virginia. The Revolutionary soldiers were pouring into all parts of the state, and Jessamine received her full share, and more than one hundred of these brave and sturdy settlers found homes within her borders.

No state could secure nobler treasure than were these Revolutionary soldiers. Their splendid courage, exalted patriotism, hardy natures, and noble characters, made them a worthy addition to any community. The self-reliance, tact and enterprise engendered by Revolutionary service, rendered them citizens of great and unusual worth. Of the rich store given by Virginia, Pennsylvania, North and South Carolina, Jessamine received an extraordinary proportion.

The most distinguished men of Revolutionary fame who came to Jessamine, were George Walker, Joseph Crockett, Benjamin Netherland, William Price, Percival Butler, William McKinney and John Price.

These were not more patriotic or more loyal to the American cause than the others, but they had in the war obtained positions which made them more prominent than their associates in the early history of the county. A brief sketch of each is properly a part of the history of Jessamine county.

Benjamin Netherland.

One of the most unique and extraordinary characters in the history of Jessamine county in its early days was Maj. Benjamin Netherland. He was born in Powhattan county, Virginia, in 1755. He went to Cuba as the agent of his father, to dispose of his tobacco crop. There learning that Sir Peter Parker was to make an attack on Charleston, he left his cargo and ran the blockade into Charleston and helped to defend Fort Moultrie against British assault. He accompanied La Fayette on his journey from Charleston in 1777 as far as Mecklenburg county, North Carolina, when the distinguished Frenchman was on his way to Philadelphia, to tender his services to Washington in behalf of American liberty. He remained at Charlotte, North Carolina until 1781, took part in the battle of Guilford Courthouse, and shortly after this he drifted into Kentucky. In May, 1782, he was at Estill station, and was with the Kentucky troops in the Estill defeat. He took part in nearly all the Indian battles from 1781 to 1784. He went with George Rogers Clark on his expedition in 1782 to punish the Indians for the wrongs of Blue Licks.

He was with General Harmar in his defeat, and with General Wayne in his victory at Fallen Timbers in 1794 and was instrumental in punishing the men who had perpetrated the slaughter at Blue Licks. After seven years' absence in Kentucky, he returned to North Carolina in 1788 and married his boyish sweetheart, Miss Theodosia Bramlette, who was a daughter of the distinguished Revolutionary fighter Col. Bramlette. He had lived in Fayette and Madison counties prior to his coming to Jessamine. After his marriage he settled on a farm five miles east of Nicholasville, and in 1793 he removed to where Nicholasville now stands, and built a hotel and called it Mingo Tavern—this house he kept until his death in 1838. The house was torn down in 1864. The author has often seen it when a boy, and the picture of it in this history is from a drawing made in 1820. He

MINGO TAVERN.

was chairman of the Board of Trustees of Nicholasville, and was prominent in its early history, and his children were the first white people born within its limits. He was the real hero of the battle of Blue Licks. Robert Wickliffe, of Lexington, whose second wife was the only daughter of Col. Todd, who was in command at the battle at Blue Licks, in a political speech in 1848 in Nicholasville said that the majority of men who escaped at Blue Licks owed their preservation to Benjamin Netherland and that Netherland was a fearless man, fruitful in resources and of magnificent courage.

Col. Robert Patterson, writing to Netherland in 1836, says, "I can not forget the part you acted in the battle of Blue Licks." At the time of this battle Netherland was only twenty-seven years old, and he went from Lexington as a member of Capt. Robert Patterson's company. In the disastrous conflict he remained mounted, and gained the ford over Licking in safety and crossed the stream unhurt. As he reached the west bank he looked back over his shoulder, and his soul was stirred with deepest emotion, and his heart filled with grandest courage as he saw his comrades struggling, swimming and plunging in the river, or rushing down the bank pursued by the savage enemy with unsheathed knives and uplifted tomahawks. He was a man of towering form, six feet two inches in height. He dismounted from his horse, and throwing the rein over his arm, in stentorian tone ordered his fleeing comrades to halt and fire upon the Indians and save those who were still in the stream. His bravery and his splendid presence restored the spirits of his fear-stricken comrades. More than a dozen men instantly obeyed his call, and facing about with Netherland and standing in line they opened a fatal and deadly fire upon the foremost of the pursuing savages. The counter attack was so sudden and unexpected that it checked the fierce pursuit of the Indians and they instantly fell back from the opposite bank. Netherland and his men maintained their position and drove the Indians to cover, while the wearied and almost despairing footmen were enabled to ford and swim the river in safety. Only a few minutes were necessary for those who could reach the stream or who were in it to pass over. The footmen as they left the bank quickly fled from the buffalo trace and disappeared in the thickets and started by circuitous routes to reach some friendly station. So soon as these distressed and exhausted or wounded footmen were enabled to secrete themselves in the dense forests, large numbers of the Indians were seen crossing both above and below, and Netherland and his comrades mounting their horses galloped along the well-worn trace, and reached Bryan Station that evening, without further loss.

Major Netherland always retained his old-time dress. He wore a cut-a-way coat, short breeches with knee buckles, and low shoes with silk lacers and silver buckles. His pants were always fastened with red bands, and his long queue was tied with a red ribbon. From his entrance into Nicholasville early in 1791 for forty years he was prominent as a leader in all its affairs. He was postmaster for about twenty-three years and always dispensed the village hospitality with a lavish hand. Every man who had fought in the Revolutionary war or in the Indian wars either in Kentucky or in the Northwest, was his friend, and none ever went from his door hungry or uncared for.

He was passionately fond of horse-racing, and owned some of the great race-horses of Kentucky in the early part of the century. He was a fair and just man in his dealings with his fellow-men. He was not averse to a "good time." as people call it, and was always, even toward the end of his life, considered "one of the boys." He opened a race track on the Willoughby place near Sulphur Well, and maintained it for many years.

In 1802 there was a quarter race on the track, and in the hearing of the crowd, Major Netherland announced that on a certain day (naming it) there would be another race for a purse of $50, one mile heats, which was "free for anything with four legs and hair on." At that time there was working on a farm a young man named Michael Arnspiger who had broken a bull to the saddle, which he rode to mill. He immediately put the bull in training and for several days gave him turns around the race track. He used spurs on the bull and when these were dug into his sides, he was accustomed to bellow. On the day of the race Arnspiger appeared on the ground with his bull. He had placed a dried hide of an ox on the bull's rump, and he carried a tin horn in his hands. He demanded of the judges the right to enter his animal, to which the owners of the horses vehemently objected, but Arnspiger answered by appealing to Major Netherland if he had not said that the race was free to "anything with four legs and hair on." Maj. Netherland admitted that he had, and explained that the bull had a right to enter. When the drum was tapped, Arnspiger blew his horn, planted his spurs in the sides of the bull, which bounded off with a dreadful bellow, with the ox-hide flapping on his sides and presenting a spectacle, combined with the noise, that had never been seen on the race track before. The horses immediately flew the track, and Arnspiger galloped home a winner. The losers contended that they were swindled out of thir money; that Arnspiger should not have been allowed to blow the tin horn, or use the ox-hide, and that but for this he could not have won the race. Thereupon Arnspiger offered to take the ox-hide off and leave his tin horn at the stand and run them from end to end. Mr. Willoughby and Mr. Netherland were judges at the next start. Arnspiger again planted his spurs into the sides of the bull with redoubled fury. The loud bellow that followed drove the horses from the track despite the exertions of the riders, and Arnspiger pulled in the second $50 purse. With the money thus obtained he purchased a blacksmithing outfit, working for many years at his trade near Wilmore, and died there in the sixties, in the 85th year of his age.

Major Netherland had a great fondness for race horses and not only ran his own horses but went to see everbody else's horses who ran in the neighborhood. The race track in those early days was on the Willoughby farm in the new field now owned by Col. N. D. Miles. Major Netherland owned a very fast horse for those days, which he called by the name of Fearnought. He had secured this horse in Virginia and brought him across the mountains. The horse had been trained in Virginia and made his first race at Fredericksburg, in 1805, beating General Tracy's horse, Indian, in three heats. In those times four mile races were run. The time given by Major Netherland was as follows:

First, 8 minutes, 29 seconds. Second, 8 minutes, 45 seconds. Third, 8 minutes, 50 seconds.

Then people believed in bottom and horses had to run long distances. This time was not up to that made by the great race horse, Lexington, at New Orleans, where he beat the world's record in 7 minutes, 19 3-4 seconds, but it was good running.

Fearnought was the special pride of Major Netherland. He ran against a horse called Bald Eagle, who was owned by Daniel Bradford, a son of John Bradford, the founder of the Kentucky Gazette, and who was for long time editor of that paper. The Alexander Willoughby referred to was a Revolutionary soldier. He came early to Kentucky and settled in Jessamine county on the Sulphur Well road. He was the father of Mrs. Catherine Shelby and died in 1837, in his eighty-fifth year.

General Samuel Hopkins was a Revolutionary soldier, a native of Albemarle county, Va. He was a distinguished officer in the Revolutionary army, and none performed more active service or enjoyed in a greater degree the confidence of Washington. He came to Kentucky in 1797 and settled on Green river, in Green county. He was a member of Congress in 1813 and '15 and was engaged in the Indian wars in the west. He and Major Netherland were great friends and General Hopkins himself had a weakness for a good horse. The following letter describing the race, is both interesting and unique:

Jessamine County, Ky., June 5, 1806.

Gen. Sam'l Hopkins,

Dear Friend: I take my seat to inform you that Fearnought is again winner of a purse of $100. In all the races which have previously been run on this track, it has been a matter of much inconvenience to the judges to make a fair decision without a fuss, which often creates unnecessary excitement throughout the day. But it did not in any manner affect the nerve of Mr. Willoughby, who was one of the judges who started the horses. He seemed to have a proper and just idea of the necessity of an even start, and nothing else but an even start would suit him, and that he gave. I wish all the other judges were as honest as he is. At the tap of the drum Fearnought and Bald Eagle darted like thunderbolts, each determined to win or die. Around the track they sped like hell cats, not a shade between them. Up the back stretch they flew like doves escaping from a hawk. At the half mile in 40 seconds, they locked around the turn. They tried it again, a slight pull before reaching the home stretch, and with renewed vigor, Fearnought in the lead. Bald Eagle renews his extraordinary power, but Fearnought comes out with unfaltering step and the race is decided in his favor. The question of championship, you will see at once, gives Fearnought the palm.

DESCRIPTION OF FEARNOUGHT.

Fearnought is five years old last grass; is a dark blood bay, 16 hands high, of superior bone and muscle, with fine limbs, lofty carriage and elastic tread; a star in his forehead, vividly lighting up a countenance expressive of great superiority; game head, curved neck; unusual depth of chest; fine, broad shoulder; beautifully inclining back, which gives him the appearance of a horse of most wonderful strength and endurance. I expect to enter him this fall for a purse of $1,000 at Fredericksburg, and the city of Baltimore and Washington. Bald Eagle is now the property of Daniel Bradford, and was trained in Maryland, and won many races there, but, I think, his career upon the turf is over.

Your friend,

B. NETHERLAND.

In another letter, written to General Hopkins in 1802, Major Netherland recites a most interesting incident. During that year a party of Cherokee Indians from North Carolina stopped all night at the Mingo Tavern, kept by Major Netherland. In the morning one of them was very sick and unable to travel and in a few days died at the hotel. He received the kindest possible treatment from Major Netherland and his family. In describing this incident Major Netherland says:

"A few days ago four Cherokee Indians from Iredell county, N. C., called at my home and remained over night. Next morning one of them was too sick to travel. All day his sufferings were severe and painful. I sent for Drs. Gale and Peter Trisler, who at once pronounced his case hopeless. After intense suffering for four days the poor Indian died. His poor, disconsolate friends were painfully grieved at the death of one of their number, who was a man of some notoriety among his people, particularly as an expert hunter, having himself killed seventy-odd deer while on the last October hunt in the Cumberland mountains. The dead body of the poor Indian was taken to the Kentucky river cliffs, eight miles south of Nicholasville, and interred in the earth after the Indian custom, but instead of filling the vault with earth, as is used with us, these poor Indians made a small frame work of wood, like a steep roof, which they put round the mouth, and reared up a heavy pile of earth, giving it the appearance of a potatoe heap. The three Indians who buried their comrade appeared bowed with grief. One seated himself on the ground, directing his face toward sunset, and extending his voice, made a great and sore lamentation. As much as I hate these wild children from the forest, I could not refrain from shedding tears when looking on them in this honest grief at the loss of one who was regarded as a good and true man. In four or five weeks after the death of their comrade, the same party, with a brother of the Indian, who died, came back and took his body in a small wagon to North Carolina, a distance of more than 300 miles, and reinterred his remains in the land of his birth among his own people. I have been much among the Cherokees of North Carolina. I consider them among the best of our Indian friends. They have strange customs. I wish I had time to give you more correct idea of their general character as compared with the other Indian tribes of our country.

"Your old crony,

" B. NETHERLAND."

Major Netherland died October 10, 1838, and was buried in his garden, which is now the lot on which the county jail is built. Mr. Jos. Wallace, a remote kinsman, has, with most commendable love and liberality and true spirit of kinship, erected a headstone over the grave of Major Netherland and that of his wife, who, in 1851, was laid beside her husband. At his death Major Netherland was accorded a magnificent military funeral. The funeral sermon was preached by Bishop Kavanaugh, who was then the Presiding Elder of the district. Gen. Leslie Combs, Maj. D. B. Price, Gen. John McCalla and Robert Wickliffe were his pall-bearers, and all the leading military companies of the county turned out to do his memory honor.

Major Netherland's experience in the battle of the Blue Licks, justified him in his subsequent love of horses.

He bred a great many fine race horses in his day, and in a letter written by him to Gen. John McCalla, in 1830, now in my possession, he begs him to come to Nicholasville on the following Sunday to dine with him and promises to show him "the damndest best three colts in the world."

Joseph Crockett.

Among the large train of Revolutionary soldiers who followed the track of empire westwardly, was Col. Joseph Crockett, of Albemarle county, Virginia. He was born in Albemarle county in 1742. He received fairly good educational advantages for that period. His father, John Crockett, came to Virginia in the first half of the century. He followed teaching as his profession and taught a high school near Charlottesville. Joseph Crockett was his oldest son.

In 1774 Joseph Crockett went as a private soldier with Gen. Andrew Lewis and was engaged in the battle of Point Pleasant. This was one of the most important of all the battles in the West. It was there that General Lewis met the Indians under the celebrated chief Cornstalk, and after a fight of nearly a whole day the Indians were put to flight.

In 1775 the county authorities of Albemarle directed that two companies be raised for the defense of the western section of the state. One company was to be stationed at Point Pleasant, where the Kanawha and Ohio rivers unite. Gen. William Russell was appointed captain of one of these companies and Joseph Crockett lieutenant. In the winter of '75 they were discharged and they were ordered to raise two new companies for the Continental army. Joseph Crockett was appointed captain of one of these companies and on the 5th of May, 1776, served in Virginia. In 1776 the regiment was marched to Philadelphia. That year he was appointed major and raised two companies for Gen. Daniel Morgan's rifle regiment. He took part in the battle of Monmouth, fought June 20, 1778, and after this battle was promoted to the rank of lieutenant-colonel, and so remained until October, 1780, when, by resolution of congress the army was reorganized and Colonel Crockett was reduced to the rank of captain. He was with Gates at the surrender of Burgoyne in '77. He was engaged in the battles of Brandywine, Princeton and Trenton, and was with Washington at Valley Forge, where there sprung up between Colonel Crockett and General Washington a warm friendship, which lasted until the end of their lives. He was wounded in the arm at the siege of Yorktown in 1782.

In 1779 Colonel Crockett was directed by the state of Virginia to raise a regiment, of which he became lieutenant-colonel, to proceed down the Ohio river to Kentucky and Illinois to assist George Rogers Clark. He raised the regiment, which was known as the Illinois or Crockett Regiment, and served for eighteen months with General Clark. He was in many of the battles with the Northwestern Indians on the Miami river, and helped to destroy Chillicothe and other towns in the northwestern territory on the Wabash. In one of the battles in which he fought he had two horses shot under him by the sharpshooters, and it was admitted that he had been in as many fights and skirmishes as any officer in the Revolutionary army.

In 1784 he moved to Kentucky and settled first between Cumberland Gap and Crab Orchard. He remained there only a short time, and moved to Jessamine county and settled on lands near the Union Mills. His son, Robert Crockett, built the Union Mills and Col. Joseph Crockett built the old stone house on the banks of Hickman creek, which is now standing and was lately occupied by Dr. Jasper, a descendant of Sergeant Jasper, who was put to death at Savannah by the British.

Colonel Crockett was appointed by Mr. Jefferson as United States Marshal for the district of Kentucky. He held this office for two terms. When the applications were read to Mr. Jefferson for this office, his eye dropped upon that of Joseph Crockett. He said, "Joseph Crockett; honest Joseph Crockett; you need go no further, he shall have the appointment." Immediately after his removal to Kentucky he at once assumed a prominent place in the development and in the government of the new state. In 1786-1790 he represented Fayette in the Virginia Legislature. He was also appointed magistrate of Fayette county in 1792, along with Percival Butler. He was a member of the first legislature from Fayette county, in 1792, '93, '94, and '95. Under the Constitution of 1792 he was elected one of the senators. These senators were chosen by electors elected for that purpose.

In 1792 a project was organized for the clearing and improvement of the Wilderness Road, under Col. John Logan and James Knox. The subscriptions for that purpose at that time would probably be the highest evidence of public spirit. Among them are the names of Isaac Shelby, for 3 pounds; Robert Breckinridge, 2 pounds 8 shillings; George Nicholas, 2 pounds 8 shillings; John Brown, 2 pounds 8 shillings; Joseph Crockett, 1 pound 18 shillings; Robert Patterson, 1 pound 10 shillings; G. M. Bedinger, 18 shillings; Samuel McDowell, 1 pound 4 shillings, and a large number of other prominent names.

He represented Fayette county in the convention called in 1788 at Danville, to consider separation from Virginia. Although at first opposed to separation, Colonel Crockett was convinced by the arguments of John Marshall of the propriety of this separation.

The question in this convention was, whether there should be a violent separation from Virginia, or whether the separation should be legal and on constitutional grounds. It was in this convention that Colonel Crockett became alarmed at the speeches of John Brown and General Wilkinson. He left his seat in the convention, hurried to Lexington and on Saturday, Sunday and Monday secured the signatures of several hundred citizens of Fayette county remonstrating against separation from Virginia without her consent, when he returned and presented this petition to the convention. After it was read General Wilkinson saw that he was in opposition to the wishes of the people and yielded to what was the inevitable.

Colonel Crockett, being then United States Marshal, arrested Aaron Burr in 1806, under proceedings by Joseph Hamilton Daveiss against Aaron Burr. Colonel Crockett's commission bore the signature of General Washington and was handed to him by La Fayette, and when La Fayette visited Kentucky in 1825 he threw his arms around Colonel Crockett at Frankfort and they wept with each other like children. Col. Joseph Crockett, Col. Anthony Crockett and Gen. Peter Dudley rode in a carriage with La Fayette from Frankfort to Lexington. Colonel Crockett introduced a large number of old Revolutionary soldiers to General La Fayette at the reception given him by Mr. Wickliffe.

As General La Fayette passed by a hotel in the parade, Maria Henderson, a little girl twelve years of age, a granddaughter of Colonel Crockett, and from Jessamine county, from the window of the hotel sang, "Hail to the Chief Who in Triumph Advances." The fresh, young voice of the little girl had a wonderful attraction for General La Fayette. He requested that the carriage should be stopped and as he listened to the song from the lips of the child, tears streamed down his cheeks. He said that it was the sweetest act of homage ever paid him.

Colonel Crockett was pensioned by the United States Government. In company with other soldiers in the Revolutionary war, he received several thousand acres of land from the government and shortly before his death his pension was increased to $600 a year. He enjoyed it only for twelve months. When visiting his daughter, Mrs. Augustine Bower, at Georgetown, he was seized with a fatal illness and died there.

The following letter written by a Revolutionary soldier to Maj. Daniel B. Price, will be interesting as it refers to many characters prominent in Jessamine county at that time.

Near Georgetown, Scott county, Ky.,
Nov. 20, 1829.

Dear Friend: I was pained that I had not the pleasure of seeing you at the burial of Col. Joseph Crockett, six weeks ago in Jessamine county. I have learned from your letter that you were very sick at the time of his burial and unable to get out of bed. He died at the home of Dr. Bower, his son-in-law. For three weeks, or more, previous to his death, he repeatedly informed his friends that he viewed himself as a dying man; that he was not afraid to meet death at any moment. A few days after he was taken with his last illness, and while he was able to walk about the room, his eye sight failed him. He took the Rev. Isaac Reed to be you and ordered him to bring your son, Joseph, to see him, as he had not seen him for some months. On my telling him that you were detained in Jessamine, but would probably be up Friday, he quietly fell into a sleep. He slept about an hour, and waked and had a severe coughing spell. It was at this time that he drew his breath with great difficulty, and the agony he was in was so great that in two hours after he had awakened from sleep he died. Capt. William Christy, Maj. John T. Pratt, Maj. William Johnson, Capt. William Smith, of Bourbon, and the Rev. John Hudson and Mr. Reed, were present in the room when he died.

When he was dying I noticed him put his head a little back, closed his eyes as if going to sleep and expired, at the ripe age of 83. His remains were taken to his home in Jessamine and buried with the honor suitable to the memory of a brave and patriotic man, who served his country bravely in the Revolutionary war. The order of procession to the grave was as follows:

The hearse with the military escort, attended by music, on each flank. The relatives, the ladies, the citizens, the fine volunteer company from Georgetown, commanded by Maj. William Johnson, with Capt. Thomas Cogar's company from Nicholasville, the whole conducted by Col. John T. Pratt, marshal of the day. At the grave the usual ceremonies took place by the firing of thirteen rounds by Captains Graves and Leslie Combs, of Lexington, who, at the head of the gun squad, fired at intervals during the services at the grave. There were present more than a thousand persons with carriages and horses. Such was the good order and decorum preserved that not the slightest accident occurred. At the close of the ceremonies the Rev. John Hudson delivered a brief address touching the high character of Col. Crockett as a citizen, neighbor and friend—a model of virtue and morality, cherished in the affections of all who knew him. Though his manly form lies low in death, his many virtues, his patriotic example, shall continue to abide in the memory of the living. Such, my dear friend, is a brief account of the burial of your father-in-law, Col. Joseph Crockett.

Very truly your friend,

B. S. CHAMBERS.

Daniel B. Price, Nicholasville, Ky.

Colonel Crockett was a man of splendid physique, six feet three inches in height, spare but muscular, dark hair, sallow complexion, with keen, piercing, black eyes; roman nose and thin, expressive lips. The many offices to which he was elected in Fayette and Jessamine counties evince in what high esteem he was held by those who knew him. He always wore a long, blue cut-a-way coat with brass buttons, with knee breeches and black silk stockings and heavy silver shoe buckles.   As was the custom among the gentlemen at that early period, he wore a cue falling down his back between his shoulders, tied with a blue ribbon.

Colonel Crockett was buried on his old home place, where had preceded him to the tomb his wife and children.   The brick house which he built in the early part of the century still stands near the grave-yard, and is the property of Mr. John Baker, formerly owned by Otho Roberts.   A few years since, his grandson, Col. Bennett H. Young, had erected around it an iron fence.

The following letter, written by Maj. Benjamin Netherland, who was then a resident of Nicholasville, will be both amusing and interesting:

Nicholasville, Ky., October 7, 1826.

My Dear Friend: I was very much pained on hearing that your cut on the leg has not improved since I was to see you in April last.   I was sorry that your wounded leg prevented you from being in Lexington last year, when the Marquis de la Fayette was given one of the greatest and grandest receptions I ever witnessed.   More than ten thousand people marched in line to receive on the big road leading from Frankfort to Lexington.   He rode in a fine four-horse carriage accompanied by Governor Desha, Col. Anthony Crockett, Col. Joseph Crockett, Genl. Peter Dudley, and many other gentlemen who rode on horseback and acted as a guard of honor in the rear of the carriage.   More than forty-six years ago I was in Charleston when he landed there in 1777, a young man from France on his way to offer his services to General Washington to fight for the liberties of the people of our country.   In Charleston he was received with becoming respect and honor, the people everywhere were loud in their praise of the young French soldier—but his reception was nothing in comparison to the reception given him by the patriotic people of Lexington last May.   When General La Fayette got into Lexington the rush of many of the old soldiers was truly exciting.   Everywhere his carriage was stopped by the surviving veterans who had served with him and Washington at Monmouth, Trenton, Brandywine and Little York.   Everyone was anxious to see La Fayette.   It just seemed that there was no other actor in the great revolutionary drama who had been so near to the heart of Washington as General La Fayette. When the great dinner given to the general in the city limits was over, I went to Mr. Wickliff's house with Cols. Joseph and Anthony Crockett to pay my respects to the young man, forty-seven years ago. I introduced to Col. William Moultry who was putting Charleston in fighting trim to resist the British fleet which I learned while in Cuba was to sail from Jamaca under Admiral Parker and bombard Charleston. I brought this intelligence which I hastened to give Colonel Moultrie, who immediately commenced putting the town in a proper state for defending every place along the harbor. On arriving at Mr. Wickliff's house Joe Crockett first introduced me to George Washington La Fayette, the son of the general. His son looked like a man who had seen much mental trouble; he seemed to be pleased at the reception given to his father, but was not a man to talk, was stiff and I thought not an intelligent man whatever, but a proud, weak man. When Colonel Crockett brought me into the parlor of Mr. Wickliff's house, General La Fayette, he introduced me as the young man "Netherland" who forty-seven years before had made him known to Colonel Moultry who in 1776 and 1777 had command at Charleston. He remembered me introducing him to Moultry and my going as far as Charlotte with him, as he went through Richmond to Philadelphia, he received me very warmly, shedding tears as he did when meeting with Anthony and Joe Crockett. He asked my age. I told him I was just in my seventieth year; he then informed me he was 69 years of age and felt that his health had greatly improved since he had revisited America. When I bid him farewell I, in company with the two Crocketts and Robert B. McAfee, lieutenant-governor, all went and bid the general a long farewell. The general shed tears and in fact every one who was present cried. Dosia, my wife, kissed the general and we separated, never to see General La Fayette again on earth. Hundreds of the people of Lexington in talking of La Fayette cried out aloud. The ladies especially shed tears when taking leave of the great friend of Washington.

Very truly your friend,

B. NETHERLAND.

Capt. Thomas W. Ashford,
  Versailles, Ky.

John Price.

Col. John Price early settled in Jessamine county in what is known as the Marble creek district. He came to Kentucky in 1788 and was one of the best educated of the Revolutionary soldiers who made the county their home. His letters show that he was man of fine mind and good scholarship and he influenced a great many of his Revolutionary friends to settle in Jessamine, Fayette and Woodford counties. He was one of the first men to respond to the call to arms in the Revolutionary war.

While born in Maryland he was descended from a distinguished Virginia family. He was severely wounded at the battle of Brandywine, September 11, 1777. He was also at Monmouth and Princeton and at the surrender of Cornwallis, at Yorktown. He died at his residence in Jessamine county on the 10th of August, 1822.

He started the agitation for the creation of a new county. He and his neighbors had been subjected to what they termed petty persecution, on the part of the constables and sheriffs, or their appointees, and as these all resided at Lexington and were not elected by the people, the inhabitants of that part of Jessamine became aggrieved at the conduct of these officers and this dissatisfaction produced the movement which finally ended in the organization of a county.

He was the first man to represent the county in the legislature and was elected late in 1798. It must have been a special election called for the purpose of choosing a representative. As the county was created on December 19th, 1798, and as the elections for 1798 under the constitution, were in May of that year, he must either have been appointed or elected as the first member from the county. A letter which he wrote to Col. Joseph Hamilton Daveiss on the 28th of August, 1799, explains much, about which there have been different statements in the county, and shows that Col. Joseph Hamilton Daveiss and others assisted Colonel Price in securing the creation of the new county.

Colonel Price affiliated with the Baptist church. He was a man of great kindness of heart and liberality. He was a friend of all who needed his help and especially of the old Revolutionary soldiers. Buried upon the old homestead, his grave was not marked. The place is now owned by a Mr. Hinds and while it is known in what enclosure he was buried, there is no stone to designate his grave.

Many of his descendants now reside in Indiana, Illinois, Missouri and in the West, and the distinguished publisher John P. Morton, of Louisville, was a grandson of Colonel Price.

William Price.

Col. William Price, who was not related to Col. John Price, was born in Fredericksburg, Va., in 1755, and came with his family to Jessamine county in 1787. Capt. James C. Price, who commanded the Jessamine Blues, at the battle of Raisin, on the 23d of February, 1813, was his oldest son, and was born while his father was absent in the American army.

Col. William Price was descended from Baptist ancestry, who emigrated from Wales to Virginia, in 1720. When a mere lad, only fourteen years of age, he had seen Revds. John Waller and Louis Craig lodged in the Fredericksburg jail for preaching the Baptist doctrine. This was before the passage of the Statute of Virginia, granting religious liberty, in the passage of which, Thos. Jefferson considered that he had achieved one of the greatest triumphs of his long career. This produced a profound impression upon his mind, and he was never able to eradicate his prejudice against the Church of England, which had been instrumental in the arrest of these preachers, and he became an inveterate enemy of that church, and never brought himself to look with complacency upon those who were connected with it. He came to Kentucky with Louis Craig and his traveling church, in 1781, and remained for three years. He then returned to Virginia, and in 1787 came back to Kentucky, settled in Jessamine county and made it his permanent home.

Colonel Price was in the Revolutionary war, from its very commencement until the end. He was a first Lieutenant in the battle of Stony Point, July 16, 1799, and at the battles of Brandywine, Germantown, Monmouth, and Princeton, he was acting as Captain. He rose to the rank of Major, and was at Yorktown

when Cornwallis surrendered October 19, 1781. He married Mary
Cunningham, in 1777, and three months after left his home and
young wife to fight the battles of freedom. His first engagement was in the battle of Brandywine, September 11, 1777, and he
did not return to his family until the close of the war. The part
which most of the Episcopal clergy in Virginia took against the
revolution, still further embittered Colonel Price against that
denomination. The following letter of his to Capt. Edward
Payne, dated December 20th, shows both his feelings to the
church, as well as to the character of the entertainments which
were given in those days. A similar invitation was written to
Col. Luke Allen, in which a like prejudice crops out:

Price's Hall, Stafford county, Va.
December 20, 1787.

Capt. Edward Payne,
    Overseer at Gunston Hall:

My Dear Sir—This note is to apprize you that I invite you
and all your Baptist friends to my house on Christmas day to
partake of a big dinner of turkey and oysters, and to conclude
with a dance at grandmother's in the evening. No Episcopalian
has been invited. Such people are too aristocratic and over-
bearing. The people who are communicants of that church try
to imitate their aristocratic brethren of England in almost every
act that they perform. I have no patience with such harpies as
the clergy of this establishment. Their titles, dignities and liv-
ings are too much like our late oppressors in the great war just
closed. They must now consider that the people of the country
now look chiefly to the practical and useful and not to mere empty
titles which serve no good purpose in a free country. What we
want in the church as well as in the state is plain, practical men,
devoted men, who know and mingle with the people as one of
themselves. We want no more English airs, no arrogance of de-
meanor among neighbors. Tell Robert Craig to bring his fiddle,
as we expect a good time generally. Tell Black Tom to come by
all means.

WILLIAM PRICE.

Colonel Price must have borne a distinguished part in the
battle of Stony Point. The following letter, which he wrote to

Maj. James Cluke, the day after this battle, will show that in that battle he acted with great courage and his conduct was commended by General Wayne himself:

                              Fort Stony Point, July 17, 1779.
To. Maj. James Cluke:

Dear Major—I wish that God would heal your wound and I could once more see you among your brave comrades. On yesterday evening, July 16th, after marching over the roughest country I ever saw, through deep swamps and narrow roads, we got within a mile of this fort, which is on the west bank of the Hudson river. It was of vast importance to our enemies and had been strengthened by every means of art that lay in their power. At night our heroic commander, Brigadier Wayne, came among us and told us that everything depended on secrecy, and, says he, "I want you men who belong to the regiments of Colonel Butler and Colonel Fleury to march with unloaded muskets and fixed bayonets; I will lead you myself," said he. The river had flooded the swamps waist deep, but when we saw our beloved General go forward, we sprang forward, and our advance of twenty men at once attacked the double palisade. When one of the red-coated sons of bitches shouted in great alarm, "Here comes the damned rebels, shoot them." He was soon knocked on the head, but a terrible fire was opened on us as we advanced through the swamps. The guns from the fort spattered mud on us as well as dirty water. Their grape and canister did not damage more than to spatter mud and water on our clothes. About this time our brave General was knocked on the head in the right temple by a spent ball. I instantly raised him up. "March on, Lieutenant Price; carry me to the fort; I will die at the head of my men." We bore him forward until we got near the center of the fort and both commands met, when the shout of victory rent the air. Our victory was complete; we carried everything so rapidly that our enemies were surprised. We lost about sixty men. Joseph Campbell, of Fredericksburg, was killed; also Private Clow and Richard Climer was killed. He was from Philadelphia, was a brave Dutchman, deeply religious. I hope he is safe in heaven. Hoping that you will soon recover from your wound, I am, your friend,

                                        WILLIAM PRICE.

He died at his residence, where he had settled when coming to Jessamine county, on the 10th of October, 1808, at the age of 53 years. He failed to reach that longevity which marked the lives of most of the Revolutionary soldiers who were transplanted to Kentucky, and especially Jessamine county.

He was a patriot of the greatest intensity and earnestness. He early introduced in Jessamine county, celebrations of the Fourth of July. He had such a celebration at his house on the Fourth of July, 1794. He invited a large number of his friends. On the fifth of July, 1794, he wrote a letter to Governor Shelby, and Revolutionary soldiers must have been abundant in those days, for he said that he had forty at his table on that occasion. The following is the communication which he made to Governor Shelby:

Fayette county, Ky., July 5, 1794.

To His Excellency, Isaac Shelby,

Governor of Kentucky:

My Esteemed Friend—I was greatly disappointed by your not coming to my house on yesterday (July 4). We had a glorious time and a big dinner. Forty men sat down at my tables, who had served in the late struggle for our freedom and independence. It was a glorious sight to behold, and I wish King George III and Lord North could have witnessed the scene in the wilds of America. On the return of this glorious birthday of our freedom from British despotism, the heart of every patriot in the late struggle may rightfully pour its highest tribute to God and the great sages and soldiers who resolved to stake their lives and sacred honor in maintaining the Declaration of Independence. Throughout the limits of our country, from Massachusetts to Georgia, the hearts of a free and happy people have been dedicated on yesterday to the contemplation of the great blessings achieved and bequeathed to us by such heroic leaders as George Washington, Israel Putnam and Nathaniel Greene. Such brave leaders took their lives in their hands, and liberty or death was inscribed on their hearts. God, in the plenitude of His beneficence, has generally chosen men qualified to resist kings and tyrants in their attacks on the rights of the people. The history of our mother country furnished full proof of this fact and our own glorious country in the late war for independence is a more brilliant illustration of the great truth that God hates all tyrants and despotic rulers, and sooner or later overthrows all such rascals in causing the people to rise up and cut their heads off.

Truly thy old friend,

WILLIAM PRICE.

P. S.—I will be at Frankfort next Monday.

The house in which he lived has been changed so as to bear no similarity to what it was when he resided in it, but the graveyard on the place is still maintained in fairly good order, and a substantial stone wall surrounds the spot where he and his loved ones rest. He had quite a number of children and some of his descendants reside in Jessamine and Fayette counties now.

George Walker.

Gen. George Walker was one of the most distinguished gifts of Virginia to Jessamine county. He was the second man to open a law office in the town of Nicholasville, which he did in 1799, Samuel H. Woodson having been the first man to open such an office. George Walker owned the land upon which Mr. Melanchthon Young now resides, and was buried in the orchard about one hundred yards from the residence.

He was a man of great learning and great enterprise, as well as great courage. Born in Culpeper county, Va., in 1763, he settled in Jessamine county, in 1794. He married Miss Rachel Coffee, of Nashville, Tenn., who was a daughter of Gen. John Coffee, who bore a distinguished part with Gen. Andrew Jackson in the Indian wars in the South and West, as well as the war of 1812. He was a mere lad when he entered the ranks of the Revolutionary army under Generals Green and Morgan, in the campaigns of 1780-81, and was at the battle of Cowpens, January 17, 1781, and Guilford Court House. He was also at the siege of Yorktown.

He was a man of noble physique and his appearance indicated his intelligence as well as his high character. His devotion to his country and its cause knew no bounds. He was appointed to a seat in the United States Senate by Gov. Isaac Shelby, to fill a vacancy.

David Meade was an uncle of Colonel Walker, his father having married Colonel Meade's sister. He was in the battle of New Orleans with the Kentucky troops, where he attracted the attention of General Jackson by his superb bravery and his splendid heroism. He was also in the battles of the Northwest and was aide to Governor Shelby at the battle of the Thames.

He died in Nicholasville in 1819, at the house now owned by Lewis C. Drake. Two of his sons emigrated to Texas and held distinguished positions. One of his sons, Andrew Walker, was a great friend of Quantrell, the celebrated Missouri soldier.

The exact location of the grave of Colonel Walker is now unknown, but in his day he was one of the most prominent and respected citizens. His youngest son, Courtney Meade Walker, removed to Oregon, where he led the life of a hunter. He died in 1886, at an advanced age.

The first public service rendered by George Walker was as one of the commissioners to run the lines between Kentucky and Tennessee, and the boundary was known as Walker's Line. Some extracts from Courtney Meade Walker's letters will be interesting as showing the condition of affairs in olden times. He says: "I was in Nicholasville in August, 1826. Harrison Daniels was a candidate for the legislature at that time. It was on the last day of the election. There were some five or six fist fights in the streets, but no one was injured or seriously hurt. I had come up from Louisville, where I had been at school. I was at the burial of Samuel H. Woodson, in 1827, at the residence near David Meade's."

Gen'l Percival Butler.

Gen. Percival Butler, was born in Carlisle, Pa., April 4, 1760. In 1778, he entered the American army as a lieutenant. He was at Valley Forge with Washington, at the battle of Monmouth, and at the surrender at Yorktown. LaFayette was such an admirer of the young man that he presented him with a sword as a token of his friendship and esteem. He married a Miss Hawkins, of Virginia. Col. John Todd, who fell at Blue Licks, married another sister. It was probably through this connection that General Butler settled in Kentucky. He came to Jessamine county in 1784, and settled at the mouth of Hickman creek and engaged in merchandise. This point was then one of great importance. The Kentucky river was the outlet for a large part of Central Kentucky, and flatboats plied up and down the stream, carrying the commerce of the country tributary to it. The rich lands lying in proximity were already producing large treasure which found markets in the East and at New Orleans. Gen. James Wilkinson had opened a large dry goods store at Lexington in 1784. Salt was carried out of the Salt river from Mann and Bullitt Licks in 1796 to Nashville, and the Kentucky river was also sending its tide of wealth to the outside world.

In 1785 a ferry had been established at the mouth of Hickman creek by the Virginia legislature, and in 1787 Wilkinson had pushed his trade down the Mississippi to New Orleans, and the mouth of Hickman at once became a center of trade.

By this date roads were cut through from Lexington to Danville, Stanford and Lancaster, and the chartering of the ferry as early as 1785 shows that a large trade crossed at this point. Prior to this date no other ferry had been established by Virginia except the one across the Kentucky river at Boonesboro (1779). The next were those at the mouth of Hickman, the mouth of Jack's creek, Madison county, at Long Lick, and two at Louisville, to the mouths of Silver creek and Mill Run.

Gen. Percival Butler remained at the mouth of Hickman until 1796, when he removed to the mouth of the Kentucky river, at Carrollton. He was made adjutant-general of Kentucky in 1792 and took part in the war of 1812, and died in Carroll county, in 1821.

His eldest son, Thomas L. Butler, was born at the mouth of Hickman, in 1789. He was an aide to General Jackson at the battle of New Orleans in 1815, being then only twenty-six years of age, and was left by General Jackson in command of the city, to protect it against outbreaks. He represented Gallatin (then comprising Carroll) county in the legislature, in 1826, and Carroll in 1848, and died at Carrollton in 1877, aged 88 years.

Gen. Wm. Orlando Butler, second son of Gen. Percival Butler, was born at the mouth of Hickman, April 19, 1791, and remained there until he was five years of age; then went with his father to Carrollton. He graduated at Transylvania University at twenty-one years of age, and at once volunteered as a private in the war of 1812, then in progress. He entered the service as a private, in Captain Nathaniel G. Hart's company, the "Lexington light infantry." Young Butler was made a corporal. This company was in the battle of Raisin, fought January 22, 1813. Captain Hart was wounded in the leg in the fight. A British officer named Elliott, who had been nursed by Hart's family during a severe spell of illness, in Lexington, offered to protect Captain Hart, who was a brother-in-law of Henry Clay, but he basely failed to redeem his promise, and Hart was massacred. In both battles at Raisin, January 18th and 22d, Butler's conduct commanded the highest praise. His courage, gallantry, and self-denial elicited universal praise. He was wounded and taken prisoner.

His heroic conduct at Raisin shows that he has had no superior in courage and chivalry in the world's history, and one event is thus told by F. P. Blair, Sr.:

"After the rout and massacre of the right wing, belonging to the Wells command, the whole force of the British and Indians was concentrated against the small body of troops under Maj. Geo. Madison, that maintained their ground within the picketed gardens, a double barn commanding the plat of ground on which the Kentuckians stood—on one side the Indians, under the cover of an orchard and fence, the British on the other side, being so posted as to command the space between it and the pickets. A party in the rear of the barn were discovered advancing to take possession of it. All saw the fatal consequences of the secure lodgment of the enemy at a place which would present every man within the pickets at close rifle shot, to the aim of their marksmen. Major Madison inquired if there was no one who would volunteer to run the guntlet of the fire of the British and Indian lines, and put a torch to the combustibles within the barn, to save the remnant of the little army from sacrifice. The heroic Butler, without a moment's delay, took some blazing sticks from a fire at hand, leaped the pickets, and running at his utmost speed, thrust the fire into the straw within the barn. One who was an anxious spectator of the event says that, although volley upon volley was fired at him, Butler, after making some steps on his way back, turned to see if the fire had taken, and, not being satisfied, returned to the barn and set it in a blaze. As the conflagration grew, the enemy was seen retreating from the rear of the building, which they had entered in one end, as the flames ascended in the other. Soon after reaching the pickets in safety amid the shouts of his friends, he was struck by a musket ball in his breast. Believing, from the pain he felt, that it had penetrated his chest, he turned to John M. McCalla, one of his Lexington comrades, and, pressing his hand on the spot, said: 'I fear this shot is mortal, but while I am able to move I will do my duty.' To the anxious inquiries of his friends, who met him soon afterward, he opened his vest, with a smile, and showed them that the ball had spent itself on the thick wadding of his coat and on his breastbone. He suffered, however, for many weeks."

He was a captain in the battle of New Orleans, December 14, 1814, and on January 8, 1815, was brevetted Major for his gallantry, and General Jackson commended his conduct in the highest terms. He was an aide on the staff of General Jackson, in 1816 and 1817, but resigned to study law. He married a daughter of General Robert Todd. He represented Gallatin county in the legislature in 1817, was elected to Congress in 1839, and served four years, refusing a re-election. In 1844 he was the Democratic candidate for Governor and reduced the Whig majority to 4,000.

On June 29, 1846, President Polk appointed General Butler a major general of volunteers, and on the same date Zachary Taylor, major general in the regular army.

On the 23d of February, 1847, the Kentucky legislature presented him a sword for his gallantry in Mexico. He bore a distinguished part in many of the battles of that war. He was wounded in the battle of Monterey in September, 1846. On February 18, 1848, he succeeded General Scott in the chief command of the American army in Mexico, and remained in such position until the declaration of peace, May 29, 1848. In that year he was nominated for Vice-President of the United States on the ticket with Gen. Cass; but they were defeated by Taylor and Fillmore. He received the full vote of his party for United States Senator in 1851, but failed of election. He was one of the six Peace Commissioners from Kentucky in January, 1861, and thereafter he remained in the quiet seclusion of his home, at Carrollton, and died August 6, 1880, in his 89th year. He rests in a sepulchre overlooking the splendid scenery where the waters of the Kentucky and the Ohio unite—a fit resting-place for him who did so much to wrest Ohio and the Northwest from the savage and to make still greater, the renown of the great commonwealth which had given him birth.

He was a man of the highest courage, truest patriotism, noblest public spirit, thorough culture and splendid talent. His poem, "The Boatman's Horn," induced by the associations and memories of his childhood on the Ohio, when listening to the large and sonorous horns the boatmen were accustomed to blow to announce their coming to the landing places on the river, is a real poetic gem:

The Boat Horn.

O boatman, wind that horn again,
 For never did the list'ning air
 Upon its lambent bosom bear
So wild, so soft, so sweet a strain.
 What though thy notes are sad and few,
By every simple boatman blown,
 Yet is each pulse to nature true
And melody in every tone.
 How oft in boyhood's joyous day,
Unmindful of the lapsing hours,
 I've loitered on my homeward way
By wild Ohio's brink of flowers,
 While some lone boatman from the deck
Poured his soft numbers to that tide,
 As if to charm from storm and wreck
The boat where all his fortunes ride!
Delighted nature drank the sound,
Enchanted—echo bore it round
In whispers soft, and softer still,
From hill to plain and plain to hill,

Till e'en the thoughtless, frolicking boy,
Elate with hope and wild with joy,
Who gamboled by the river side
And sported with the fretting tide,
Feels something new pervade his breast,
Chain his light step, repress his jest,
Bends o'er the flood his eager ear
To catch the sounds, far off, yet near—
Drinks the sweet draught, but knows not why
The tear of rapture fills his eye;
And can he now, to manhood grown,
Tell why those notes, simple and lone,
As on the ravished ear they fell,
Bind every sense in magic spell?
There is a tide of feeling given—
To all on earth—its fountain, Heaven,
Beginning with the dewy flower
Just ope'd in Flora's vernal bower,
Rising creation's orders through
With louder murmur, brighter hue,
That tide is sympathy; its ebb and flow
Gives life its hues of joy and woe;
Music, the master spirit that can move
Its waves to war, or lull them into love;
Can cheer the sinking sailor 'mid the wave
And bid the soldier on, nor fear the grave;
Inspire the fainting pilgrim on his road,
And elevate his soul to claim his God.
Then, boatman, wind that horn again!
Though much of sorrow mark its strain,
Yet are its notes to sorrow dear.
What though they wake fond memory's tear?
Tears are sad memory's sacred feast,
And rapture oft her chosen guest.

BOATMAN'S HORN.

First Settlers.

John Hunter, Jacob Hunter and Samuel Hunter came to
Jessamine county in the spring of 1779. Jacob was the oldest
and was born in 1753. They first stopped at Boonesboro in 1778
and were employed by Elias Hite, son of Abraham Hite, who
was at that time engaged in the surveying of lands in Kentucky.
The father of these young men died at Boonesboro. They had
two sisters. They had been employed by Mr. Hite as chain-
carriers, and they all settled close to each other on Hickman
creek. The following letter shows when they were dismissed:

Thursday, April 1, 1779.

Dear Father: Dismiss the chain carriers, John Hunter,
Samuel Hunter and Jacob Hunter; pay them six shillings per
day for three months' services on Boone and Hickman creeks.

ISAAC HITE.

Tell Mr. Douglas to go at once to Boonesboro.

Here, in 1780, was born Joseph Hunter, who was the first
white child born in the present boundary of Jessamine
county. Joseph Hunter lived to be quite an old man.
He died in 1858. The old home of these first settlers embraced about 900 acres of land, which has now been in cultivation
120 years and is still fertile and productive. The old house for
a long time was the property of John Portwood, who was a son-
in-law of John Hunter. The farm is situated about six miles east
of Nicholasville on the pike leading to Boone's Ferry.

When John Portwood died, Dudley Portwood, his son, sold
a part of the farm containing 200 acres to Jessamine county for
the erection of a poor house.

The Hunter homestead was built of brick and is still standing,
and was erected about 1798. One of the bricks in the chimneys
has this date upon it.

Jacob Hunter left Jessamine county and went to Owen
county, where he died after attaining the extreme age of one
hundred years.

Samuel Hunter settled some miles above these other two

KENTUCKY PIONEER'S DRESS.

brothers, on Hickman creek, and they were unquestionably the first white men who ever undertook a permanent settlement in Jessamine county. They did not build forts or blockhouses, and were doubtless driven in about 1782, when the Indians were so determined in their assaults on the Kentucky settlers.

Early Settlers on Jessamine Creek.

The early settlers on Jessamine creek were mostly German Protestants who came in large part from Pennsylvania and Maryland, with a few from Virginia. The following letter written by Dr. Peter Trisler to Rev. David Zeisberger in 1794, from Jessamine county, will prove valuable, historically:

Jessamine Creek, September 4, 1794

Dear David: I am exceedingly sorry that you did not come along with your father during his recent visit to this delightful country. The sun shines brighter in this country, and the skies are more blue, than the damp, moist atmosphere at the mouth of the Cuyahoga. A good school is needed among us, and I invite you once more to leave that inhospitable country of savages and cold winds.

Faithfully yours,

PETER TRISLER.

From most reliable records Rev. Jacob Rhorer was the founder of the first Moravian church on Jessamine creek, in 1794, and the building was used as a Moravian church by the Rhorer family up to near the beginning of the Civil War.

The following are the names of the early settlers who were of German parentage and belonged to the Moravian Church, or "United Brethren": Arnspigers, Alcorns, Cormans, Bowmans, Bruners, Earthenhousers, Easleys, Funks, Fraziers, Grows, Gilmans, Goforths, Hiffners, Howsers, Harbaughs, Horines, Ritters, Rices, Masners, Zikes, Ketrons, Waggamans, Warmslys, Overstreets, Quests, Yosts, Hoovers, Trislers, Turks, Turpins, Shreves, Veatches, Vantresses, Naves, Cogars, Crows, Cooleys, Cawbys, and Schmidts. Nearly all of these names were in the list of German settlers in the western part of Jessamine county, who were largely the followers of John Huss. They were men of great common sense, good judgment, honesty, a high sense of morality, and great lovers of freedom, and their descendants still reside in that part of Jessamine county which their ancestors in the early history of the state settled.

In 1884 John Cawby had a Bible which was printed at Wittenberg in 1440. This Bible was brought from Germany to Maryland in 1780, by Peter Trisler, who, in 1794, settled in the present limits of Jessamine county, where he died April 22, 1821. This old Bible was the property of Mrs. Nancy Horine, who was a grandaughter of Dr. Trisler.

Dr. Peter Trisler was born in Wittenberg, Germany, in 1745. He came to Hagerstown, Maryland, when a very young man, and settled on Jessamine creek in 1791. When he came from Germany he brought the old Bible above referred to, and this book contained records of a large number of the families above named. From this stock German settlers have gone throughout the West and South, and they usually became men of thrift, energy, character and brains. Some now in Illinois and many in Missouri have carried away with them the splendid qualities of these early settlers, and in their new homes have shown the sterling qualities of their ancestors, who did so much to create and promote the best interests of the new state they helped to found in the then wilderness of Kentucky.

Names of those who settled in other parts of Jessamine from 1782 to the close of the century:

Archibald Bristow; Manoah Singleton; Elder Michael Rice; Jacob Howser; David Watson, Sr.; Jacob Sedowski, afterward removed to Bourbon county; James McKinney; Jeremiah King; Col. Jos. Crockett; Abraham Howser; Jacob Rhorer; John Welch; Jacob Bruner; James Overstreet; Chris. Mason; Wm. Moss; Jno. Thornton; Patrick Watson; Fielding Pilcher; Shadrach Pilcher; Samuel Rice; Minor Young; Rev. Jno. Hudson; Jeremiah Dickerson; Wm. Fletcher; Wm. Bowman; John Two Nine Scott; Col. Byrd Prewitt; Jno. Johnson; Jno. Lowry; Thos. Caldwell; Col. Geo. Walker; John Lewis; James Duncan; Chas. Duncan; Jonas Davenport; James McCabe; Jacob Rice; Rev. Nathaniel Harris; Col. Wm. Price; Col. Jno. Price; Major

Netherland; Benj. Blackford; Benj. Adams; Jno. Todd; Robt. Campbell; Abraham Cassell; Francis Lowers; Thos. Shanklin; Robt. Shanklin: Daniel Mitchell; Thomas Rowland; Thomas Overstreet.

Black's Station.

It is strange that, from the time of the settlement at Harrodsburg in 1774 down to 1779, there were no stations established in Jessamine county. In Mercer, Boyle, Fayette, Woodford, Madison, Scott and Franklin, numerous stations were erected, but with all the richness of the land in Jessamine county, none came to found a fort within its midst. There were surveys made in the county during this time, one of which, the Abram Hite survey of 2,000 acres on Marble creek, was both permanent and important, and discussed in the fort at Harrodsburg in 1774 and 1775. A Mr. Black established a station on what is known as the G. B. Bryan farm, half way between Nicholasville and Brookline on the Harrodsburg turnpike. It was on the old trace which led through the county along the waters of Jessamine creek to the waters of South Elkhorn. There were several large boiling springs in the locality, and as these were always in demand for settlements, Black located his station there. It was composed of several cabins, and the land was originally part of what is known as the "Craig Survey," and was subsequently owned by Archibald Logan, who was a rich tanner and had an establishment in Lexington.

Logan conveyed this land to his daughter, Mrs. Hord, when he left Jessamine county in 1829, and the house known as the Patterson House is where Logan lived. Mrs. Hord conveyed the place to her daughter, Mrs. Worley, and she conveyed it to others, and it is now owned by the Bryan's heirs.

Beginning with 1783, this station became quite an important one, and was one of the stopping places for those who followed the trace from Mercer and Boyle to Franklin and Woodford counties. The difficulty in obtaining water in this general section was very great, and Joel Watkins, in his diary, says: June 24— "Forded river at mouth of Hickman; after travelling seven or eight miles on the road that leads from the river to Lexington I turned to the left of said road and crossed a water course called East Jessamine; after leaving the said creek, the land is very level and of a very pretty mulatto soil and the growth is black and white oak, hickory, and some walnut and sugar trees, and the under-growth hazel nut and red bud, till I arrived at West Jessamine. I proceeded up said river to head, the land altering as I proceeded up said creek until I came near the head springs, the land there appearing very rich till I struck the waters of South Elkhorn. This day I passed several good farms, and especially John Craig's, badly watered between the two Jessamines, so much so that people settled only along the said creeks." This scarcity of water was doubtless one of the reasons for establishing the station at Black's.

Watkins says August 18, 1889: "Passed Dick's river at Mc-Guir's, from thence we proceeded to Curd's Ferry on Kentucky, which is at the mouth of Dick's river—the latter we forded—(here the cliffs are of amazing height); we proceeded towards Lexington about eight miles; we turned to the left of said road past Black Station on the waters of Clear creek, proceeded on-ward, the land lying very well, but the growth indicating the rock being nigh the surface of the earth; we crossed several forks of Clear creek; we came to Captain Woodfolk's mentioned on page 22; from this place the land continued very slightly, both soil and Growth, to Mr. Watkins', at which place we arrived about dark—received very kindly."

He also says, August 24: "Monday, after breakfast with Mr. W., set out for the south side of Kentucky river, agreeing with the aforesaid gentleman at parting to keep up a literary cor-respondence, past Black Station again and crossed the two forks of Jessamine and arrived at Kentucky river at the mouth of Hickman, which I forded, and arrived at Mr. Walker's at two hours besun."

It will be seen that the trace along by Black's Station was the road usually traveled by those who passed from Garrard and Mercer and Boyle to Woodford and Franklin.

Another station in Jessamine county was built by Levi Todd a little northwest of Keene—its exact location can not now be de-termined—it, is, however, laid down upon Filson's map, but was abandoned. This was a fort. The road from Harrodsburg to

Lexington doubtless passed by Black's Station, and from this on to Todd's Station. There was also another route by which they crossed the river to the mouth of Hickman, followed Hickman for some distance, and then turned northeast towards Lexington, then their route followed Hickman for several miles, then struck East Jessamine and followed it to its head at Mrs. Horine's on the Southern Railroad, about a mile east of Nicholasville, and from this over to the headwaters of Jessamine, and from this along the general route of the Lexington and Harrodsburgh turnpike to Lexington. This is shown by deposition of David Williams, which was filed in the case of Manson's Executors vs. Craig Williams, in which Williams deposes as follows:

"He was well acquainted with Hickman's creek from a small distance above the survey, 'Abram Hite,' to the head of the creek, and that the east fork of Jessamine was as well known to the people of Harrodsburg as Hickman's creek was. The east fork of Jessamine lay more out of the course generally taken by hunters in traveling from Harrodsburg to the waters of the Licking; they commonly fell on main Jessamine above the mouth of East Fork; thence up the main Jessamine spring; thence crossing the waters of Hickman to Boone's creek, and over to the head of Stroud's creek, where there were roads leading down most of its branches to the Salt Licks. It was also common to pass by main Jessamine above the East Fork and by Todd's station on the waters of Hickman to go to the headwaters of South and North Elkhorn. This deponent, with others, frequently took this road to avoid large canebrakes."

The Last Indians.

The high cliffs, covered with dense forests of cedar and other timber, along the Kentucky river, and their utter inaccessibility, rendered them excellent hiding places for the Indians who disturbed the settlers as late as the end of 1792. No great incursion of the Indians into Kentucky happened after the battle of Blue Licks, in 1782, but predatory bands, consisting of four or five members, both from the south and from the north, gave the settlers great disturbance and uneasiness and murdered a great

many women and children.   Shortly after the battle of Blue Licks
the people abandoned the forts and scattered out in their log
cabins over the state.   Fear of Indian raids had been removed
and the immense tide of settlers which came into the state during this period took up lands in every part, but as late as 1792
many people were killed in Garrard, Lincoln, Madison and Jessamine.   On July 6, 1793, Major Benjamin Netherland wrote the
following letter to Governor Shelby, which gives a contemporane-
ous account of these troubles:

"Mingo Tavern, Fayette county, Ky.,

"July 6, 1792.

"To His Excellency, Isaac Shelby,

"Governor of Kentucky:

"Dear Sir—Your letter of the 29th of June, was handed to me
on yesterday by John Wilson.   I tender to you my hearty, warm
thanks for the good opinion you express concerning my poor
services in the defense of our beloved country.   To enjoy your
confidence and friendship may well be considered a distinguished
honor, and I shall at all times consider it a pleasure to be of service to you.

There have but few depredations occurred in these parts of the
county,   Last year it was reported three men were killed by a
party of Shawnees.   They were pursued, overtaken and two of
them were killed the following day at Boonesboro.   About three
months ago two Indians crossed the Kentucky at the mouth of the
Dix river, and came among the settlers, as they said, for trading.
I was not pleased at seeing such treacherous enemies, and gave
orders to Tom Lewis and his father to keep a watch on them.
They spoke English very well and were trying to make the impression that they were our best friends.   When they left the
next morning they met one of the settlers named Michael Hiffner,
who had been to see Thomas Rowland, who settled on a planta-
tion some miles above.   The Indians told Hiffner he must let
them have his horse.   This he refused, when he heard the snap of
a gun.   He at once jumped from the horse and stabbed the Indian to the heart.   He then turned upon the other, who shot him
in the arm and ran off into the timber.   Hiffner, being a good Indian fighter and a brave and active man, pursued him, and before

the Indian could reload his gun Hiffner caught him and knocked his brains out with a club, and threw his body down the high cliffs into the river. The body of the Indian he stabbed to death was buried. A party of Wyandots killed a man at the mouth of Jessamine last spring. At the various crossings Indian tracks have been discovered. At Paint Lick two years ago two men were killed by this same party of Indians. It is my opinion that if 50 mounted men were employed to scour the Kentucky river cliffs during the fall, I feel sure no more of our people would be ambushed and killed. These hills and cliffs, Major Whitley says, are good hiding places for Indians to do us much injury. I must urge you to appoint Tom Wilson captain and lieutenant of this end of the county. He is young and active and can run like the wind, and such service would be in keeping with his nature, which is daring and full of adventure. I would seek the place myself, but I have so long neglected my private affairs that it would be ruinous for me to put my affairs into the hands of others, who seek their own interest to the neglect of mine, besides I have now the high and responsible duties of husband and father, which I can not throw aside without doing great injustice to the innocent who look to me for protection as husband and father.

"Your old friend,

" B. NETHERLAND."

All sorts of "varmints" were plentiful in the days of the early settlers. Bears and rattlesnakes were in great abundance. On the farm of Mr. Alexander Willoughby, near Sulphur Well, one of the great curiosities was a place known as "Rattlesnake Spring." When the land was first settled this spring was a great resort for these snakes. The water issued from a large crevice in a limestone rock, overlaid by a bold bank. Near the spring was a cave. Major Netherland, who visited the place in 1796, says: "In the fall of the year they would crawl from the cave to the spring and enter the crevice of the rock, where they remained torpid during the winter. When the warmth of spring revived them they would emerge from the crevice and the cave and bask in the warm sun. At this season they fell an easy prey to the destroyer. Henry Allsman, who is now living on this portion of Mr. Willoughby's land, told me he and his family have killed hundreds of them in the last week. He would pile them up on a log heap and burn them. By this wholesale slaughter, this enemy of God and man was extirpated, and in another season of spring and summer nothing will remain of that representative of the transgression but his hateful name."

The man Allsman here referred to was the father of the notorious Andrew Allsman, who caused General McNeil to shoot ten innocent men at Palymra, Mo. He was born on this farm in 1805 and left home in 1829. Allsman boasted on the streets of Palmyra of causing the death of these men. The next day after he made this dreadful confession his dead body was found hung and riddled with bullets. He had been put to death by Col. Joe Porter's men in the neighborhood.

The First Powder Mill

Erected in Jessamine county was located on Hickman creek, near the old Union Mill. The old powder houses remained there as late as the year 1850. These powder mills were owned by Richard Laffoon, but the powder house was erected by Robert Crockett, and after he left the country, it fell into the hands of the Laffoons. It was struck by lightning and destroyed in 1837.

The first paper mill in Jessamine, was erected on Jessamine creek at the old Glass Mills by Thomas Bryan in 1837, and he carried it on until 1848.

The first burr mill-stones ever imported to Jessamine, came from France in 1837, and were used by Bryan in what is known as the Henry Glass Mills.

The First Mill.

The first mill built in Jessamine county was constructed by Meredith Wright, father of Mr. Robert Wright, who still lives in Nicholasville at the advanced age of eighty-one years. Meredith Wright was the first millwright in the state, and the mill he built was Haydon's Mill, afterward run by Mr. Gavin Steele. Mr. Wright also built the Union Mills and the Torbett Mills. He was among the earliest settlers in Kentucky, and came from

ANCIENT PAPER MILL AT GLASS MILL.

Culpeper Courthouse, in Virginia, and immediately settled in Jessamine county. His mills were used generally by the early settlers, and the one used by David Trabue in Jessamine county was among the first and most primitive. The process of grinding was very slow; each man's or boy's grist was ground in its turn, and sometimes a wait of twelve hours was required before the flour could be taken home.

Thomas Berry, brother of Joseph and Lewis Berry, ran the paper mill on Jessamine creek, where the character of paper made was good for the opportunities of manufacture. It was deep blue and broadly lined, but it was smooth, with a good polish, and held the marks distinctly.

In 1825 James Wilson owned and ran a powder mill on Clear creek. The power used was horse power, and the mortars and pestles were operated by this power. Powder was then worth $1 a pound.

At this time a fine flour mill was operated also on Clear creek by Mr. Campbell Steele, who was the grandfather of Wm. L. Steele, of Nicholasville, and Mr. John Steele; and a hominy mill was operated by Samuel Ruffner on Clear creek. The pestles were operated by horse power.

Early Houses.

House building in Jessamine county in early days was not a very expensive or protracted work. The houses were rude and simple structures of hewn logs and the chinks stopped with mud or filled with stone and then plastered with mud on the outside. The roof was made of clap-boarding about three feet long and four inches wide, and along these were placed poles supported by blocks of wood and these were weighted so as to hold the clap-boarding in place. There was rarely more than one window, which was at the side of the door. In early days it had no glass but was closed by a wooden shutter made of heavy oak boards. The floors were made of logs or puncheons hewed smooth on one side with an adze. The logs were generally split to a convenient size and length, and then hewed flat. The doors were made of riven boards fastened together with wooden pins to wooden

PIONEER CABIN NEAR TROY, KY.

slabs. These doors always had the latch on the inside and a hole was bored above the latch about 4 inches, through which a leathern string passed and so fastened to the latch on the inside. When this string was taken in there was no way to open the door from the outside. In the morning the string was passed back from the inside so that any party who desired to enter could raise the latch. From this comes the Kentucky proclamation of hospitality, "You will always find the latch-string on the outside." The chimneys were made of logs plastered with mud. The back and jambs were either covered with mud or stones were placed on the inside to keep the heat from setting them on fire. The fire places were often 10 or 12 feet wide, and while they consumed an enormous quantity of wood, they made jolly good fires, which lent cheerfulness and comfort to the whole house. Weatherboarding was not used until about 1815. Some of these houses are still standing in the county, and in some of the brick houses which were erected in early times, the doors were made without nails. One of the earliest brick houses erected in Jessamine county was that of William Shreve, which was built in 1793 and is now owned by Mrs. John Simms, a short distance west of the Cincinnati Southern depot, and it is still in a good state of preservation.

The First Vineyard.

John Frances DeFoure was a native of Vevay, Switzerland, and planted the first vineyard west of the Alleghanies, in Jessamine county in 1796. The land was patented by William Hazelrigg in 1785. The place is ten miles southeast of Nicholasville, and is the land on which Col. Percival Butler lived when Gen. Wm. O. Butler was born in 1791. Col. Percival Butler had moved to this section because the Indians were less dangerous than in the northwest territory. The DeFoures, purchased the land from Colonel Hazelrigg, who lived and died in Bourbon county. They afterwards settled in Vevay, Indiana, and named the county Switzerland. They were very successful in Indiana, and became very wealthy. The deed and agreement between the DeFoures and Hazelrigg is recorded in Deed Book 1, page 34, in the Jessamine county clerk's office.

STONE HOUSE AT UNION MILLS, BUILT 1863.

The land chosen did not suit the varieties of the grape introduced. Hybridizing and crossing had not yet developed the excellent varieties of grapes which can now be grown in all parts of the United States. The European grapes were not adapted to the soil of Kentucky. All other fruits in the early settlement of the state, were produced in perfection. The cherries from Virginia and Pennsylvania, the apples and peaches from Virginia and North Carolina, and the pears from Virginia grew with marvelous rapidity, and were free from all diseases, and in twenty years after the settlement of Kentucky magnificent orchards were abundant in all parts of the Commonwealth. The Janet or Jeniton, the Limber Twig, the Horse apple, the Spice apple, the Pryor Red, Morton's Pearmain, the summer apple, propagated by slips brought over the mountains or produced from seed; found in the virgin soil of Kentucky, a vigor and an abundance of crops which satisfied the fullest wants of the new communities; but the grapes found wild in the forests of either Virginia or Kentucky were not utilized, or domesticated, and for a long while but few grapes were grown.

The Kentucky Vineyard Association was organized in Lexington in 1799, and seven hundred and fifty acres of land "lying in the big bend of the Kentucky river near the mouth of Hickman creek," were secured as the site for planting the vineyard. Great expectations were created. There was supposed to be no limit to the products and production of the state and if Europe could grow grapes, it was confidently assumed Kentucky could do likewise and better. The announcement of the association declared that, "in less than four years, wine may be drunk on the banks of the Kentucky, produced from the European stock."

The experiment was a dismal failure. Down in the swamps of North Carolina on the banks of the Catawba river was then growing the splendid Catawba grape and on the islands in James river in the midst of the forests and dense thickets the Norton's Va. (Virginia seedling) was yearly producing prolific crops, either of which, if transplanted to Kentucky, would have produced a vintage which would have done all the promoters of the Kentucky Vineyard Association desired and prophesied, but these early grape growers went to Europe rather than unto the

CROZIER'S MILL, ON JESSAMINE CREEK.

forests of America for their plants, and misfortunes were the result.

Another vineyard was started by some Swiss settlers on the banks of Jessamine creek near the Crozier Mill, but these, after some years of cultivation of the European varieties, abandoned their vines and homes and sought success in more congenial climes.

James DeFoure, who was at the head of the vineyard at mouth of Hickman creek, after his failure there, had the sagacity to discover that the European varieties were not adapted to this portion of the country. Alexander, a gardener for Governor Penn, had propagated before the war of the Revolution, a grape now called by his name, which was thought to be the celebrated grape of the Constantia colony from the Cape of Good Hope, but which in reality was a native variety. It was called also the Cape grape. DeFoure planted this vine at Vevay, Ind., and made the first successful attempt to establish a vineyard in America. His experiments in Jessamine county at least showed him the true path to success and wealth at Vevay.

Kentucky Pioneers.

God always provides men for occasions. In emergencies they invariably arise to fill the measure of the hour. Men are fashioned by their surroundings and they must be judged by the same standard.

The settlement of Kentucky and its wresting from the savage, made an unusual demand upon the Ruler of the Universe. It required a man unknown in the past history of the human race. It must be a man devoid of fear, filled with love of adventure, with an instinct of freedom as strong as that of the eagle; as self-reliant as the king of beasts, as hospitable as the Arab—who in the mighty desert despises the yoke of the oppressor and who protects with his life the guest who sits at his board; as patriotic as the Roman, as enterprising as the Carthaginian, as fearless as the Saxon, as defiant of death as the Turk; and, with all these, the subtle instincts of the Indian and his heroism under misfortune.

The Virginia cavalier, with his superb gallantry, ennobled by his lofty, gentlemanly instincts, would not meet the requirements. The Pennsylvania settler, with his indomitable patience and unfailing courage, fell short of the demands, and the sturdy Scotch-Irishman of North Carolina, with his unquenchable love of freedom backed by his superb bravery and uplifted by his abiding faith in God, was not equal to what the time and circumstances exacted of the men who should undertake the seemingly impossible task of conquering Kentucky.

As we turn backward one hundred years to commemorate the character, lives and virtues of our forefathers and to understand their sacrifices, their valor and their splendid achievements, let us briefly picture their surroundings.

These Kentucky pioneers were to conquer a land four hundred miles away from help or succor. It was an untrodden forest, with no roads or path except such as the buffalo in his migrations had trampled through the canebrake, or beasts of prey had traced in their seach for food. It had no human inhabitants, and its defense was by common consent imposed upon the savage red men, who claimed as their lands that vast country which stretches from the great lakes in the Northwest to the waters of the Tennessee, the Cumberland, Ohio, and Mississippi rivers; covering an area of over 300,000 square miles. No survey had marked its lines; he who traversed the solitude and depths of the forest must rely upon the stars, or nature's marks upon the trees, as his guide. All supplies must be carried on pack-horses or pack-men; powder and lead were to be transported over six hundred miles; not a single blade of wheat or stalk of corn as yet had sprung from its virgin and fertile soil. He who entered its domain must always be prepared to meet an alert, savage, brave and merciless foe. The cooing of the babe, the wail of defenseless women, or the appeal of the helpless prisoner, found no sympathy or response in the foe who defended this land. Death by the tomahawk or at the stake was the punishment the Indian meted to those who invaded his beloved hunting ground. As he asked and expected no quarter for himself, he gave none to his white foe. By day and by night the merciless warfare was to be waged. The coming of the morning sun only quickened and vitalized anew his barbarous plans, and its departure at night only gave time for more relentless resolve to drive out the intruder.

What race, what country, could produce men for such a task?

The settlement of Kentucky and its possession and the maintenance of the white man's supremacy was a part of God's plan to make the colonies free and to form in America a republic—a government of the people by the people, which was to be the great beacon light of freedom and the vanguard of mankind for the establishment in the world of true national liberty.

The thousand pioneers flung out into the wilds of Kentucky, with their log stations and forts, close by the homes of the savages, whom England was arming and teaching to slay white men and white women and white children—with their skill as woodsmen, with their courage as soldiers, and with their endurance as frontiersmen, and with their fierce hatred of the barbarous Indians, were worth ten thousand men on the Atlantic under leaders as great as even Washington, Greene, or La Fayette.

These Kentucky pioneers stayed savage invasion of Virginia and Pennsylvania. They kept back the herd of marauders and murderers, which in the wilds of Ohio, Indiana, and Illinois, longed for an opportunity to imbrue their hands in white men's blood, and the savage wrath which would have poured itself with irresistible tide over the settlements of the upper Ohio, Monongehela and the Kanawha, turned its savage and bitter force upon the stations in Kentucky. The thousands of brave and noble men, and still braver women, who from 1775 to 1783, died in the Kentucky wilderness, surrendered their lives to protect Virginia and Pennsylvania and stood the red men at bay, while the colonists were enabled to fight and defeat the British soldiers along the Atlantic coast.

Creation of the County of Jessamine.

1798 was the banner year for the creation of new counties. In 1792 seven had been formed, in 1793, one; in 1794 two, in 1796 six had been formed, and in 1798 thirteen were made, of which Jessamine was one, and the thirty-sixth in the state. It was carved entirely out of Fayette, and given one representative in the Legislature; while Fayette county retained six representatives, the number to which it had before the separation been entitled. The inequality of representation had not then been so fully recognized as afterwards. The whole population of Fayette county at the time of the division was about 18,000. Jessamine took off at least one-fourth of the population of Fayette and was given one member, while Fayette, with only three times the population of newly made Jessamine, had six, or twice the voice in legislation that was given her newly sent out daughter.

The creation of some counties was fought for years, but that of Jessamine produced but little hard feeling. Fayette had always been generous in the partition of territory. With 264,000 acres, after some protesting and legislative discussion, she surrendered 101,000 of it to create another county. Doubtless the retention of her six representatives had something to do with acquiescence in the division.

The men in the Senate those days, were men of wide, broad views. They were chosen not by districts, but from the state at large by the Commission formed for that purpose under the terms of the Constitution of 1792. The Senate then consisted of only eleven members. The Senator representing Fayette was James Campbell. In the House, Col. Robt. Patterson, John McDowell, John Parker, Walter Carr, Thos. Caldwell, ———— McGregor,

These were wide-gauge men, and private interest was subordinated to public interest and local benefit.

The real cause leading up to the formation of the county, was some friction between the officers of Fayette county and the people in the Marble creek neighborhood.

New counties were already being rapidly formed. Starting with nine in 1792, by the beginning of the session of 1798, sixteen new ones had been created, five of which—Scott, Shelby, Clark, Franklin and Montgomery—had been created close to Fayette.

Col. John Price was then a resident of the Marble creek district and he set about securing the formation of a new county. His influence with the Revolutionary soldiers, who then constituted so large a share of the legislators, was very strong. The battle over the act (creating the new county) continued from November 15 to December 19, 1798.

The journal of the House shows that the petition for the act, signed by the citizens demanding such an act, was on November 9, 1798, read and referred to the proper committee. The copy of the record and the extracts from the minutes of the Palladium tell the story of the struggle. They are as follows:

Journal.

Page 24.   Thursday, November 15, 1798.

Resolved, that the petition of sundry inhabitants of Fayette county, whose names are thereunto subscribed, setting forth that they labor under great inconveniences from their detached situation from their present seat of justice; and praying that the said county may be divided, agreeably to certain lines therein proposed, is reasonable.

The said resolution being read, was ordered to lie on the table.

Pages 80-81.   Tuesday, December 18, 1798.

Several petitions from sundry inhabitants of Fayette county, in opposition to the division thereof, were presented and ordered to lie on the table until the end of the present session.

The house then took up the bill for the division of Fayette county.

Page 85.   Wednesday, December 19, 1798.

Mr. Slaughter, from the joint committee of enrollments, reported that the committee had examined the enrolled bill entitled "An act for the division of Fayette county," and that the same was truly enrolled. Whereupon the speaker signed the said enrolled bill.

Ordered, that Mr. Slaughter inform the senate thereof.

Extracts from the Minutes of the Kentucky Legislature of 1798, in the Palladium.

November 9, 1798. A petition from Fayette praying for a division of that county, was read and referred to the proper committee.

November 20. Several reports were made and the following petitions were read and referred to the committee on propositions and grievances: A petition praying that a division of Fayette county may not take place.

November 23. The following bills were reported and read a first time: A bill for the division of Fayette.

November 24. In committee of the whole went through the bill for the division of Fayette, which, after some amendments, was ordered to be referred.

November 26. A bill for the division of Fayette was read a third time and passed. Yeas 24, Nays 15.

December 4. Concurred in the senate's amendments to the bill for the division of Fayette.

December 18. Several petitions from Fayette against the division of that county, were laid on the table to the end of the session.

Took up the bill for the division of Fayette with the governor's objections, which were agreed to.

Some very important assistance must have been rendered in securing the necessary legislation for the creation of the county by Col. Joseph H. Daveiss; for, in a letter written to him eight months after the passage of the act, Col. John Price proceeds to thank Colonel Davis for his services in this regard.

At this time Colonel Daveiss was a resident of Frankfort and later was United States District Attorney for Kentucky.

Extracts from Acts of the Legislature.

CHAPTER CXLIII.

An Act for the Division of Fayette County.

Approved December 19, 1798.

Section 1. Be it enacted by the General Assembly, That from and after the first day of February next, all that part of the county of Fayette, included in the following bounds, to wit: Beginning on the Woodford line, where it strikes the Kentucky river, near Todd's ferry; thence along said line half a mile north of John Allin's military survey; thence to the seven-mile tree, on Curd's road; thence to the eight-mile tree on Tate's creek road; thence along said last mentioned road to the Kentucky river; thence down the Kentucky river to the beginning, shall be one distinct county, and called and known by the name of Jessamine.

Sec. 2. A court for the said county shall be held by the Justices thereof, on the fourth Monday in every month (except those in which the court of quarter sessions are hereafter directed to be held) after said division shall take place, in like manner, as is provided by law in respect to other counties, and as shall be by their commissions directed.

Sec. 3. The Justices to be named in the commission of the peace for the said county of Jessamine, shall meet at the house of Fisher Rice, in the said county, on the first court day after said division shall take place, and having taken the oaths prescribed by law, and a sheriff being legally qualified to act, the justices shall proceed to appoint and qualify a clerk, and shall, together with the Justices of the court of quarter sessions for said county, fix upon a place for holding courts therein; then the courts shall proceed to erect the public buildings in such place; and until such buildings are completed, shall appoint such place for holding courts as they may think proper; provided, always, that the appointment of a place for erecting the public buildings shall not be made unless a majority of the Justices of the said courts concur therein.

Sec. 4. It shall be lawful for the sheriff of the county of Fayette to collect and make distress for any public dues or officers' fees, which shall remain unpaid by the inhabitants of the county at the time of such division, and shall be accountable for the same in like manner as if this act had not been made.

Sec. 5. The court of Fayette shall have jurisdiction in all actions or suits in law or equity, that shall be depending therein at the time of such division, and shall try and determine the same, issue process ,and award execution thereon.

Sec. 6. The court of quarter session for the said county of Jessamine, shall be held, annually, on the fourth Monday in January, March, July and October.

Sec. 7. The said county of Jessamine shall send one representative to the General Assembly, and the county of Fayette shall retain six representatives.

This act shall commence and be in force from and after the passage thereof.

5

From Vol. XI. of the Statute Law of Kentucky, printed at Frankfort in 1810.

CHAPTER CCIII.

An Act to Amend the Act, Entitled "An Act for the Division of Fayette County."

Approved December 19, 1799.

Whereas, it is represented to this General Assembly, that disputes have arisen between the inhabitants of the counties of Fayette and Jessamine, in ascertaining the true line of division; and also in the collection and manner of appropriating that part of the levy which was levied by the County Court of Fayette, on the inhabitants now in the county of Jessamine; for remedy whereof—

Section 1. Be it enacted by the General Assembly, that the dividing line run by the surveyor of Jessamine county, is hereby ratified and confirmed.

Sec. 2. And be it further enacted, that the County Courts of Fayette and Jessamine, shall, on their respective parts, in the month of March, next, appoint, each, a commissioner, who are hereby authorized to examine the records of Fayette county, and enquire into the situation of levies and appropriations heretofore made by the County Court of Fayette; and if upon such examination, it shall appear to the said commissioners, that there is, or ought to be, a deposit, amounting to more than the claims given into the said County Court of Fayette, the said court of Fayette is hereby required to pay to the court of Jessamine county, for the use of said county, their proportion of said deposit.

This act shall commence and be in force from and after the first day of February next.

The establishment of the new county demanded a name.

Up to this time the thirty-five counties created had all been named for soldiers, pioneers, or a statesman, with one exception, and that was Ohio county, the thirty-fifth, which was named for the great river which marks the northern boundary of Kentucky for 700 miles and had been called by the Indians, the Ohio, "The Beautiful River." Cumberland was called for Cumberland river, but the river had before been named by Dr. Thos. Walker for the Duke of Cumberland. Such names as Jefferson, Fayette (La

Fayette), Lincoln, Nelson, Mercer, Madison, Mason, Woodford, Washington, Scott, Shelby, Logan, Clark, Hardin, Greene, Franklin, Campbell, Bullitt, Christian, Bracken, Warren, Garrard, Fleming, Pulaski, Pendleton, Boone, Henry, Gallatin, and Muhlenberg, represented a full share of the patriotism, glory, bravery, wisdom and exploits of the people of the United States prior to 1798, and, with so many great heroes still unrewarded, it required both determination and courage to break away from the long line of precedents and call the county by the simple and beautiful name of a flower.

To Col. John Price was undoubtedly given the privilege of naming the new municipality.

Jessamine creek—one hundred years ago a stream of large volume and great beauty—rises near the line of the R. N. I. & B. Railroad, close to the station called Nealton and about half a mile from where the Nicholasville & Versailles turnpike crosses, and on the land now owned by Pleasant Cook, Esq. Along its banks grew the jessamine in richest profusion. This flower was found in great abundance in many parts of the territory embraced by the new county. The name had been given to the creek by the pioneers, and the beauty of the plant and the beauty of the name so impressed the early settlers that they called this beautiful stream Jessamine creek. It is about twenty miles long and empties into the Kentucky river.

Colonel Price asked that the new county should be called Jessamine.

The county, always full of romance, in some way heard the story of Jessamine Douglas, which was to the effect that Jessamine Douglas, the beautiful daughter of a Scotch settler, was one day sitting upon the bank which overhangs the source of this creek, and while, in maidenly contemplation, gazing into the depths of the water, an Indian cautiously and silently stole upon her and sunk his tomahawk into her head and then tore her beautiful auburn locks from her head, with his scalping knife.

This story is given the flavor of truth by its insertion in Collins' History of Kentucky. See Vol. 2, page 399. The author goes on to say that the land about the head of the creek was settled by the father of Jessamine Douglas. There is no foundation for that pathetic and dramatic incident. The land at the head of Jessamine creek was not settled by Douglas, but by Michael Cogar, and this historical tradition has not even a shadow of foundation.

The letter of Col. John Price, quoted below, written within eight months of the legislative creation of the county, settles, beyond all cavil, that the county was called from Jessamine creek and the flower, and not from Jessamine Douglas. The story of the beautiful Scotch girl and her tragic end, has been told so often and has been so honestly and faithfully believed by the people of the county, and it has in it so much of that tragic and bloody character which marked Kentucky's early history, that it is both ungenerous and unkind to destroy and disrupt the faith which for nearly one hundred years has reposed with unfaltering trust in the pathetic story.

As Colonel Meade did not come to Jessamine county until 1796, and as both the East and West Forks of Jessamine creek were known and traveled in 1774 and 1775 and on down to 1790, and lands described and surveyed by the creek, and its course and meanderings laid down on Filson's and other maps and plats long prior to 1790; it is impossible for the creek to have been named for Jessamine Douglas, who, under no circumstances, did she come with Colonel Meade, could have arrived in Kentucky prior to 1796. The Williams deposition, the Watkins journal, and Filson's map show that Jessamine creek was a well known and named stream prior to 1789.

The Price Letter about the Formation of the County.

Barbour Home, Jessamine county,
November 13, 1820.

My Esteemed Friend: I have read your favor of October 6th with much pleasure. The county of Jessamine was surveyed by my friend, Maj. Frederick Zimmerman. I think he commenced his work in May, 1796, but the county was not organized as a county until February 14th. In August the next year I was chosen as a member of the General Assembly by the county—without opposition.

The name Jessamine was selected from a flower that grows on many creeks in the county.

The villainy practiced in the Marble creek neighborhood by the constables and other petty officers of Fayette county, induced me to make an effort to form a new county, as I had known for several years that it was becoming impossible for my neighbors to get along on peaceable terms with officers who took pleasure in arresting and putting in prison men and women for the pitiful sum of $5. The only bed of straw, the only horse, the only cow, or pig of a neighbor, was leveyed on and sold at Lexington by the sheriff, but we now have a new set of officers and they are much better men than the others, who have so long annoyed my neighbors with their villainy.

Present my compliments to Mr. Bowman and John Marshall.

Your obedient servant,

JOHN PRICE.

Col. John Price induced many of his Virginia friends to settle in the Marble creek neighborhood. The following letter to Lewis Tapp will be extremely interesting, as he has many descendants in Jessamine county:

Lexington, Ky., May 10, 1805.

Dear Sir and Friend: I have received yours of April 2d. I take great pleasure in informing you that if you have a desire to leave Virginia and settle in Kentucky I would advise you to pay a visit to this portion of Kentucky. Jessamine county was formed eight years ago. I settled in the limits of the county in 1788. The population is 5,400. The surface of the land for the most part gently undulating, rising here and there into hills and moderate elevations. The timber is white ash, hickory, hackberry, elm, white oak, also white and black walnut. Besides this variety of timber in the county, cedar trees, yellow poplar, beech and cherry is scattered over various parts of the county. The principal creeks in the county are Hickman and Jessamine. There are also numerous smaller streams well distributed throughout the county. You can buy good land in this town for $20 per acre and in Elkhorn first-class land is worth from $10 to $12 per acre.

As I am just in the act of going to Nashville in Jesse Cogar's flat-boat at Frankfort, I trust you will make us a visit soon.

Your old friend,

JOHN PRICE.

Lewis Tapp, Staunton, Augusta county, Va.

In response to this invitation Lewis Tapp came to Kentucky and settled in the Marble creek neighborhood, four miles from the residence of Colonel Price. He raised a large family of great respectability, and died in 1822. Tapp's Branch is named in memory of him.

On the 22d day of April, 1799, an order was entered fixing the seat of justice for Jessamine county at the place now occupied by the town of Nicholasville. The following order, entered by six of the justices of the peace, determined the county seat:

"At a court began and held for the county of Jessamine at the house of Jonas Davenport in said county, on Monday, the 22d day of April, 1799,

"Present, ——— Lewis, Thos. Caldwell, Gab'l Mattison, Geo. Walker, Jas. Johnson and ——— Price, gentlemen justices.

"Ordered that the seat of justice for Jessamine county be permanently fixed on the lands of Thos. Caldwell and Chefley Gates on the Hickman road."

The blank before the name of Lewis should have been filled with William, and the blank before the name of Price should have been filled with the name of William.

As there were nine justices, it required five for a majority.

The original act creating Jessamine county, directed that the location of the county seat should be determined only by a majority of the justices. William Scott, Hugh Chrisman, and John Freeman were not present at the time of the entering of this order, but Thos. Caldwell, one of the justices who voted, was joint owner with Chesley Gates of the twenty-five acres which had been laid out by Rev. John Metcalf, on the 16th of September, 1798.

The county had not been formed at the time of the first survey of Nicholasville, but was only created on the 19th of December, three months afterwards; nor had the town of Nicholasville been officially recognized until the 26th day of August, 1799. On that day, proceeding under the statutes of Kentucky then in force for the establishment of towns, another order was entered, on the motion of Thos. Caldwell and Chesley Gates, which is as follows:

At a court begun and held for the county of Jessamine at the court house thereof on Monday the 26th day of August, 1799.

Present, Will Lewis, James Johnston, Geo. Walker and John Lewis, gentlemen, justices.

On the motion of Thomas Caldwell and Chesley Gates it is ordered that a town be established on their lands lying on the Hickman road, at the place where the seat of justice for said county is established, to be called and known by the name of Nicholasville and bounded as follows to wit: Beginning at a stake in Caldwell's field running W. 12 deg. E. 87 poles to a stake; thence S. 78 deg. E. 36.84 poles to a stake; thence S. 12 deg. W. 42 poles to a stake; thence S. 78 deg. E. 14 poles; thence N. 12 deg. E. 2 poles; thence S. 78 deg. E. 3 poles; thence S. 12 deg. W. 5 poles; thence N. 78 deg. W. 17 poles; thence S. 12 deg. W. 42 poles; thence N. 78 poles W. 36.84 poles to the beginning. And it is further ordered that Joseph Crockett, William Shrieve, Richard Young, James Johnson, Gabrl. Madison, William Robards, Nicholas Lewis, James Davenport, Patrick Gray, Phil. Webber and Chesley Gates be appointed trustees of the said town.

These trustees were simply appointed for the benefit of the land owners. It was their duty to make disposition of the lots in the town of Nicholasville, which now for the first time was officially recognized as the name of the county seat; so that in celebrating the centennial of Nicholasville on September 16, 1898, it is a celebration of the centennial of its survey, rather than of its first official existence and recognition.

The contest in regard to the location of the seat of justice began even before the creation of the county by legislative authority. The establishment of a new county had been under discussion throughout the territory for quite a while. The petition which had been prepared for the legislature and the agitation of the question concerning the existence of a new county, had been more or less discussed by the people within the limits of the proposed county. It was difficult, of course, to determine exactly where the line would run, but the tremendous bend in the Kentucky river—which forms almost a horse-shoe—rendered the location of the county line very easy, as it was only necessary to run from the Kentucky river on the one side, to the Kentucky river on the other side, in order to cut off a county of reasonable proportions.

Quarter Session Judges.

The first session of the Court of Quarter Sessions was held at the house of Fisher Rice, in the county of Jessamine, on the 25th day of March, 1789. Governor Garrard commissioned Joseph Crockett, William Shreve and Richard Young as justices of the Court of Quarter Sessions.

The Court of Quarter Sessions then heard all matters except criminal matters, and these were heard in the District Court at Lexington. These three gentlemen were all present at Fisher Rice's on the said day, and they unanimously appointed Samuel H. Woodson, clerk of the Jessamine County and Quarter Session Court. Mr. Woodson immediately entered upon the discharge of his duties, with Joseph Crockett as his security, his bond being in the sum of $1,000. Joshua Lewis was on the same day appointed by the Court of Quarter Sessions state's attorney to prosecute causes for the Commonwealth within Jessamine county.

The first lawyers to qualify in the county for the practice of law were Joseph Lewis, William McDowell, Samuel Venable, and Fielding L. Turner. These were all on that day qualified for practice in the Quarter Session Courts. Fielding L. Turner was the father of the Hon. Oscar Turner, so long a distinguished member of Congress from the First District of Kentucky. He removed from Kentucky to New Orleans, where his son Oscar was born in 1829.

On the following day, March 26, 1799, the first session of the court was held, the members of the court having qualified on the previous day.

The house of Fisher Rice was used as a place for holding Quarter Session Courts for several years. Courts were also held at the house of Samuel H. Watson, the clerk of said court, who then lived on the farm now the property of the Shelys.

In those days it was necessary to appoint commissioners to value certain lands taken by the sheriff under execution. John Hawkins, Patrick Gray, Joseph Chrisman, John McKinney, and Jonas Davenport were appointed said commissioners, and this was the first order ever made by court of record in Jessamine county.

The second grand jury of Jessamine county empaneled in

the summer of 1799, had for its foreman Manoah Singleton, and among its members were Francis Lowens, Benjamin Netherland and Samuel Rice. The first indictment for selling whisky was found at this term of court against William Patterson, and the information on which this presentment or indictment was found was given by two members of the grand jury, Frances Lowens and S. Walters.

The first man who ever took out license to keep a tavern in Jessamine county was Maj. Benjamin Netherland. A free negro, Bob Speed, was also a prominent caterer in those days, and he also took out a license to keep tavern, and some of the most prominent men, especially among the lawyers, have dined at his tavern, which was at a corner on Main street immediately opposite the court house.

First Court.

The first court held in Jessamine county was on the 25th of February, 1799. The members of the court assembled at the house of Fisher Rice, who lived in the field opposite the Kleber Price place, and where Mrs. Bridget O'Connell now lives. The record says: "At said time and place commissions were produced from Governor Garrard, directed to William Lewis, Thos. Caldwell, William Scott, Gabriel Madison, George Walker, William Price, James Johnson, John Lewis, John Berry, Hugh Chrisman and John Freeman, appointing them Justices of the Peace in and for the county of Jessamine, whereupon William Lewis, Esq., first named in the commission aforesaid, administered the several oaths prescribed by law, to Thomas Caldwell, William Scott, Gabriel Madison, George Walker, William Price, James Johnson, John Lewis, John Berry, Hugh Chrisman and John Freeman; and Thomas Caldwell, Esq., administered the said oaths to William Lewis, and then the court was held for the said county."

"Present the gentlemen within named. Charles West, Esq., produced a commission from the Governor, James Garrard, appointing him sheriff for the county aforesaid, which, being read, the said West took the several oaths prescribed by law, and, together with Major Dickenson, Frances Lowens, Patrick Gray and

John Scott as sureties, executed their bond to the Governor of the Commonwealth, in the penalty of $3,000, conditioned as the law directs for the due performance of duties."

The court then proceeded to the appointment of a clerk, one Samuel Hughes Woodson, who was appointed Clerk, pro tem., who, thereupon, took the several oaths prescribed by the laws of this state, and the Constitution of the United States, and, together with Joseph Crockett and Andrew McGill entered into bond to the Governor in the penalty of $1,000, as the law directs, which bond was ordered to be recorded."

"County Surveyor, Frederick Zimmerman, produced in court a commission from Governor Garrard, appointing him surveyor of this county, whereupon he executed bond in the penalty of $2,000, with James Curtin and Frances Lowens as securities, conditioned according to law. He took the several oaths prescribed by the laws of this state and the Constitution of the United States."

At this meeting the first bridge ever constructed in Jessamine county was ordered to be let. The minutes says:

"John Lewis and Benjamin Bradshaw are appointed to let and contract for the building of a bridge on Curd's road, near the ferry, which contract to be made by letting to the highest bidder." Curd's Ferry had been established at the mouth of Dick's river by the general legislature in 1786. Daniel Mitchell presented his commission as coroner, and qualified as such.

The first lawyers admitted to practice in the Jessamine County Court were Joshua Lewis and Fielding Turner, who separately produced in court, on the above day, their license, properly authenticated, as the law directs, and were, thereupon, admitted to practice.

First Circuit Court.

The Jessamine Circuit Court was organized in 1803, and its first order was the appointment of a clerk. Samuel H. Woodson received this appointment, and held the office until 1819, when he resigned. The following orders will show the Constitution of the court, and also the first petition filed in the court:

"April Circuit Court, 1803.

"Be it remembered that in pursuance of an act of the General Assembly, entitled, 'An Act to establish Circuit Courts, and an act entitled an act to amend an act entitled an act to establish Circuit Courts,' the Honorable Samuel McDowell, Circuit Judge, attended at the court house of the county of Jessamine, on the 18th day of April, 1803, being the third Monday. Present, the Honorable Samuel McDowell, Circuit Judge.

"It is ordered that Fielding L. Turner, Esq., be appointed clerk, pro tempore, to this court, who, thereupon, took the several oaths prescribed by law, and executed his bond, with Samuel H. Woodson and Joseph Crockett his security in the penalty of £1000, conditioned as directed by law.

"It is ordered that Samuel H. Woodson be appointed clerk to this court, and that the pro tempore appointment made by the court this day, be discontinued, and, thereupon, the said Samuel H. Woodson took the several oaths required by law, and executed his bond, with Joseph Crockett and William Lewis his securities, in the penalty of £1,000.

First Order Entered in Civil Action.

"At a Circuit Court, began and held for the county of Jessamine, at the court-house thereof, on the 18th day of July, 1803: Present, the Honorable Samuel McDowell, Circuit Judge, and Richard Young, Esq.:

James Dunn,

vs.

Nicholas Lewis.

Debt.

Be it remembered that heretofore, that is to say, on the 13th day of June, one thousand, eight hundred and two, James Dunn, by Wm. McDowell, his attorney, applied for and obtained from the clerk's office of the late court of Quarter Sessions for the county aforesaid, the Commonwealth's writ of capias ad respondendum, which, together with the motion of plaintiff, by his attorney aforesaid, it was ordered that the said Deft. should appear at the next rules, enter special bail and plead to the plaintiff's action, or that judgment would be granted the plaintiff for the debt in the declaration mentioned and what damages he hath sustained in the premises and a writ of enquiry awarded him to have the same assessed by a jury of the bystanders at the next court."

      *   *   *   *   *   *   *

"Jessamine county, Sct.:

"James Dunn, by his attorney, complains of Nicholas Lewis in custody, etc., of a plea that he render to him the sum of seventy-two pounds, current money, current money of Kentucky, which he owes and unjustly detains, for that, whereas, the said defendant on the thirtieth of May, 1800, at the parish of Kentucky, and county aforesaid, by his certain note, in writing, sealed with his seal and to the court now here shown, eighteen months after the date aforesaid promised and obligated himself to the plaintiff to pay him the sum of thirty-six pounds, for the payment of which said sum the said defendant bound himself in the penal sum of seventy-two pounds like money, yet said defendant not regarding his obligation hath not paid the said sum of thirty-six pounds, although often required, by means whereof an action hath accrued to have and demand of him the said sum of seventy-two pounds, but the said defendant, to pay the same or any part thereof, although often required the same to pay, hath hitherto refused, and still doth refuse, wherefore the said James Dunn says he is injured and hath sustained damage to the value of 72 pounds, and therefore, he sues, etc.   Wm. McDowell, A. P.; Jno. Doe and R. Roe, P. P."

First Will.

The first will recorded in Jessamine county was that of Charles Weber. It is only interesting because the first of its kind ever placed upon the records:

First Will, recorded August, 1779.

"In the name of God, Amen.   Charles Weber, of Jessamine county and state of Kentucky, being in sound mind, praised be

God for the same, do give and dispose of all my worldly goods and estate in a manner and form as follows:

"First, my desire is that all my just debts be paid by my ex· ecutors, hereafter mentioned, and in the following manner: First I wish my mare and colt to be converted to my debts, and if they should not be sufficient, my negro fellow, Booker, is to be hired for the balance till paid, as my executors think most expedient. Then the said negro to be hired on till the profits amount to sixty pounds. The first forty pounds arising is to be delivered to my brother William Webber, for his own use and his heirs forever. The other twenty pounds to be given to my brother, Philip Weber, for his own use and his heirs during life, and then the said negro to be delivered to my brother John Webber, for his use and his heirs during the life of the said negro, or the said John Webber or his attorney.

"Applying for the same, I do also give and bequeath unto my brother Archie Webber, my negro boy by the name of Bill, to him and his heirs forever. I also appoint and ordain James Owens, and Robert Cohoun, of Jessamine county, executors of this, my last will and testament, desiring that the acting executors to my estate shall, in lieu of my expenses to them, recover with my other debts that is to be paid, twenty dollars each for their services in cash out of my estate.

"In witness whereof I have hereunto set my hand and affixed my seal this the seventeenth day of June, one thousand, seven hundred and ninety-nine. Signed, sealed and published, and do declare this to be my last will and testament, revoking all other wills before named by or for me.

"CHARLES WEBBER. (Seal.)

"Rosin Brashers,
"Jacob Rice,
"Peter Akins."

The First Marriage.

Jesse Hughes and Mary Nicholson were married by Nathaniel Harris on March 14, 1799.

The First Baptist Meeting-house.

It is difficult to establish the exact location of a Baptist church in the very earliest settlement of the county near Clear creek. This was the church at which Lewis Craig frequently preached; it is near what is now known as the Jack Cunningham property, or the Fisher place. It was called Mount Moriah, and in early times was a very important burying-ground. Joel Watkins, in his diary, mentions the fact of having attended services at that point several times, and there seeing large congregations. It was established about the same time as the Ebenezer church, but the latter is undoubtedly the oldest church organization in Jessamine county.

County Judges under the Constitution of 1849.

Alexander Wake, served eight years; W. S. Scott, died in office; John A. Willis, appointed, served from 1858 to 1859; Henry J. Campbell, elected, and served four years; Richard Ferguson, served one term; Melvin T. Lowry, served four years; James G. Bruce, served one term, died in office; Tucker Woodson, elected in 1872, died in office in 1874; W. H. Phillips, present County Judge, has held the office for twenty-three years.

County Attorneys: John Dishman, John S. Bronaugh, Wm. R. Welch, Wm. Byrd Woodson, Geo. R. Pryor, Benjamin P. Campbell, Benjamin A. Crutcher, John H. Welch, E. B. Hoover, N. L. Bronaugh, J. Willard Mitchell.

Under the Constitution of Kentucky in 1799, the oldest Justice of the Peace was made Sheriff. Charles West, first Sheriff; Bartholomew Kinnard, deputy; Benj. Nicholson; Thos. Butler, deputy; Lewis Singleton, Andrew McCampbell; James H. McCampbell; John Perry, Sr.; James Wilmore; Campbell Wilmore; Harrison Daniel; W. P. Daniel; William Bronaugh; W. P. Daniel; Jerry Dickerson; Newton Dickerson; John Butler, deputy; M. T. Lowry; Thomas E. West, his deputy; Geo. T. Chrisman.

Members of the Kentucky Senate and House of Representatives.

Senate of the Commonwealth of Kentucky: Joseph Crockett, 1800-1804; William Bledsoe, 1806-1810; George Walker, 1810-1814; George I. Brown, 1829-1834; William Clark, 1838-1842; Tucker Woodson, 1842-1846, 1853-1857; A. L. McAfee, 1869-1873; E. R. Sparks, 1882-1886; Thos. R. Welch, 1896-1898. From Jessamine and Woodford counties, Wm. Vawter, 1808; Richard C. Graves, 1850.

House of Representatives, Commonwealth of Kentucky: Joshua Lewis, 1799, 1803, 1804; John Scott, 1800; George Walker, 1805, 1807, 1808, 1809, 1810; William Price, 1801, 1802; John Hawkins, 1806, 1811; William Caldwell, 1812, 1813, 1814, 1815, 1816, 1818, 1820, 1822; Wm. Walker, 1817; Samuel H. Woodson, 1819-25; James Clarke, 1820; Richard E. Meade, 1822; George I. Brown, 1824, 1829, 1832, 1850; Harrison Daniel, 1826-27; John Cunningham, 1828; Courtney R. Lewis, 1830; David M. Woodson, 1831; Dr. J. W. S. Mitchell, 1833-34; Tucker Woodson, 1835-36-37-40; George S. Shanklin, 1838-44-61-65; Alexander Wake, 1839; George T. Chrisman, 1841; James McCampbell, 1842-45-55-57; James H. Lowry, 1843; Joseph W. Thompson, 1846; Joseph C. Christopher, 1847-49; John M. Reynolds, 1848; James C. Wilmore, 1851-53; Larkin Fain, 1853 55; Allen L. McAfee, 1857-59; Wm. Fisher, 1859-61-65-67; Thomas T. Cogar, 1867-71; James H. McCampbell, 1871-73; died December 25, 1872, was succeeded by Wm. Brown, 1873; N. D. Miles, 1874-75; Samuel R. Overstreet, 1875-77; Dr. John C. Welch, 1871-78-79-80; J. N. Mattingly, 1881-82; E. T. Lillard, 1883-84; Thomas A. Davis, 1885-86; W. T. Jones, 1887-88; J. H. Welch, 1889-90-91-92; George W. Goode, 1893-94; R. S. Perry, 1895-96; C. A. Wilson, 1897-98.

Nicholasville.

On Saturday, September 16, 1798, Rev. John Metcalf took the initial steps to locate Nicholasville. At the time of the location of the town he called it after Hon. George Nicholas. At that time several roads, well-located, converged at the point. The settlers

from Jessamine and Hickman creeks, which were then the most
thickly populated parts of the territory embraced in Jessamine
county, were in the habit of traveling between these two creeks.
The road which then ran to Lexington ran substantially on the
line of the turnpike and its traces are still distinctly visible to the
eye at various points along the turnpike. This was true of the
roads which ran from Nicholasville and what is known as Russell's tavern. In the location of the turnpike, very little of this

WM. O. BUTLER.

old line was used. This was equally true of the road to Sulphur
Well, but the roads crossed at that time north and south and east
and west, exactly where Main street and Maincross street now in-
tersect each other.

The inducing causes which led to the location were, first, four
large springs, which were presumed then, to be never-failing.
These all were within the limits of the twenty-five acres laid out
into the town, and second, to the fact of the road passing from
Lexington and Danville, and from East Hickman to Jessamine,

crossing at right angles at the point. Little Jessamine, or East Jessamine, was then a stream of more importance than now. Rising about a mile above and fed by other streams along the line, it became quite a volume for a creek by the time it passed through the borders of the newly laid out village.

It was quite a while after the town was established before much trade centered within its limits. The people who first lived in the town were farmers in the immediate neighborhood.

There was no post-office in Nicholasville for several years after its location. The mails were carried on horseback between Lexington and Danville and Lancaster and Harrodsburg. Its location was not made without clashes of personal interest. Samuel H. Woodson, who was then a lawyer, desired to establish the town where the Shely place now stands, about one mile south of the present location, while Frederick Zimmerman sought to have the town established about three-quarters of a mile north, on top of the hill, just beyond the Duncan farm. It required several years to get the matter finally settled, and it was largely due to the great influence as well as the persistent efforts of Rev. John Metcalf that the town was laid out in its present location.

A large proportion of the settlers in Nicholasville were from the state of Virginia, and a few from North and South Carolina.

Nathaniel McLean, who married Catherine Blackford in Morris county, New Jersey, was a brother-in-law of Benjamin Blackford. McLean built the first log cabin in Nicholasville on the lot now owned by Mr. Burdine. Blackford himself had settled on the farm just north of Nicholasville, now owned by his grandson, Robert Duncan, in 1783.

John McLean, Associate Justice of the United States Supreme Court, lived for quite a while in his youth on the Duncan farm. When four years old his father moved to Morgantown, Va., and thence came to Nicholasville, Ky., and subsequently moved to Warren county, Ohio. He remained in Jessamine until he was about sixteen years of age. In 1812 he was eected to Congress from the Cincinnati district. He refused the nomination for the United States Senate in 1815, but was elected a Judge of the Supreme Court of Ohio, in 1816. In 1821 he was appointed postmaster general and in 1829 he was appointed Associate Justice of the United States Supreme Court. He was a

6

man of great ability and great force of character. He delivered a dissenting opinion in the Dred Scott case, declaring that slavery was contrary to right and that it had its origin in power alone, and that in this country it was sustained only by local law. He died in Cincinnati on the 4th of April, 1861.

Within the memory of persons living, there was an old well dug by Judge McLean's father on the Duncan place. It was east of the house about 200 yards.

The next settler in the town was Maj. Benjamin Netherland. Shortly after the battle of Blue Licks, in 1782, he put up a log cabin on the lot now occupied by the county jail, and adjoining it shortly afterwards, another log cabin. This was subsequently replaced by the Mingo tavern. The tavern house he erected in 1793, and it was still used by him as a hotel at the time of his death, in 1838. Previous to October, 1801, there was no post-office nearer to Nicholasville than Lexington. On the first of September of that year Major Netherland wrote to the postmaster general urging the establishment of a mail road from Lexington, Nicholasville Lancaster and Harrodsburg, and by way of Frankfort and Richmond.

Joseph Habersham, of Georgia, was postmaster-general. He wrote the following letter to Major Netherland:

"Your letter was received. Enclosed you have an advertisement, inviting proposals for carrying the mail from Nicholasville to Lexington, Frankfort, Lancaster and Richmond, and I shall be glad to receive yours. Mr. Clay has recommended your appointment to the office of postmaster of Nicholasville, and I have decided upon your appointment unless you decline, and wish to avoid the trouble. I am

"Your obedient servant,

"J. HABERSHAM, P. M. G."

This letter Major Netherland answered as follows:

"Nicholasville, Ky., Sept. 21, 1801.

"Your favor of the 4th of August came to hand while I was in Lexington, with enclosed advertisement for carrying the mails from Nicholasville to Lexington, Frankfort, Richmond, Harrodsburg and Lancaster. It is the earnest wish of all the inhabitants of this county that a postoffice be established in Nicholasville, which is twelve miles from Lexington, over a totorous mud road, in winter. If it should be thought expedient to establish a post-office in the village and my name annexed to it, I will accept. I am, sir,

"Your obedient servant,

"B. NETHERLAND."

In answer to this Major Netherland received the following letter:

"Washington City, Sept. 20, 1801.

"Major Benjamin Netherland:

"From information I have received I conclude it will be agreeable to you to accept the office of postmaster at Nicholasville. You will receive herewith two packets containing a copy of a law for regulating postoffices, with forms and directions, a key for unlocking the mail portmanteau, a table of postoffices, and the necessary blanks. The enclosed bond you will be pleased to execute with sufficient surety or sureties and then return the same together with a note, after they have been duly certified by the Justice of the Peace, before whom you shall take and subscribe them. When they are received at this office a commission will be duly forwarded. You can commence business as soon as your bond is executed and forwarded, if you think proper

Your obedient servant,

"J. HABERSHAM, P. M. G."

It is evident that these two letters crossed each other on the post road, between Washington and Nicholasville. Major Netherland remained postmaster at Nicholasville for more than twenty years, and kept the postoffice in the Mingo tavern.

Col. George Nicholas and Rev. John Metcalf were close friends. Four years before Nicholasville was located he wrote Colonel Nicholas the following letters:

"January 14, 1794.

"Hon. Geo. Nicholas:

"I have lately received from you two of your kind letters and would have answered them before now, but I have taken charge of Bethel Academy, and have been so confined for the last two weeks in fitting up suitable places of abode for some of my pupils that I have greatly neglected my private affairs, and especially that portion of them which you are attending to in Lexington."

　　　　　　　　　　　"Jessamine county, Ky., Sept. 16, 1798.
"Hon. Geo. Nicholas:

"It afforded me great happiness to hear that you had returned in safety and health to your family and friends.　I expected to hear from you more frequently, but, I suppose, the multiplicity of care and busines prevent your devoting much of your time to letters, save what you wrote to me and Joseph Crockett.　But now that you have arrived at home I shall expect to hear from you soon and as often as usual.　I must inform you that I have named our county seat Nicholasville in honor of you.　I was all day laying off three streets to-day, and my nerves are very much affected by the severe labors in the wet weather.　These being the circumstances under which I write you this hasty note, I fear it will have but poor claims upon your time, but I can not help it.
　　　　　　　　　　　　"Your friend,
　　　　　　　　　　　　　　"JOHN METCALF."

The contest about the location of the county seat must have been carried on for some time and quite vigorously.　On the 7th of October, 1803, Mr. Metcalf wrote the following letter:

"Charles West, High Sheriff,
　　　　　"Jessamine county:

"My Dear Sir—I write to assure you that we have succeeded, amid much foolish opposition from Samuel H. Woodson, County and Circuit Court Clerk, and Mr. Frederick Zimmerman, County Surveyor, in locating our county seat.　Mr. Woodson wanted to locate the town near his residence, one mile south of the first survey, which I made six years ago, including twenty-five acres. Mr. Zimmerman wanted the town to include the residence of Fisher Rice, which is one mile north.　I am now convinced that through your efforts and Mr. Caldwell's and mine, I have defeated Mr. Woodson and Mr. Zimmerman in their foolish opposition to the present location, which is more suitable and more

convenient to roads east and west to the Kentucky river. A supply of good water was another great advantage which we had over
the other two places. There are four good springs of water that
never run dry. This convenience to good water, more than any
other consideration, caused me to select this location in preference
to the other places. I thank you for the assistance you gave me
in defeating a claim as foolish as it was selfish. I am pleased to
learn that Mr. Zimmerman, as 'legal surveyor,' has surveyed
the present site, which was legally recorded last year (1802). We
have twenty heads of families erecting houses on a number of lots.
Come and see me soon."

First Charter.

The first charter of Nicholasville was passed in 1812, and is as
follows:

CHAPTER CCCCIV.

An act authorizing the trustees of the town of Nicholasville
to sell real property in said town, under certain restrictions:

Approved February 8, 1812.

Section 1. Be it enacted by the General Assembly of the
Commonwealth of Kentucky, that the trustees of the town of
Nicholasville, in the county of Jessamine, shall have power to
levy a tax on the real property in said town, in proportion to the
value of lots, not exceeding one hundred cents for every hundred
dollars; and the trustees, or a majority of them, shall have power
to cause an assessment to be made of the lots in said town, in order to enable them to fix the sum to be paid by the proprietors or
occupants of the lots, provided, however, that a majority of the
trustees shall concur in levying the tax.

Sec. 2. And the trustees, or a majority of them, may appoint
some fit person to collect the tax; and should the owner or occu-
pant, refuse to pay the tax for the space of three months after the
amount of the tax is fixed as herein provided, in that case the
collector shall, after giving thirty days' notice by advertisement
at three of the most public places in said town, expose for sale the
lot or lots, or so much thereof, as will be sufficient to pay the tax
and cost of sale; but the owner or owners of the lot or lots, his,

her or their heirs, executors or administrators, shall have twelve months from the time of sale of the lot or lots, or parts of lots, to redeem the lot or lots, or part of lots, by paying to the purchaser the amount of the lot or lots, or part of lots sold, with 100 per cent thereon; and the collector shall be entitled to 7 per cent on the amount of the tax collected under this act.

Sec. 3. And the trustees of the town shall have full power to convey to the purchaser, by deed or deeds of conveyance, the lots, or parts of lots, sold under the provisions of this act, and not redeemed within the time allowed for redemption, which shall vest in the purchaser, his, her or their heirs, or assignee, or assigns, all the right, title and interest of the owner, or owners, in and to the lot or lots, or parts of lots, saving, however, to infants, femes covert, and persons of unsound minds, a right to redeem within three years after their several disabilities shall be removed, or come of age; provided, however, that the collector shall not be allowed to sell any lot or part of a lot where sufficiency of personal estate can be found on such lot or lots, or parts of lots, to satisfy the tax due; which the collector is hereby authorized to seize and sell.

Second Charter.

The second charter of Nicholasville was passed in 1823. It was as follows:

CHAPTER DXLVII.

An Act to Regulate the Town of Nicholasville.

Approved November 18, 1823.

Section 1. Be it enacted by the General Assembly of the Commonwealth of Kentucky, that the free, white male inhabitants of the town of Nicholasville, who shall have attained the age of tweny-one years and upwards, shall meet annually in each year, at the court-house in said town, on the first Monday in May, and elect seven trustees for said town, which trustees shall possess the qualifications hereinafter mentioned; and a majority of them so elected, shall be sufficient to constitute a board, who shall be, and they are hereby, authorized to make such by-laws for the government and regulation of said town as to them shall seem proper, not inconsistent with the Constitution and laws of this state. The said trustees shall have full power and authority to impose a poll tax annually, on the male inhabitants of full age, not exceeding one dollar each.

Sec. 2. Be it further enacted, that the said trustees shall appoint their clerk or any other officer they may think proper, who shall continue in office for and during the time for which the trustees, who appointed them, shall remain in office, and the said trustees shall have power and authority to remove any officer by them appointed, for neglect of duty or malfeasance in office, and appoint any other instead of the person so removed.

Sec. 3. Be it further enacted, that the trustees of said town or a majority of them shall have full power and authority to levy a tax annually, on the real property in said town, in proportion to the value of the lots in their improved state, not exceeding one hundred cents for every hundred dollars' value, and the trustees or a majority of them, shall have power to cause an assessment to be made of the value of the lots in said town by some person or persons, appointed by them, in order to enable them to fix the sum to be paid by the proprietors or occupants of said lots; provided, however, that a majority shall concur in laying the tax.

Sec. 17. Be it further enacted, that the said trustees shall, before they can recover any fine or fines for a breach of their by-laws or ordinances, have a fair copy of their by-laws set up at three of the most public places in said town at least three weeks.

Sec. 19. Be it further enacted, that it shall be the duty of the trustees, annually, at the August County Court of Jessamine, to make a settlement with the County Court and pay over any moneys that may be on hand, to their successors, and in case of failure the County Court is hereby authorized to summon them to appear at their next or succeeding term to make a settlement and to enter up judgment against them for any sums that may appear against them and award executions thereon.

Sec. 20. Be it further enacted, that the first election under this act shall be held by two Justices of the Peace, for the county of Jessamine, and the Clerk of the Board of Trustees, at the time said election takes place.

Sec. 21. Be it further enacted, that all laws of a special nature heretofore enacted, applying to Nicholasville, be, and the same are hereby, repealed from and after the first general election under this act.

The first election was held on the 31st of May, 1824. A certificate of this was in the following words: "We do certify that we have this day caused an election to be held for trustees of the town of Nicholasville, agreeably to an act of the legislature of the state of Kentucky, approved the 18th of November, 1823, when the following gentlemen were duly elected trustees for the said town for the ensuing year, namely: B. Netherland, Sr., Harrison Daniel, Levy L. Todd, Wm. Perkins, John Messick, James Lusk, Wm. Cox. Given under our hands this 31st day of May, 1824.

"GEORGE BROWN, JOHN DOWLING,

"Two of the justices of the peace of Jessamine county.

"Attest: H. Daniel, clerk B. T. T. N."

A meeting of the Board of Trustees of the town was held on the 19th day of June, 1824, at Mingo Tavern. On that day the report of James Wolmore, Waddell G. Bruce and Benjamin Netherland, Jr., as commissioners, and W. G. Bruce was allowed $2 as assessor for making out a list of taxable property in the year 1823, and B. Netherland, Jr., was allowed $105 for services as assessor for one year. The tax rate was fixed at 30 cents on each $100 worth of value on the valuation fixed by the commissioners. On the 27th of September, 1824, another meeting was held, when the treasurer was directed to pay Wm. Overstreet $10 for his services as town sergeant and market master, and Wm. Campbell, who was the father of the late Henry J. Campbell, county judge, who died in 1866, was allowed $15 for his services as town sergeant for six months.

An ordinance on the subject of dogs was also passed. It was known as a by-law and declared "That any person in the town of Nicholasville who shall keep more than one dog or bitch shall be fined $1 for every twenty-four hours he shall retain the same after the 10th day of May next," and that it should be the duty of the town sergeant to enforce this by-law on all alike. It was also ordered that Wm. Cox be allowed $13 for whipping thirteen slaves, according to the by-laws of the town, and that the treasurer be authorized to pay the same.

In the days of slavery in Kentucky all the towns and county seats adopted ordinances or by-laws preventing negro slaves or free negroes from visiting the towns after the hours of 10 o'clock, either in the streets or collecting on street corners or at the kitchens of others than their owners. If they had a written permit from their owners stating their business in town after 10 o'clock at night they were permitted to go free and were not arrested and whipped. The author remembers when a boy very often to have used his father's name to a great many of these permits in the town of Nicholasville for his slaves, and in return to have received numerous pies and cakes and frequently bundles of stick candy, which the grateful recipients of the order brought back as an assurance of their gratitude and as the means of securing further indulgences.

The following list of property for the year 1831 affords curious reading:

The report of the Commissioners appointed to value the houses and lots and slaves in the town was received, adopted and ordered to be recorded, which is done as follows:

1	$ 45	29	$ 800	56	$ 125	86	$ 300
2	45	30	300	57	110	87	200
3	45	31	125	58	75	88	600
4	50	32	125	59	1,800	89	40
5	150	33	225	60	60	90	400
6	45	34	450	61	65	91	800
7	55	35	1,800	62	175	92	75
8	55	36	2,000	63	750	93	75
9	30	37	800	64	1,500	94	500
10	30	38	1,500	65	750	95	125
11	30	38½	750	66	1,600	96	600
12	500	39	800	67 & 68	3,000	97	600
13	75	40	2,700	70	3,800	98	600
14	400	41	2,500	71	2,000	99	160
15	800	42	2,000	72	1,500	100 & 101	950
16	175	43	3,000	73	600	102 & 103	2,150
17	70	44	2,500	74	1,500	104	300
18	60	45	900	75	900	105	60
19	60	46	500	76	1,400	106	70
20	50	47	1,200	77	1,800	107	60
21	65	48	400	78	300	108	700
22	200	49	400	79	600	109	800
23	150	50	650	80	600	110	50
24	50	51	250	81	700		
25	50	52	200	82	125		$68,065
26	50	53	750	83	100		
27	300	54	250	84	150		
28	30	55	575	85	250		

NEGRO SLAVES.

Henry Burch, man and woman . . . . $ 700
B. Netherland, Sr., boy, girl, woman and child 1,050
The same, administrator of P. Netherland, woman 300
James Norvell, woman, child and 2 men 600
B. Netherland, Jr., man, woman and child 900
Wm. Shreve, 2 men, 2 women and 3 children 1,550
David Crozer, 1 woman, 2 girls 800
Thos. J. Brown, 1 man, 1 boy, 3 girls, 1 woman 1,905
Robt. Young, 1 boy 350
James Lusk, 1 girl 300
James Hill, 2 women, 2 girls 900
David Majors, 1 girl 300
Henry Ball, 1 girl 200
James McCabe, woman, girl and boy 725
Charles M. Davenport, man, woman and child 800
James L. Peak, 1 girl 275
John Downing, woman, boy and girl 650
William Campbell, 1 boy 200
William White, woman and 2 children 600
Alex Wake, 2 women, 2 boys and girl 1,000
George Cunningham, woman 250
Henry Metcalf, woman and man 700
Joseph Carson, girl 325
James C. Wilmore, girl 225
Jerome B. Sparks, boy 350
James Mars, 1 girl 225
Richard Reynolds, girl 300
Levi L. Todd, woman and girl 350
Joseph Maxwell, 2 girls 600
Samuel Rice, man, woman and girl 450
　　　　　　　　　　　　　　　　　　　　　　　　$17,880
　　　　　　　　　　　　　　　　　　　　　　　　68,065

Total value lots and slaves $85,945

TITHES.

Henry Burch, B. Netherland, Sr., Robt. McMurtry, James Norvell, B. Netherland, Jr., James Downing, Emmanuel Messick, William Shreve, Woodson Dickerson, David Crozer, George W. Elley, J. M. Spraggins, Miller Messenner, Ezekiel Burch, George Davenport, Robt. Young, David Shook, John W. Bourne, Churchill Faulconer, Wm. Faulconer, Charles Gibson, James Hill, David Majors, James Majors, Henry Ball, James McCabe, Jas. L. Peak, Chas. M. Davenport, George B. Nelson, Joseph Rutherford, Henry R. Roland, William H. Mathews, Jas. Lusk,

David Bowman, John Downing, William Campbell, Alex. Wake, George Cunningham, Henry Metcalf, Joseph Carson, James C. Wilmore, Jerome B. Sparks, James Mars, Richard Reynolds, Joseph Maxwell, Samuel Burch, Samuel Rice, William Cox, Joseph Easley, Levi L. Todd, T. J. Browning. Total, 51.

DOGS.

	No.		No.
H. Burch	1	Wm. Campbell	2
James Norvell	2	Alex Wake	1
B. Netherland, Jr.	1	G. Cunningham	1
E. Messick	2	Henry Metcalf	2
Wm. Shreve	1	Elizabeth Buskett	2
Jas. Downing	1	Joseph Carson	1
T. J. Brown	6	Metcalf's Charlotte	2
Robt. Young	1	James C. Wilmore	1
Frie Fanny	1	Jerome B. Sparks	1
Jas. Hill	2	Jos. Maxwell	1
David Majors	1	Samuel Burch	2
C. M. Davenport	2	Wm. Faulconer	1
Sucky East	2	Samuel Rice	1
John Downing	1		
B. Netherland, Sr.	4	Total No. dogs	46

VALUE OF TAXABLE PROPERTY IN NICHOLASVILLE.

1858	$246,300
1874	261,075
1882	336,260
1888	566,920
1892	799,475
1894	853,600
1898	976,860

Various other legislative enactments were passed from time to time, until 1884 the town first had authority to choose a Mayor, together with a Board of Councilmen. In that year, Hon. John S. Bronaugh was elected first Mayor of Nicholasville; he served eight years, but declined re-election. He was on every hand regarded as a most valuable official, and brought the affairs of the town into splendid condition. He was succeeded by Dr. Charles Talbert, who served two years, and he by William L. Steele, the present Mayor.

Under the Constitution of Kentucky, of 1890, providing for the classification of all the towns and cities of the state, Nicholasville became a city of the fourth class.   It has now a population within its limits of over 3,000.

At the close of its centennial year, its Mayor and Councilmen are as follows :

Mayor—William Steele, grandson of Samuel McDowell, born 1843.   Councilmen—Jephtha D. Hughes, born in 1852; Charles Mitchell, born in 1856; Frank Smith, born in 1870; Charles Evans, born in 1852; Andrew McAfee, colored, born in 1861; Adam Adcock, born in 1851.

No city in Central Kentucky has grown more rapidly or has more beautiful streets or a better city government.   The little village of 1798, with a few straggling log houses has become in 1898 a thrifty, energetic and enterprising city of 3,500 people, with 8 miles of streets, with handsome residences, with imposing public buildings and with every comfort and convenience which enter into modern city life.

Upon the 100th anniversary of its existence, the following are the physicians in Nicholasville :

Dr. Chas. Mann, Dr. Joshua S. Barnes, Dr. Thomas R. Welch, Dr. Wm. H. Fish, Dr. Jos. A. Vanarsdale, Dr. D. A. Penick, Dr. William H. Mathews.

And the following constitute the members of the local bar :

John S. Bronaugh, N. L. Bronaugh, James W. Mitchell, John H. Welch, George R. Pryor, Everet B. Hoover.

George Nicholas.

On the occasion of a centennial which Nicholasville celebrated on September 16, 1898, the history of the man for whom the county seat was called, becomes profoundly interesting.

George Nicholas was born August 11th, 1753, in Williamsburg, Va.   His father was Robert Carter Nicholas, a prominent lawyer, a member of the Virginia House of Burgesses (Legislature), connected with the Colonial Government of Virginia, and Colonial Treasurer.   He became a captain in the Continental army, and practiced law in Charlottesville after the war.   Of the Virginia Convention, called to consider the Constitution of the United States, he was a member, and he ably and earnestly advocated its adoption, which prevailed by a vote of 88 for and 78 against, and that only after a lengthened and even acrimonious discussion.

This ratification was made by the convention on June 26th, 1788; Virginia being the tenth state to adopt the instrument.

On October 24th, 1788, Colonel Nicholas advertised in the Kentucky Gazette, as follows:

"Richmond, Va., Oct. 24th, 1788.

"I propose attending the General Court in the District of Kentucky, as an attorney, and shall be at the next March term, if not prevented by some unforeseen event."

He came in the following year and settled in what is now Boyle but was then Mercer county. (Boyle county was not established until 1842.)

As Harrodsburg and Danville were, in pioneer days, places for the most important conventions, and the seat of the county, it was doubtless for the purpose of being near the seats of justice which induced Colonel Nicholas to find a home in Mercer.

The act admitting Kentucky as a state was passed June 1st, 1791, but it was not to go into effect until June 1st, 1792.

In December, 1791, a convention was elected to meet in Danville April 3d, 1792, to frame a State Constitution. George Nicholas was one of the men elected a member of this convention from Mercer county. He was the greatest lawyer in this body. His experience as a member of the Virginia Convention, in the discussion of the Constitution of the United States, and his superb legal training, combined with his logical and analytical mind, and his power of accurate statement, made him the man of and for the occasion.

In his fortieth year, in the full tide of his mental and physical powers, and with a ripe judgment, the result of military, civil and judicial experience, combined with a peculiarly philosophical and analytical mind; it was both reasonable and proper that he should be the dominant spirit of the body. Experience subsequently showed that many of the provisions of the Constitution adopted at his suggestion, were not adapted to the conditions surrounding Kentucky. It only remained in force seven years, and was then, by almost the unanimous will of the people, set aside in 1799.

No forty-five men ever assembled together who were more patriotic and who more faithfully endeavored to discharge the trust confided to their keeping. Benjamin Logan, Alexander Bullitt, Robert Breckinridge, David Rice, Samuel McDowell, Caleb Wallace, were a part of that distinguished convention, and in that period of Kentucky's history, they represented a courage, fidelity, patriotism and loyalty to the people which reached the highest limit of human attainment.

The perfect knowledge Colonel Nicholas had obtained of the Constitution of the United States and his admiration of its provisions, created by his splendid defense of it in the Virginia Convention, were largely used in the creation of Kentucky's first Constitution. His superb legal attainments, his varied knowledge, his judicial mind, his unbounded patriotism, and his thorough conception of the true principles of government, made him an unquestioned leader in such a body.

The Constitution was framed and adopted in seventeen days, and in thirty days from the assembling of the convention a Governor was elected, and in sixty days a Legislature assembled under its provisions.

Colonel Nicholas was married to Mary Smith, of Baltimore. One of her brothers, Samuel Smith, was a member of the House of Representatives and United States Senator for twenty-nine years, and another, Robert Smith, was Secretary of the Navy under President Jefferson, and Secretary of State under President Madison. One of his sons, S. S. Nicholas, was one of the most distinguished lawyers of the state. He was a Judge of the Court of Appeals, Judge of the Louisville Chancery Court, and one of the Commissioners appointed in 1850 to revise the laws of Kentucky. His youngest daughter, Hetty Morrison, was the wife of Hon. Richard Hawes, of Paris, Ky., at one time Provisional Governor of Kentucky, while under the control of the Confederate States; and he represented the Ashland District in Congress, 1837-1841. He opened a law school at his own house, and taught gratuitously such men as Joseph Hamilton Daveiss, John Rowan, Martin D. Hardin, Robert Wickliffe, William T. Barry, Isham Talbott, and John Green. He moved to Bath county in 1794, to which his interests in the old slate furnace, which was operated from 1790 to 1839, and was for nearly 50 years one of the great industries of the state. Later he came to Lexington to devote himself to the practice of law.

In 1799 he was elected Professor of the Law Department then added to Transylvania University, then in the zenith of its glory, but he died shortly afterwards, in July, 1799, in his forty-sixth year.

The capital of Jessamine is named, as will be seen, from one of the really great men of his period. It was called for Colonel Nicholas through the partiality of Rev. John Metcalf, who held the highest admiration for Nicholas, and who had known him in Virginia, before his removal to Kentucky.

Militia of Jessamine County.

Even to the soldiers who participated in great battles in Mexico or the recent war there was never any military experience which left so charming memories as that of service in the old state militia, commonly known as the "Corn Stalk Militia." It was called the Corn Stalk Militia because there were no arms for the troops and very frequently they used corn stalks in the place of guns. The state militia grew up with the early settlement of Kentucky. In those times every man was a soldier and was ready to respond to such call as might be made in defense of his home or in punishment of the Indians, who had invaded the state.

From 1775 down to 1793, every able-bodied man was of necessity connected with some military command. A while after the Indian peace of 1794, the militia organization slackened a little, yet it never died out as a state institution until after the Constitution of 1849-50 was enacted.

Up to that time every male citizen from the age of twenty-one to forty-five was to report for duty at all drills, in default of which a fine was adjudged.

Jessamine county had two regiments, formed in different parts of the county, and they were required to assemble in the spring for battalion drill. In September they had what was called a "big muster," which was a brigade drill, called in that day "The Evolution of the Line."

Nicholasville, the county seat, as the central point, was selected for this army movement. The uniform of the officers, from briga-

ATTENTION!!
8th Regiment K. M.

COMPANY ORDERS,
1832.

Mr.

SIR: You are hereby notified to attend the following Musters in the present year, viz:

REGIMENTAL MUSTER on the 10th of October, at Nicholasville, 10 o'clock.

BATTALLION MUSTER on the 3th of May, at Nicholasville, 10 o'clock.

COMPANY MUSTER on the 2d Saturday in April, at 2 o'clock, P. M.   Parade in the Academy Lot, Nicholasville.

Court of Assessment, the last Monday in October at Nicholasville.

No guns required.   By order of

W. F. SHELY, Captain.

JAS. SWITEZEN, O. Sergeant.

MILITIA NOTICE, 1832.

dier-general down, consisted of epaulets, sword, red sash, high hats with plumes tipped with white, and a black cockade on one side. The great day in the county was the big muster, and from all parts of the county, not only the soldiers but the citizens came to Nicholasville, and these military officers were as proud and well satisfied with their appearance as any army officer equipped with gold and tinsel, under the forms prescribed by General Miles of the present day.

The drills were great occasions and were especially attractive to the boys, who would post themselves along the roads and watch the incoming of the officers. Standing on the fences and on high steps they would wait with keen zest for the uniformed men, and as they would see an officer coming up in his splendid attire, they would yell out with delight and enthusiasm: "Here comes a muster man." The band was not composed of scientific musicians or many pieces; it included a tenor and bass drum and a fife, all of which were played by the negroes.

The band would begin the march around town playing martial airs, early in the morning, and they would march up and down the streets and thrill the crowds with their soul-stirring strains. First, the musicians, then the companies would fall in.

After marching around the town, the musicians would halt at the court house, the music would cease and the orders would be given:

"Fall in, Captain Crozier's Company; fall in, Captain Hoover's Company; fall in Captain Rohrer's Company."

And so on, until all the companies of the regiment had been called and had taken their places in the line.

When the line had been formed, the captain would go up and down and dress the men with his sword or cane. After the alignment of the companies, they would form in regiments and move in column to a field or pasture near the town. At the head of this cavalcade would march Brigadier-General Horine. The troops would move along without keeping step, some with umbrellas raised, some with coats, some without coats, and many smoking, and the brigadier-general commanding would have his cob pipe in his mouth—thus unconscious of his military position and unconscious of his military bearing, as he sat on his horse with his back bent and his head inclined forward.

7

UNION MILLS, HICKMAN CREEK.

On reaching the field, the great and striking maneuver would be to form a hollow square. The use of this by the British troops had impressed it upon the soldiers' minds as a most important accomplishment. It took a long time to get the square formed and sometimes took a still longer time to unform. After squaring and unsquaring, the command would come to parade rest and then would be extended an opportunity for notices to be given by the farmers—such as "farms for sale or rent, stock for sale, or lost live stock." After this the square would be formed again and from this a battle line would be stretched; then a counter-march would be ordered.

On one occasion General Horine had his command in line of battle, but not remembering to reverse or about face when they had almost reached a high worm fence which enclosed a thirty-acre field, he called out: "Pull the fence down or climb it." As, under the orders of the commanding general, it had been left discretionary with them what course to pursue, they pulled the fence down.

After two or three hours of drilling they would march back to town and were dismissed.

Small boys and all the idlers about town moved up and down with the line and became as profoundly interested in the evolutions as the soldiers themselves.

These occasions were always splendid opportunities for great profit of the vendors of watermelons, ginger cake, and sweet cider. Few Jessamine men of that day will forget Aunt Milly Howard and Aunt Fannie Mason as they sat at their tables and dispensed such ginger cake and fried chicken and fried ham as the world has never surpassed.

Notwithstanding the slackness of the Corn Stalk Militia in Jessamine county, there were organizations of special companies which acquired great proficiency in drilling and were not only efficient but beautifully uniformed.

One of these companies, raised by Capt. George S. Shanklin, attained great skill and was thoroughly drilled, as much so as any modern militia.

Capt. Thompson Worley had a cavalry company which was perfectly trained. The men had good horses, took pride in them, and while they had nothing but sabres and flintlock pistols, they performed cavalry evolutions in a most creditable manner.

Capt. William R. Kean organized an infantry company known as the Jessamine Grays. This command for a long time had great celebrity. The uniform was of gray cloth, with frock coat, the breast of which was ornamented with silver braid, and had silver stripes down the sides of the trousers. The hat was of black leather with a drooping red and white plume.

Capt. J. D. Hill was in command of this company for many years. He was succeeded by Capt. Tucker Olds, of Nicholasville. The company was long the pride of the citizens of the county and it was not disbanded until near the beginning of the late war.

Patriotic Celebrations.

The early settlers on the Fourth of July were accustomed to have patriotic celebrations. They invited each other to their homes and in sumptuous repasts and neighborly communion celebrated the important events, not only in their own history, but in the history of their country. In 1794 Col. William Price had such celebrations at his house. As early as 1802 formal meetings were held to glorify the Fourth of July. There are in existence now the minutes of a meeting called on the 12th of June, 1802, to take formal action upon the celebration of the Fourth of July for that year. The following copy of the doings of that meeting will show the character and nature of the ceremony:

At a meeting of the citizens of Nicholasville on the 12th of June, 1802, Maj. Benjamin Netherland in the chair, Col. John Price, secretary, it was resolved, that the 26th anniversary of the Independence of our beloved country be celebrated on the Fourth of July next in Nicholasville. Thereupon, a committee of arrangements was appointed, who, in accordance with the resolutions of the meeting, present the following as the order of the day:

Procession.

1st. The Military Jessamine Blues, under Capt. James Price and Lieutenant Caldwell, will be drawn up between the residence of the Rev. John Metcalf and Mrs. Dillard's gate, in double file, with music on their right, will move down Main street, when the procession will be formed by each class, or division, falling in the rear of its preceding class, or division, according to the subsequent arrangement, the front class falling in the rear of the military.

2nd. Rev. Mr. Metcalf's school children in the following order: No. 1, at the Methodist Episcopal church, Rev. John Metcalf, marshal; No. 2, at the quarter session court house, Col. John Price, marshal; drawn up in front of the school room of Mrs. Nancy Lafevers, with their right on Main street.

4th. The ladies dressed in white, at Downing & Evans' store, with their right on Main street, Michael Horine, marshal.

5th. Ladies of the town and vicinity, citizens and farmers of the county, in double file, at Mr. Metcalf's corner, with right on Main street, near Mr. Netherland's stable lot, Benjamin Hughes, Stephen Frost, Col. John Mosley, marshals.

The procession will move off at slow time at nine o'clock, a. m., to the woodland east of the town where the ceremonies of the day will proceed in the following order:

First. Prayer by the Rev. John Metcalf.

Second. Music.

Third. An address by the Rev. John P. Campbell.

Fourth. Music.

Fifth. Reading Declaration of Independence by Samuel H. Woodson.

Sixth. An oration by Rev. Robert Stewart.

Seventh. Prayer by Rev. John Shackelford.

The procession will again form in the same order and return to town, dispersing at the points where they joined the procession in the morning and in the same order.

Michael Horine, Col. John Price and William Caldwell are appointed marshals.

The ladies and gentlemen of Jessamine county are most respectfully and earnestly invited to celebrate our Independence like patriotic men whose fathers were engaged in a bloody civil war for seven years.

Many of the old soldiers who served their country in the armies of Washington and Greene are among us and will be pres-

EBENEZER PRESBYTERIAN CHURCH, ON CLEAR CREEK.

ent and participate in celebrating the 26th anniversary of the freedom and independence of our country.

John Price,
Col. Wm. Price,
Hugh Chrisman,
Michael Horine,
John Metcalf,
Joseph Crockett,
Robert Crockett,
Caleb McDowell,
Committee of Arrangements, June 12, 1802.

The Michael Horine referred to in these proceedings, was an
uncle of the late Henry Horine and John Horine. Michael Horine married a sister of General Muhlenberg, a Revolutionary
soldier, and for whom Muhlenberg county, in this state, is named.
He settled in Jessamine county in 1799 and afterwards moved to
Ohio, in 1808, where he became principal of a female school.

The Hugh Chrisman mentioned is the ancestor of the large
Chrisman family in Jessamine county. He was born in Rockingham county, Va., in 1769, and died in 1849. His son, General
Henry Chrisman, long lived in Jessamine as one of its most distinguished citizens and died in 1876. He lived on Hickman
creek, a few miles from Nicholasville.

Men in Indian Wars Antedating 1812.

James Hemphill, an uncle of Andrew Hemphill, served under
General Wayne in the campaign against the Indians, and was in
the battle of the Fallen Timbers, August 20, 1794; Terrence Mc-
Grath, who was the father of the late horseman, Price McGrath,
lived in Jessamine county, and was also in that campaign. In
this battle General Wayne relied upon the charge of the Kentucky
mounted infantry to draw the fire of the Indians, and then sent in
his foot men, with the bayonet, before which the Red Men precipitately fled. The blow inflicted secured peace and forever stopped
Indian incursions into Kentucky.

Price McGrath, the son of Terrence McGrath, was born in
Nicholasville, and in his boyhood learned the tailor's trade. He

subsequently moved to Louisville, and while there he became interested in the horse business, which he so successfully managed, and afterward founded his splendid breeding establishment for race horses in Fayette county, near Lexington.

Soldiers in the War of 1812.

Jessamine county sent soldiers to the war of 1812, commanded by the following captains: Capt. Jas. C. Price, Capt. Mason Singleton, Capt. Richard Hightower, Capt. Patrick Gray, Capt. Thos. Lewis, Capt. Robt. Crockett, Capt. Augustine Bower. Quite a large number of Captain Price's company were killed at the battle of the River Raisin, while Capt. Thos. Lewis' company was in Dudley's defeat at Fort Meigs, May 15, 1813, and there lost a large number of its members, who were either killed during the fight or murdered by the Indians after the surrender.

The following letter, written by a member of Captain Bowers' company in the battle of the Thames, will be of interest to those whose ancestors were engaged in that fight. It was written by Nathaniel Adams, who died some years since in Pulaski county, and was the maternal uncle of S. M. Duncan. There are parts of it that relate to purely personal matters, which are omitted from the text as published:

MR. ADAMS' LETTER TO MISS NANCY STINSON.

Put-In-Bay, on the Shore of the Great Lake.
Oct. 15, 1813.

My Dearest Nancy:

I reached this muddie den of a village on Monday, the 11th. I was in the battle on Tuesday, October 5th, and was not hurt by the bullets of the British and Indians, though I was in very great danger, as the company I was in formed the second line when Colonel Johnson made his men charge the enemy. The Indians raised a loud yell and opened a severe fire on our advance. About seventy or eighty red-coated British soldiers and an equal number of Indians opened a heavy fire on us again, emptying eighteen saddles, killing twelve and wounding more than thirty of our men in the front line. Captain Bowers rushed up in a moment and ordered our company to advance instantly. Our men rushed forward in a rapid gallop over the front line of the British, who stood their ground like men who preferred being shot down rather than surrender. Our company killed several British soldiers who had surrendered, and who attempted to escape. When we dispersed their army in the charge, we captured over five hundred prisoners. I saw a large Indian wandering along the river with two guns and a bag of fried fish. I called the attention of Captain Bowers to the Indian, who, to all appearances, was going to steal a horse that belonged to one of Colonel Trotter's men. Captain Bower ordered three of the men to catch him. All three of us dashed at him. He raised one of the guns and fired; the ball came very close to my left ear. Instantly John Doolin shot him dead. He had fried fish in a dirty bag, and six scalps were in the bag, separated from his dinner of fish by a dirty, old towel, which was marked by stains of blood. We scalped him and left him lying on his back. John Doolin wanted to cut a razor strap from his thigh, but I objected to this and as we were picking up our wounded and sending them across the lake, I saw no more of the Indian.

War of 1812-1815.

The War of 1812 was one in which Kentucky figured more prominently than any other state. The warlike spirit had been undaunted by Indian aggressions on the frontier from 1783 down to 1811, when the men of Kentucky fought at Tippecanoe, and where the brilliant and popular Joseph Hamilton Daveiss and other gallant Kentuckians gave their blood for the defense and preservation of the Northwestern territory. Kentucky, off and on, had in this war over 25,000 soldiers. She gave some of her noblest blood in the battles it produced and manifested a patriotism and valor which gave her increased renown. To this war Jessamine county sent, first and last, 600 soldiers.

England had never accepted gracefully the result of the Revolutionary War. The Northwestern Indians were fed and maintained by the British officials in Canada. They wore British clothes, used British guns and knives and traded with and for British gold. The war was brought about by a series of events, but there were two principal causes:

HEAD OF JESSAMINE CREEK.

First. England claimed the right to stop and examine, anywhere on the high seas, American vessels engaged in commerce,
and to take from such vessels all British subjects.

"Once a subject, always a subject," a favorite maxim of John
Bull, was interpreted in the most offensive sense and any man
who was supposed to be an Irishman, Scotchman, etc., was taken
and forced to serve in the British navy, even though he was an
American citizen. Diplomacy, always slow to redress wrongs,
was in these cases extremely tardy, and thousands of American
citizens were thus relentlessly forced to serve a country whose
allegiance they repudiated. The necessities of the English
government were very great. Its navy, greatly increased by the
war with the French people led by Napoleon, could only be maintained by impressment, and these American ships were most attractive places for that sort of work. It took the news of these
seizures a long time to reach home, and then a long time to get
to the State Department, and then there was a long correspond-
ence before even a hearing could be obtained. In the mean time,
the men were in the navy and driven by the lash or other more
dreadful punishment to this hateful service.

Second: The United States, in the thirty years that had
passed since the Revolutionary War, had built up a large ocean
carrying trade. England, through the blockade of European
ports, claimed the right to seize all American ships and cargoes
bound for any blockaded port in Europe (and they were nearly all
blockaded) unless these ships, going to or returning from such
ports, first entered an English port and registered and obtained
license to prosecute their voyage.

With such claims on the part of any government, war could
not long be avoided, and so on the 18th of June, 1812, Congress
declared war.

As soon as the news of the war reached Kentucky and before
the President's requisition came to the Governor, volunteer companies all over the state rushed to offer themselves to the Governor. Kentucky's quota was 5,500 of the 100,000 called for.
Weeks before the actual declaration of war had been made, re-
cruiting offices had been opened and war meetings throughout
the state gave assurance that however lukewarm New England

might be, Kentucky would give the government the heartiest support.

By August the 14th, the Kentucky quota was ready. Jessamine sent two full companies and scattering soldiers into other commands.

One of these companies was commanded by Capt. James C. Price, a son of Col. William Price. The other was commanded by Capt. Patrick Gray. The roster of these two companies was as follows:

Roll of Capt. James C. Price's Company.

Lewis' regiment, Kentucky Volunteers. War of 1812.

Captain—James C. Price. Lieutenant—William Caldwell. Ensign—Daniel Bourne. Sergeants—William E. Price, David Richardson, John Shanklin, John Scott. Corporals—Nathaniel H. Caldwell, John Ficklin, Solomon Smith, Elisha Williams.

Privates—Barkleye, William; Barr, George; Bennett, James; Brice, John T.; Brown, Thomas; Carlton, Isaac; Carlton, Noah; Carlton, George; Callender, Jacob; Conner, Rice; Daugherty, John; Dedman, James; Easley, Pleasant; Edwards, Thos.; Elkin, Benj.; East, Elijah; Finney, James; Forset, James; Forsee, Stephen; Farrow, John; Goin, John; Haggard, John; Hicks, James; Hews, Charles, Hushman, Matthew; Kindred, Edward; Krickbaum, John; Lewis, Wm. A.; Moss, Pleasant; Morgan, W.; McGrath, Terrance; McConnell, M. G.; Neal, George; Netherland, John; Overstreet, W.; Rice, Joseph; Rice, Geo. W.; Richards, Alexander; Ramsey, John; Richardson, Robt.; Scott, Joseph; Scott, Joseph; Simmons, David; Skeene, William; Taylor, John; Underwood, Edward; Woodson, Obediah; Wilson, Thos.; Ward, William; Webber, Benj.; Walker, James; Ward, Geo. S.; Young, Joel; Young, Richard.

Roll of Capt. Patrick Gray's Company.

Lewis' regiment, Kentucky Volunteers. War of 1812.

Captain—Patrick Gray. Lieutenant—James Fletcher. Ensign—James Clark. Sergeants—William Sechrest, Thomas

Reed, John Batts, Geo. Chrisman. Corporals—Robt. Dunwiddie, Sam'l Huckstep, James Norrel.

Privates—Anderson, Oliver; Armstrong, Livy; Arnett, John; Bagwell, Cary; Bishop, John; Brown, Samuel; Bradshaw, Smith; Burk, Benj.; Campbell, James; Cardwell, Sam'l; Cardwell, James; Cary, Melford; Clark, Geo. W.; Croslin, Benj.; Downes, Penore P.; Dickerson, Wm.; Dickerson, David; Elmore, Edward; Howard, Achilles; Hopkins, Thos.; Hutcherson, Sam'l; Hunter, Chas.; Jeter, Henry; Jimerson, David; Jimerson, Wm.; Jimerson, John; Johnson, John; Kennady, Wm.; Lana, Henry; Leon, Moses; Lusk, James; Marshall, James; Marshall, Wm.; May, Lindsay; Messick, Nathan; Morris, Henry; Myers, John; Miller, Francis; McClure, Martin; Nevens, Henry; Newal, Armstrong; Patterson, John; Pilcher, Louis; Read, Peter; Robinson, Michael; Rusk, Robert; Sales, Thos. P.; Spencer, Absalom; Spiers, Greenbery; Summers, James; Summers, Thos.; Smith, Peter; Stype, John; Shelton, Thos.; Thompson, Pitman; Venable, Hamden S.; Waters, Lewis; Wallace, James; Whorton, Joseph; Wallace, Abraham; Welsh, Alexander; Willis, John; Willis, William; Wager, Absalom.

These companies were part of the 5th Kentucky Regiment, commanded by Lieut.-Col. William Lewis and Majors Joseph Robb and Benjamin Graves. The other companies constituting the regiment were those of Captains Hart, Hamilton and Megowan from Fayette, Captain Williams, from Montgomery, and Captains Martin and Brassfield from Clark. They were ordered to assemble in Lexington on the 14th of August. They were enlisted on the 15th at Georgetown.

An immense concourse, estimated at 20,000, greeted the soldiers of this regiment at Lexington. Revolutionary sires, hoary with age, wives whose hearts were filled with apprehension and dread, sweethearts whose trustful and tearful eyes told the story of love for men in the ranks, children who looked with strange wonder upon the brilliant scene of these uniformed soldiers passing in review before the vast and sympathetic crowd, came from far and near to say good-bye and god-speed to the country's defenders. Each company paraded in its own uniform, and each vied with the other in evolution and manly

CLEAR CREEK CHURCH.

bearing. None surpassed the Jessamine Blues under Captain Price and the other Jessamine company under Captain Gray, and the vast crowds of their fellow citizens felt a just pride at their splendid appearance as they marched so promptly at their country's call.

They formed on Water street in Lexington and then marched into Main street and from thence out to the Georgetown road. They marched only about four miles and then camped for the night and next day went into camp at Georgetown. The Lewis Regiment was reinforced by those of Col. John M. Scott and Col. John Allen, and they were formed into a brigade under Gen. John Payne.

On the following Sunday the brigade was reviewed by Gov. Charles Scott and Generals John Payne and James Winchester. After the review the soldiers and the crowd assembled and listened to an address from Henry Clay and a sermon from the eloquent Dr. James Blythe, who was then president of Transylvania. Mr. Clay reviewed the causes of the war and set forth the many and unbearable grievances which had forced the government to declare war, and closed with an appeal to the troops to remember that Kentucky was renowned for the bravery of her people and that they must remember that they had both the glory and the prestige of Americans and Kentuckians to maintain. The vast crowd departed after these patriotic, soul-stirring words and the soldiers went into camp, and a few days after marched to Newport to receive their arms and equipment. The most of the march was made in drenching rains, which were ominous of the hardships and misfortunes which awaited them in the campaigns upon which they had entered.

Dudley's Defeat.

A part of the Jessamine troops were in what was known as Dudley's defeat, which was fought on May 5, 1813, on the left bank of the Maumee river, opposite to Fort Meigs, a few miles south of Toledo, Ohio.

Col. William Dudley's regiment was part of Gen. Green Clay's brigade of Kentucky volunteers. After leaving Newport, they had a fatiguing march for men and ammunition, and they found these on approaching the open boats lodged on the left bank of the Maumee river, within hearing of the cannon of Fort Meigs, where General Harrison was then besieged by the British and a large force of Indians.

At twelve o'clock on the night of May 4th, when General Harrison was informed of General Clay's approach, he directed General Clay to land 700 men on the west side where the British were, charge their batteries, spike their cannon, and immediately return to their boats and cross over to the American fort. The remainder of Clay's troops were to land on the east bank and force their way into the fort by sorties from the garrison. Dudley's regiment was ordered to perform the first service. They were successful in the beginning, but the bravery of the Kentuckians and a misunderstanding of orders drew them into an ambuscade where they were cut off and surrounded by overwhelming numbers, and the apparent victory was turned into dreadful defeat.

When the Kentuckians landed they marched at once toward the battery. This battery was taken without a struggle. It was left in possession of two companies, but it was shortly after taken by the British and forced to retreat to their boats and cross the river, when they reached Fort Meigs in safety.

The Kentuckians advanced and charged the Indians, and after seeing that they were outnumbered they attempted to retreat to the battery. They found this no longer in possession of their friends, but manned by British soldiers in large numbers, who opened fire upon them. Arriving without order and being taken completely by surprise, they were compelled to surrender or be shot down. They surrendered. They were robbed by the Indians, who inflicted blows upon the prisoners at their pleasure. Most of the Americans were stripped of their clothes, and they were told by the British soldiers that the Indians intended to make them run the gauntlet, and just before the Americans reached the fort, the Indians taking advantage of their helpless condition, whipped and bruised and killed them as they pleased. A large number of them were shot down and scalped. One Indian shot four prisoners and scalped them in the presence of their comrades, and in the presence of the British officers these Kentucky troops were subjected to all sorts of indignities, and even murdered.   Captain Lewis was killed in the battle, together with a number of the men from Jessamine county.

Battle of the Thames.

The blundering and misfortunes and the disasters which attended the War of 1812 in the Northwest, in the end took a turn. The American arms were at last to receive some reward.   The great naval battle fought on Lake Erie, on the 10th of September, 1813, had destroyed the British fleet under Captain Barclay; not a single ship escaped.   The gallant Perry had grandly accomplished his task and told his own story of the victory and success in those glorious words, "We have met the enemy and they are ours."

More than a hundred Kentuckians who knew nothing of ships and had never sailed on any water but rivers, volunteered to serve on the vessels under Perry, and they deserved part of the credit for that superb victory.

General Proctor and his Indian allies under Tecumseh, after the destruction of the British fleet, were safely shut in upon English soil.   General Harrison was not slow to avail himself of the effect this naval victory had secured, and he at once crossed into Canada and commenced his pursuit of Proctor and Tecumseh.

The horses of the Kentucky troops were corralled on the Michigan shore; they were surrounded by brush and trees cut down and pickets driven so as to make a complete enclosure. When the pursuit was determined upon it was impossible to secure guards for the horses and camps other than by draft.   No man was willing to accept such inglorious service unless by compulsion.

The capture of the British vessels enabled General Harrison to make an immediate crossing and with five brigades of Kentuckians and 120 United States regulars, he landed on the Canada side on the 27th of September.

Col. Richard M. Johnson's Kentucky mounted infantry was the only cavalry in the invading army.   It was a splendid regiment of thirteen companies and contained nearly 1,400 men.

REMAINS OF STONE MILL AT KEENE.

With this regiment was detailed one of the Jessamine companies under Captain Bower.

The river Thames is a small stream rising in Canada east of Detroit and emptying into Lake St. Clair. About forty miles east of Detroit there was a small Moravian settlement, and after a dreadful and tiring march of a week, late in the afternoon of October 5, 1813, the American army was in such close pursuit that Proctor and Tecumseh were forced to offer battle.

Proctor had 600 British regulars and Tecumseh had 1,500 Indians. They were formed along the river bottom, with Tecumseh on the left, and there awaited the approach of the American army, which was composed almost entirely of Kentuckians. Governor Shelby had abandoned his duties as governor and assumed the place of commander-in-chief of the Kentucky forces. Both he and General Harrison had upon their staffs some of the most brilliant men of the state—Geo. Walker, William T. Barry, John Speed Smith, Gen. John Adair, J. J. Crittenden and Percival Butler.

Colonel Johnson had during the previous months trained his regiment to charge on horseback, and so soon as General Harrison learned that the British were formed in open order he directed Colonel Johnson to charge with his regiment mounted.

Colonel Johnson discovered that the front of the British regulars was too narrow for the use of all his men. He divided his regiment, gave half of it to his brother, James Johnson, Lieut.-Colonel. Colonel Johnson called for an advance guard of twenty men to move in advance of the troops. He had promised the wives and mothers and sweethearts and friends of his troops, when they assembled at Stamping Ground to start for the war, that he would in every way protect their lives in the campaign on which they had entered with him. He conceived the idea that if he could draw the fire of the Indians upon an advance guard, that the main force could charge and ride over the enemy's line before it could reload, and that, though he might sacrifice the twenty men he would save heavy mortality among the remainder of his force.

It was a heroic thought, and it was carried out in a heroic way. Nineteen men gallantly volunteered to ride with Colonel Johnson in advance on the enemy; of these only ten are known.

The advance was placed under the command of Col. William Whitley, who was a private in Captain Davidson's company. Of the members only the following names are known: Lieut. Samuel Logan, Coleman's company; L. L. Mansfield, Stucker's company; Benjamin Chambers, quartermaster; Robert Payne, Stucker's company; Dr. Samuel Theobald, Coleman's company; William Webb, Stucker's company; Garrett Wall, forage major; Eli Short, forage master.

Lieut.-Col. Johnson at once charged the British regulars. He passed through their line, then turned and fired upon them in the rear. They immediately surrendered. Col. Richard M. Johnson, with half the regiment, with the advance guard in front, charged the Indians who at once poured in a deadly fire upon the advance guard, all of whom were either killed, wounded, or had their horses shot under them, except Dr. Samuel Theobald, of Lexington. The brave and heroic William Whitley was killed at the first fire on the advance guard.

In these later days, when acts of heroism are applauded with such vigor and enthusiasm, it is well to remind the world of such deeds as those of Gen. William O. Butler and Johnson's advance guard at the river Thames. These lose nothing in comparison with the conduct and courage of any men of any age.

Proctor's regulars were all captured, the Indians were routed, Tecumseh was killed, his force was scattered, and peace in the Northwest was at once assured. Proctor himself abandoned his men, his carriage and baggage, and fled precipitately from the field. His guilty conscience smote him as he heard the Kentucky hosts on entering the battle, with mighty shout cry out, "Remember the Raisin." He knew that his perfidy and barbarity deserved the death that the comrades of the murdered heroes of Raisin would inflict upon him, and like a coward he fled from the just wrath of the American soldiers.

In this splendid battle a large number of the men from Jessamine participated, and part of its glory belongs to those who composed the Jessamine troops.

The accompanying letter written by a Jessamine man who participated in this conflict will be both interesting and historical:

"Bass Island, Lake Erie, October 10, 1813.

"My Dear Father: I have only time to inform you and my friends that I am now confined to my bed with severe rheumatism in my legs. I am unable to walk, but am very kindly treated Frenchman who served in our armies under General Washington and received a severe shot in the left hip joint at the battle of Princeton, he has lived in this dreary country thirty years engaged in fishing on the lake. Our company under Captain Bowen was in the battle of Thames river on the 5th. A cannon ball killed Captain Bowen's horse in the beginning of the battle, but he soon got another one much stronger and active than the horse he brought from home. After Commander Perrie gained the victory on the lake, the Barbarian Proctor abandoned the post at Malden and took a position on the river Thames. His rapid movements, we have learned since the battle, was very annoying and displeasing to his Indian allies. This morning Captain Bowen called to see me in company with Captain Danfield of the British army. I heard Captain Danfield say that the Indian chief Tecumsey was very mad at General Proctor for leaving his Indian brethren exposed to the vengeance of our soldiers. Danfield said that he heard the Indian chief address Proctor in very severe language about his leaving Maldens. It was also stated by the English officer that Proctor was fairly outgeneraled by Harrison and was unable to escape with all his baggage, being hard pressed by him in every move up the Thames. After a great deal of heavy marching and loss of sleep both armies met in the vicinity of a Dunkard settlement called Moravian town, which was deserted, not a human being in it when the fight took place October 5th. The battle did not last very long, but it was fierce and savage. The Indians under their Chief Tecumsey were in possession of a thick woods, who, with the British infantry had formed their line of battle on ground which gave them some advantage over our troops. When the fight opened I saw Gen. Harrison with Commodore Perrie who was in the battle and was acting as aid, he and Captain Butler, Colonel Cass who was a very large man had the post of honor and led the front line. Colonel Johnson, of Scott county, with the mounted men was ordered to charge at full speed, and break their line. Johnson

PLACE OF COL. WM. PRICE'S BURIAL.

rushed along the line hat off and gave command in a loud voice that now was the time to fight, and in an instant his mounted men including Captain Bowen's company were rushing on the lines of the enemy. At first our horses recoiled on receiving the heavy fire from the British and Indians, yet it was only momentarily, the voice of Colonel Cass and our Colonel Trotter was heard amid the roaring of musketry, the enemy run in every direction, we were completely victorious. Governor Shelby whose presence on the field was greeted by thousands. The Indian chief Tecumsey was killed, over 500 of the enemy were taken in by our men, 80 of the English were killed and over 100 Indians were left on the field. Come to Newport after me and bring three feather beds in the wagon, as I can not bear jolting.   Your son,

"GEORGE T. CHRISMAN.

"Hugh Chrisman, Jessamine Co., Ky."

The following extracts from a letter, written by John Netherland, who was a son of Maj. Benjamin Netherland, will prove interesting and show how the men from Jessamine acted in the battle of the Thames:

"On the Thames, October 7, 1813.

"My Dear Parents: I never wanted to see you so badly in my life. After the massacre of so many of the company of the brave Captain Price at the river Raisin, I succeeded in making my escape, after running seventeen miles in snow over two feet deep. I joined the main body of the army under General Harrison and served with Colonel Johnson in the battle which took place day before yesterday. I stood on the shore of lake Erie on Sunday, the 10th of September, and saw Captain Perry whip hell out of the British fleet on the lake. As soon as they were whipped on the water, General Harrison made us all get on board of the ships of Captain Perry and sailed to Canada. When the army landed we marched in pursuit of the d—d murderers and cutthroats. We came up with them at the river Thames on the 5th of October, gave the devils a sound thrashing and took over seven hundred prisoners and shot to death five Indians for breaking their paroles five days before the battle. It took old Governor Shelby a long time to keep our company from scalping twenty

English soldiers for giving rum to the Indians and furnishing them with guns and powder to murder our people.   We are now burying the dead and will leave here as soon as we can hunt up all who are wounded and unable to get home.   When I come home I can tell you of as much suffering in this army as you ever suffered in the Revolutionary War.   I must say that every man and officer from Jessamine was game and did his duty without fear or favor.   Billy Caldwell and Lieut. Ebenezer Price, brother of Captain Price, was like a mad bull in battle.   He was brave on all occasions and he and Billy Caldwell could hallo louder than any men in the army.   They were ever ready to fight.   I send you this letter by Noah Carlton, who goes to Newport and who will send it to you from Lexington. Don't let brother Ben go frollicking about on my horses.   Before I left home he was in the habit of letting the young women have my horses to hunt grapes and persimmons on Hickman creek.   I will be at home in five weeks.

"Your oldest son,
"JOHN NETHERLAND."

Jessamine County Soldiers who Battled at Thames.

Jessamine county had two companies in the battle of the Thames, fought June 13, 1813. The two companies were mounted men and were in Col. George Trotter's regiment. Capt. Gustavus Bower commanded one of these companies. He was born near Fredericksburg, Va., in 1786 and settled in Nicholasville in 1810, as a physician. When the War of 1812 was declared he raised the following company, which was in the battle of the Thames:

Captain—Gustavus Bower.   Lieutenant—Bartholomew Kindred.   Ensign—Smith Bradshaw.   Sergeants—Joshua Hightower 1st, R. Michael Bower 2d, Peter Withers 3d, Robt. D. Overstreet 4th.   Corporals—Geo. T. Chrisman 1st, Reuben Bennett. 2d, Wm. Wilson 3d, Benj. Bradshaw, Jr., 4th.

Privates—Allison, Jno.; Bird, Jno.; Bourne, Daniel; Bradshaw, Benj.; Bustard, David; Campbell, Jno.; Campbell, Wm.; Carroll, Jno.; Cobb, Thos.; Connor, Rice; Connor, Wm. R.; Corr, Jas.; Casby, Chas.; Casby, James; Crockett, Jno. W.;

Crutcher, James; Davenport, Jno. F.; Davidson, Richard; Davis, James; DeMoss, Asa; Dickerson, Fontaine; Dickerson, James; Dougherty, James; Duncan, James; East, James; Fitzgerald, Francis; Fassee, John; Gilman, James; Gray, David; Haggard, Jno.; Hawkins, Thos.; Higbee, James H.; Higginbotham, Jesse; Hunter, Davidson; Johnson, John G.; Lewis, Daniel; McCarly, Dennis; McConnell, Andrew; McCune, Jno. L. P.; McDaniel, Thos.; Miles, Benj.; Miles, James; Murrain, Wm.; Pennington, Saml.; Moss, Wm.; Powers, Samuel; Reynolds, Wm.; Rice, Thos. N.; Richards, Alexander; Robertson, Michael; Scott, James; Shaw, John; Shearer, Caleb; Shelton, Wm.; Sike, David; Smith, Adam; Smith, Alexander; Stipe, David; Stipe, Henry; Stipe, Jacob; Taylor, Samuel; Taylor, William; Thompson, Alex.; Thornton, Elijah; Trister, Peter; Turner, Robt.; Walker, Reuben; Wallace, Thomas; Walters, Thomas; Ward, Geo. S.; Welch, Alexander; Willis, Drury; Wilson, W. M. S.; Woods, James; Zimmerman, John.

Capt. Mason Singleton, of the Keene neighborhood, also raised a company which was in Trotter's regiment. The following is a list of the company:

Capt. Mason Singleton's Company.

Captain—Mason Singleton. Lieutenant—Benj. Williams. Ensign—Thomas Haydon. Sergeants—Joel Turnham 1st, Wm. Scott 2d, Jesse Hayden 3d.

Privates—Sallee, Edward; Burton, Thos.; Conklin, Hugh; Ellison, Thos.; Evans, Andrew; Ficklin, Thomas; Frost, Jno.; Gatewood, Gabriel; Hampton, Stephen; Haydon, Ezekiel; Haydon, Jno.; Holloway, Samuel; Hughes, Chas.; Hundley, Jno.; Lambkins, Daniel; McVey, Jno.; Moore, Joel P.; Morrow, Jno.; Moseley, Ewd.; Neal, Jno.; Proctor, Isaiah; Proctoi, Thos.; Reed, Phillip; Reynolds, Drake; Rice, Richard; Richardson, Jesse; Poper, Jesse; Schofield, Samuel; Sharewood, Wm.; Singleton, Lewis; Smith, James; Smith, Wm.; Starr, Henry; Steel, Darbey G.; Webster, Christopher; Wells, Jacob; Williams, Elijah; Williams, Thos.; Willis, Lewis; Wilson, Nathan; Wilson, Alex.; Woods, Richard; Woods, Christopher; Young, Lewis; Fizer, Jacob; Jenkins, Henry.

WOODEN BRIDGE OVER KENTUCKY RIVER, AT MOUTH OF HICKMAN CREEK.

These captains, as well as their men, all acted a courageous and handsome part in the battle. Captain Bower, after the war, married a daughter of Col. Joseph Crockett, and went to Georgetown to practice medicine. He subsequently removed to Palmyra, Mo., where he died in 1869.

The following is also the list of the company of Capt. Richard H. Hightower, in 17th United States, engaged in the War of 1812:

Captain—Richard Hightower. 1st Lieutenant—Thomas C. Graves. Sergeants—Lucius C. Pleasants 1st, Benj. Segar 2d, Jesse Denilhess, 3d.

Privates—Acton, Wm.; Alison, Jno.; Andrews, Robt.; Barton, Karswell; Bates, Alfred; Black, Beverly A.; Blythe, William; Byron, Jno.; Camp, Wm.; Carter, Jno.; Casey, Joshua; Cesgar, Thos.; Childers, Thos.; Cooly, Jno.; Cook, Matthew; Craig, Walter; Davis, William; Delaney, Willis; Denore, Baldwin; Dobbs, Jno.; Dyne, Andrew; Emmerson, Wm.; Farrow, Isham; Fisher, Jno.; Fowler, James; Fowler, Thos.; Gentry, Zebedee; Gohagen, Wm.; Goodlett, Wm.; Grindstaff, Isaac; Ingsley, Jas.; Hanley, Thos. H.; Hobson, Bennett; Hope, Geo.; James, Saml.; Johnson, Wm.; Lane, Jno.; McCarty, David; McDaniel, Wm., McKenzie, Jno.; Martin, Jas.; Mathews, Philip; Maxwell, Jno.; Mayfield, Sutherland; Morgan, J.; Murphy, David; Murrane, J.; Murrane, Mark.; Murrane, Tom; Pagget, James; Pagget, Thos.; Pogue, Jno.; Prewitt, Edmund; Price, Jno.; Ralston, Alex.; Reed, Adam; Reed, Robt.; Scroggins, Wm.; Shaw, Jno.; Shimp, Geo.; Shover, Simon; Smith, Richard; Stewart, Rice; Sumerfield, Ephraim; Thompson, James; Tiller, Jno.; Walker, Jeremiah; Webb, Adam; White, Chas.; Williams, Silas; Winchester, Peter; Wood, Jno.

Roll of Capt. Robert Crockett's Company.

Roll of Capt. Robert Crockett's Company, Kentucky Mounted Volunteer Militia—Commanded by Lieut.-Col. James Allen. War of 1812.

Captain—Robert Crockett. Lieutenant—John C. Morrison. Ensign—Henry Lindsey. Sergeants—Jonathan Robinson, 1st, Alexander Logan, 2d, William Mead, 3d, John Lawny, 4th.

Privates—Armstrong, Samuel; Bank, Ephraim; Baxter, Samuel; Brownlee, John; Bobb, William; Butler, Samuel; Bond, Cornelius; Crockett, John W.; Crockett, Samuel C.; Carr, Thomas; Cloud, Sam'l G.; Decreet, Joseph; Duncan, James; Dougherty, James; Fracher, Charles; Fink, John; Fracher, John; Gaunt, William; Harrison, Jos. C.; Jewet, Matthew; Logan, Samuel; Moore, Angus; Messock, Isaac; McCall, William; McCornell, William; Parmer, James; Rankin, Adam; Roberts, John; Ramsey, Robert; Royall, William; Smith, John; Tadloer, Andrew; Talbot, Jonathan; Venable, James; Villers, George; Wardlow, John; Walker, Matthew; Young, Leavin.

Roll of Capt. Thomas Lewis' Company.

Roll of Capt. Thomas Lewis' company of infantry of the Kentucky Militia, detached—Commanded by Lieut.-Col. William Dudley. War of 1812.

Captain—Thomas Lewis. Lieutenant—George S. Herndon. Ensign—William Sally. Sergeants—William Moss 1st, Henry King, 2d, William Roach, 3d, Newton H. Tapp, 4th. Corporals —William Dunn, 1st, Thomas Payne, 2d, Eliphalet Roan, 3d, George Doxen, 4th.

Privates—Acres, Larkin; Aldridge, Joshua; Anderson, James; Attsman, Henry; Baker, Lewis; Ball, Henry; Baxter, James; Bourne, John; Bowman, John; Brockman, Aaron; Brooner, Davis; Brown, Samuel; Buskitt, David; Busley, William; Butler, Wm. W.; Castle, John; Clark, James; Cromwell, Oliver; Davis, Jarred; Dunnegan, David; Easley, Obediah; Fisher, James; Frazier, Jeremiah; George, Ellis; Green, James; Green, John; Hampton, Thos.; Hendricks, Michael; Hitt, Elias; Houser, Isaac; Hughes, Thomas; Hunter, John; Hynes, Alexander R.; Keen, John; Lewis, Adam; Lockhart, Silas; Masterson, Moses; May, Solomon; McAtee, Abednego; McCune, Samuel; McDaniel, Alexander; McDougal, James; Mifford, Joseph; Moon, Zachariah; Morris, Jesse; Morrow, James; Moss, Pleasant; Myers, Jacob; Mutter, William; Ritter, Michael; Romans, John; Ronyan, Francis; Rutherford, Archibald; Rutherford, Jesse; Rynolds, Samuel; Sandusky, Jacob; Scanlan, Travis; Scott, Matthew T.; Sergeant, Wm. B.; Shannon, Jacob;

Shrewsberry, Nathaniel; Simpson, Nathaniel; Skewens, Clayton; Spencer, Charles; Starr, Christopher; Starr, John; Ateward, John; Tapp, Nelson; Taylor, Conrad; Twindle, Alexander; Triplett, Fielding; True, John; Truit, John; Ungles, Hillery; Wallace, Thomas; Waters, John; Williams, Lewis; Williamson, Richard; Wilson, James; Wilson, William.

The subjoined names were taken from recent transcripts furnished by the War Department:

Baum, Whitfield; Baines, Zachariah; Beeler, Henry; Brown, Joel; Bunds, Geo. S.; Burchum, Jos.; Corn, James; Corn, Hiram; Davis, James; Damele, Spencer; Dixon, Geo.; Dornell, William; Erwin, Stephen; Fitzjarrell, Silas; Fizer, Jacob; Gardner, Francis; Hanes, Simeon; Jack, Andrew; Kendrick, Michael; Lee, Achilles, musician; Lowry, Stephen; McClain, James; McMillen, William; Mofford, James; Overtums, Garland; Parish, Price; Pierson, Allen; Paxton, Joseph; Pilcher, Shadrach; Rankins, John; Right, Jonathan; Singleton, Daniel; Smith, John; Stewart, Gehew; Stewart, William; Walker, David T.; sergeant; Walker, Matthew; Wallace, Robert; Wallem, John; Wilsom, Gabriel.

River Raisin.

General Hull, in command of the Ohio troops, on the 16th of August, 1812, surrendered at Detroit. His army composing the army of the northwest, together with Detroit, had been turned over to the British. This conduct aroused the keenest indignation. No sooner had the news reached Kentucky than all the volunteers that the state and government desired pressed forward at once and offered themselves for the purpose of wiping out the disgrace which General Hull had inflicted upon the American army.

The two troops from Jessamine county in the regiment of Colonel Lewis, marched from Cincinnati towards Detroit and finally reached Fort Winchester. Here their baggage was transferred to canoes upon the Maumee river. The road was difficult and long. The troops, starting from home with their summer clothes, had not yet been provided with their winter outfit, and this amid the fierce climate of the northwest presented most serious

COURT HOUSE, NICHOLASVILLE.

difficulties. In a little while the provisions failed and for fourteen days the Kentucky troops subsisted on hickory roots, elm bark and the beef of a few cattle, which were killed in a half-starved state. In the midst of the winter a supply of warm clothing was received, and this gave the troops new courage and animation.

A small force of regulars had been united with the Kentuckians in this march. The Kentuckians received their winter clothing first, and it was quite a while before the regulars were supplied, and, with the chivalry and generosity which marked men of that period, these gallant Kentuckians demanded that the regulars should be exempted from camp duty, and all military service required should be performed by them.

On the 8th of January they were ordered to march to the rapids. Upon reaching this point the officers were informed that in the village called French Town, the inhabitants were terrified at the approach of the English and the Indians. French Town is on the River Raisin, a small stream emptying its waters in Lake Erie. General Winchester promptly sent forward Colonels Lewis and Allen, with six hundred men. They reached the River Raisin on the 18th of January, 1813, and met the combined English and Indian force, about 500 strong, under Major Reynolds, of the Canadian militia, and drove them from the place. The people of French Town were delighted with the result. A few days before they had feared the tomahawk of the Indian, and now they rejoiced at the presence of their Kentucky defenders. Those who had been assigned to march with Colonel Lewis's regiment were delighted that glory was placed in their grasp, while those who remained behind felt as if a great sorrow had come into their lives.

On the 21st of January, 1813, General Winchester moved forward and reinforced Colonels Lewis and Allen. This reinforcement consisted of 300 regulars, commanded by Colonel Wells. Colonel Lewis, who was an experienced officer in Indian service, had posted his troops in an enclosed garden, with an open field on his right. Colonel Wells outranked Lewis as an officer of the regular army, as Lewis was only a volunteer, and he demanded the position on his right. This placed Colonel Wells in the open field, while Lewis and Allen still remained in the enclosed garden, with a picket fence as their protection. Colonel

Lewis strongly insisted that Colonel Wells should be placed in the same garden on his left, but General Winchester, yielding to the exactions of the regular army officer, ordered that Colonel Wells be placed in the open field on the right.

General Proctor, who was in command of the British at Malden, pushed forward with all his force. He prepared for an assault on the dawn of the 22d. It was hardly light, when, with his artillery covering his right, and both his flanks protected by Indian marksmen, he advanced upon the Americans. But no sooner had he reached within musket shot of the Kentuckians, than he was met by such galling and incessant a fire that part of his army fell in confusion. Discovering the exposed position of the army under Wells, the British general rushed forward all his force against him. Volley after volley of musketry broke the stillness of the morning air, and the whoop of the Indians and the cheers of the Kentuckians sounded on every side. But the 300 regulars could not withstand the assault of the entire British force. After the battle had lasted twenty minutes, General Winchester saw that he must relieve Wells and place him within the enclosure occupied by General Lewis. The moment an order was given for this purpose the British and Indians redoubled their forces and pressed the Americans so hard that the line fell in disorder. A panic seized the regulars and they rushed towards the river to cross the rapids, where the remainder of the Kentucky army was in camp. The British and Indians pursued them, tomahawking and scalping all who came in their way.

General Winchester, although incompetent, was brave. He endeavored to reform his men. Colonels Lewis and Allen each took a company of fifty men, rushed out of their enclosures, and did their best to check the defeat and rout. Nothing would avail; nothing could prevent the disaster. Colonel Allen was killed and General Winchester and Colonel Lewis taken prisoners. The two Kentucky companies that had come with the regulars were swept away. It was here that the Jessamine troops interposed with superb courage and bravery. Captain Price was killed, together with a large number of his company. Some fell by rifle balls, some were scalped, others were left to perish in the cold.

In the fight thus far Proctor had lost one-fourth of his force, but he was delighted to know that General Winchester was among the prisoners. Sending for General Winchester he recounted the savageness of the Indians, and the difficulty which he would have in restraining them if the battle was continued. He said that he could set fire to every house in the village and this he would probably have to do and that as a result the innocent women and children would be massacred by the Indians. He then asked General Winchester to direct his men to surrender. General Winchester consented to advise surrender, but when the message was carried to the Kentuckians and handed to Major Madison, who was the ranking officer after the capture of Colonel Lewis, informing him that he and the Kentuckians with him had been surrendered by General Winchester, Major Madison refused to recognize General Winchester's authority to command his surrender while a prisoner, and declared his determination to die with the Kentuckians unless favorable terms of surrender were given.

At last General Proctor entered into an agreement that all private property should be respected, that sleds should be sent the next morning to remove the sick and wounded to Amherstburg, that the prisoners should be guarded from the savages and that the side arms of the officers should be restored to them next morning. Major Madison finally did reluctantly surrender. He was induced to do this by the failure of ammunition.

That night the prisoners, 600 in number, were carried to Amherstburg. They were put in a wood-yard, exposed to a pelting rain, without sheds or blankets or fire. Instead of the sleds, which were to come for the wounded, came 200 savages, who rushed in the houses where the wounded lay and killed them, scalped them and set the houses on fire. In the smouldering ashes the bones of 64 men were consumed.

The bodies of the Americans were denied sepulture and were left a prey to the animals of the village. Afterwards they were placed in the ground and the following summer, when the American army passed the same way, their bones were again exposed. They were buried once more, but there went up from the heart of every Kentuckian the stirring cry of "Remember the Raisin."

The night before this awful battle Captain Price had written to his father-in-law. He had a premonition of his death.

HIGH BRIDGE OVER KENTUCKY RIVER AT MOUTH OF DICK'S RIVER.

Capt. James C. Price was the father of the late Kleber F. Price, of Jessamine county, who died at his residence, above Nicholasville, in 1864. The accompanying letter of Captain Price was addressed to his wife, and was, doubtless, the last letter he ever wrote to his family. He was killed in the battle of Raisin, January 22, 1813. He was a gallant and chivalrous soldier and a man of noble and generous impulses. His body was never recognized and his remains, with those of his compatriots, who died in that dreadful conflict, rest in unmarked graves, in the soil of the state they died to redeem and defend. He commanded the Jessamine Blues, which was one of the most noted military companies in its day. The uniform was blue, with light facings, and was considered, in those days, a marvel of beauty.

"In Camp, near Raisin River,
"Jan. 16, 1813.

"Dear Susan: I have only time to inform you that we ex-"pect to have a battle tomorrow with the British and Indians. "On the eve of battle I have believed it proper to address you "these lines. As you are aware that the object nearest to my "heart is your welfare and that of my children, and so far as I "have been able I have provided everything in my power for "your comfort and that of my children. I feel in no unhappy "mood about my girl children; I know they are in your com-"pany at all hours of the day. You know where they visit and "who are their associates. My only son, I feel a great interest "in his future life and welfare. Early impressions are lasting "and often, perhaps always, tend to give a permanent cast to the "leading principles of the heart, and to the general character of "the mind. Teach my boy to love truth, to speak truth at all "times. He must not be allowed to associate with children or "other persons who indulge in swearing or misrepresentations. "He must be taught to bear in mind that 'an honest man is the "noblest work of God;' he must be rigidly honest in his dealings. "He must be taught to attend church every Sabbath. Never "allow him to run about on Sabbath days, fishing. Teach my son "the habits of industry. Industry and virtue are twin brothers, "but indolence and vice are closely connected. Indolence leads to "every vice and every other evil. Industry leads to virtue and

"every other good.   Not a day must be lost in teaching him how
"to work, and the great principles of our holy religion must be
"on all occasions impressed on his mind.   It may be possible I
"may fall in battle and my only boy must know that his father,
"next to God, loves his country, and is now risking his life in de-
"fending that country against a barbarous and cruel enemy.   Be
"sure and teach my son, with Pope, to say and feel that—

"Vice is a monster of such frightful mien
"As to be hated needs but to be seen.
"Yet seen, too oft, familiar with her face,
"We first endure, then pity, then embrace.

"Teach him these lines of the great poet; they will do him
"good when he grows older.   Pray for me that you may be with
"me once more.
"Your affectionate husband,
"James C. Price.

"Susanah Price,
"Near Nicholasville, Ky.

"Post Script.—The snow is two feet deep, the crust is very
"hard and we walk over it and ride upon it on horseback.   We
"often sleep under such deep snow, we cover up in our blankets
"and we sleep warm during the night.   Eb. has been sick, but is
"now on duty.   "J. C. P."

In Camp, Near Newport, Ky.
February 20, 1813.

Mrs. Mary Price:

You will, long before this reaches you, have received the painful intelligence of the death of your brave and gallant son, Capt.
James C. Price, who was killed and scalped by the Indians on
the morning of January 22d.   He had been engaged in a
severe skirmish early on the morning of the 17th.   At ten o'clock
he was ordered by General Winchester to bring in all the wounded
men and carry them in all the sleds beyond the reach of the Indians.   In the discharge of this duty Captain Price and myself, at
the head of fifty men of our company, were attacked by a large
body of Indians, who had concealed themselves in the timber, on
the river bank.   The Indians had succeeded in breaking the crust

of the deep snow a mile above our camp, on the river, which was the only road through which we could reach the command of General Winchester, who had retreated about three miles, and was awaiting the arrival of General Harrison. As soon as the Indians opened a heavy fire on us we returned their fire and continued a rapid retreat to the main army, under General Winchester, over the only road on which the Indians, under their chief, Tecumseh, had early on the morning of the 18th succeeded in breaking the thick crust of the snow, which was two feet deep. In this trap we were caught. In getting away from the river many of our men were killed, and scalped before we got out of the deep snow. Captain Price was shot in the right shoulder by a musket ball, which disabled his right arm; he was attacked by three Indians; he ran his sword through the heart of one of them, but was soon overpowered, killed and scalped. Eight of our company, besides Captain Price, were brutally massacred; more than thirty got away and reached the command of General Winchester in safety. I had five bullet holes in my hat and clothing. The force of General Winchester was 350 and we were attacked again early on the morning of January 22d by a large force of British and Indians. We were completely routed and all of our army taken prisoners. General Proctor, the British commander, suffered the savages to kill and scalp more than twenty of our soldiers after we had surrendered. About twelve o'clock we were marched off. Dr. Todd and Dr. Augustine Bower of our regiment were left with the sick and wounded. About sunrise the next day, instead of sleds coming to convey the sick and wounded to Malden, a large body of Indians made their appearance, painted black and red. They began to plunder, and the sick and wounded were scalped. One Indian had the scalp of Captain Price. I, being next in command of the company from Jessamine, the savage showed the scalp to me, but I knew he was lying for Captain Price was very baldheaded on the top of his head. The few who were able to be sent to Malden were saved, but all who gave out were killed on the way and were left lying on the road in the deep snow. General Proctor, after he had promised us protection before our surrender, never named, nor did he pay any attention to our sick and helpless soldiers. General Winchester and Major Madison repeatedly told him of it, but he paid no atten-

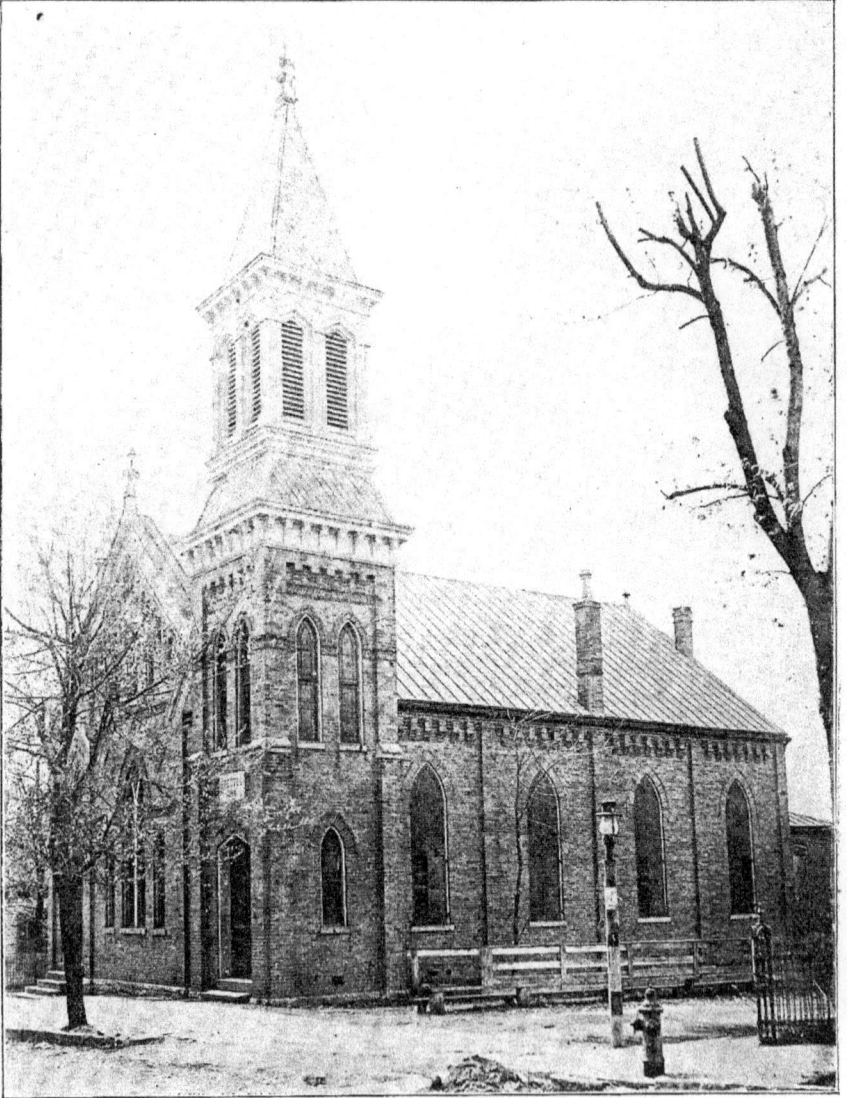

NICHOLASVILLE CHRISTIAN CHURCH.

tion to them whatever. Capt. Elliott, a cowardly British officer, said to Major Madison and Winchester, in my hearing, that "the Indians were very excellent surgeons and ought to kill all the officers and men." I have, as you well know, passed through a terrible winter in suffering for our country. We have all been exchanged, and will be at our homes the tenth of March. I rejoice that we have done our duty to God and our country. Ebenezer is now lieutenant in my place. Look for us on the tenth.

Your friend and neighbor.

WILLIAM CALDWELL,
Acting Captain of the Blues.

Conduct of the Kentuckians at Raisin.

The conduct of the Kentucky troops under their own officers evinced the highest order of courage and gallantry. They were worthy of the state whence they came and worthy of all the expectations of those who had sent them to this war.

General Winchester, in speaking of the Kentucky troops, said: "On them too much praise can not be bestowed. Assailed by numbers greatly superior, supported by six pieces of artillery constantly employed, they gallantly defended themselves with small arms alone for over four hours of constant battle. No troops ever behaved with more cool and determined bravery, from the commanding officer down to the common soldier. There was scarcely a single abandonment of duty. At last, when their ammunition was nearly exhausted and they were surrounded by the enemy, greatly superior in numbers and the means of war, they surrendered with a reluctance rarely to be found on similar occasions."

Had the regulars under Colonel Wells sustained themselves as did the volunteers under Lewis and Allen, the awful tragedy of the Raisin would have been avoided, and instead of defeat and massacre and broken faith, there would have been a glorious victory. The Kentuckians beat off Proctor and his Indians. "At ten o'clock in the morning," says Butler, in his history, "Proctor, finding it useless to sacrifice his men in a vain attempt to dislodge this little band of heroes, withdrew his forces to the heights, intending to abandon the contest or to await the return of the Indians who had pursued the retreating party. The loss sustained by our men was inconsiderable and when Proctor withdrew they employed the leisure it afforded them to take breakfast at their posts."

Their surrender was only obtained by Proctor taking advantage of General Winchester's capture and by basely misrepresenting a message which he had sent to these Kentucky troops within the enclosure.

Civil War.

At the commencement of the Civil War, the people of Jessamine county were divided in sentiment, and many of its citizens took up arms both in the Federal and Confederate armies.

Company K, of the 20th Regiment, Kentucky Infantry, commanded by Col. Sanders Bruce, was almost altogether composed of Jessamine county men, and they were in the service three years.

Andrew McCampbell, captain, resigned June, 1862; Charles R. West was elected captain May 24, 1863, served three years; George W. Baker, first lieutenant, resigned in 1862; Ben Thornburg, Joseph Lewis, afterward William L. Steele; Samuel M. Anderson was made first lieutenant September 29, 1862; Allen A. Burton and S. T. Corn, now of Corlinville, Ill., were first and second lieutenants; William Plumblee, first sergeant; Levi Reynolds, second sergeant; Oliver Davis, first corporal; Jonathan White, second corporal.

Names of Men of the Company:

Albertson, Adam; Bailey. E. Hayden; Bailey, Robt.; Baker, Benedict; Barnes, David; Barnes, Geo. W.; Brennan, John; Bright, Benj.; Brown, S. S.; Brumfield, James; Bruner, Tilford; Bruner, M.; Burch, James; Burgess, Wm.; Coleman, Francis; Courtney, Jno. F.; Crow, Zebedee; Dean, Wm.; Dobson, Elias; Dobson, Pleasant; Easley, Jno. T.; English, W. T.; Fain, Jno. K.; Foster, Frank; Foster, James; Gifford, Jabez; Gilride, Thos.; Green, Corydon B.; Henderson, S. M.; House, Benj.; Hockersmith, Edward; Howard, James W.; Hunter, Jos. W.; Hersey, Jno.; Land, James; Land, Robt.; Letcher, Alex.; McKane.

James; McMurty, Robt. L.; Masters, Frank; Masters, Henry W.; Murphy, Chas.; Phillips, Dr. H. H.; Plumbly, Wiley; Preston, Alfred; Preston, Samuel; Ramsey, Samuel; Ramsey, Jno. F.; Reynolds, Henry; Reynolds, James; Reynolds, W. H.; Rhorer, Hardin; Riley, Henry; Sharp, Thos.; Short, James M.; Thornbro, Robt.; Tredway, David; Tredway, Wm.; Turpin, Jno.; Walters, Bluford; Walters, Geo.; Woods, Jess.

The following is a list of the colored soldiers who served in the United States Army in Company L, Fifth Cavalry, Capt. J. S. Caldwell, Bowen's Regiment, J. S. Brisbin's Brigade:

Allen, Dudley; Anderson, Jefferson; Ballard, Wilson; Balard, Geo.; Berry, Chas.; Bowen, James; Baggs, Geo.; Burley, Frank; Berry, Edmund; Bell, A. Travis; Brown, Richard; Brown, David; Brown, Sidney; Brown, Sandy; Bowles, Jack; Blackburn, Chas.; Bush, Jos.; Black, Jacob; Brown, Perry; Bryant, Green; Burnside, Jno.; Campbell, Alexander; Carter, Jos.; Carson, Wm.; Clay, Ambrose; Clay, Henson; Coleman, Samuel; Davis, David; Denny, Ben; Douglas, Ned.; Favors, Jos.; Fry, Louis; French, John; Gable, Green; Grodon, Marion; Dr. Garnett; Gatewood, Thos.; George, Lewis; Garvin, Henry; Gess, Frank; Hamilton, Henry; Hamilton, Perry; Hamilton, Sanford; Hanson, Robt.; Howard, Adam, (died 1882, 99 years old); Hood, Daniel; Hunt, Jack; Jackson, Alex.; King, Hiram; King, Milo; Kyle, Orange; McConnell, Geo.; McDowell, Bacchus; Mason, Robt.; Massie, Jos.; Martin, Edward; Moran, Anderson; Oldham, Thos.; Overstreet, Burd; Owsley, Branch; Peniston, James; Priest, Stephen; Ridgeley, Dick; Scott, Alfred; Scott, Charles; Scott, King; Smith, Jos.; Smith, Wm.; Spillman, Alex.; Stout, Isaac; Stuart, John; Thomas, James; Thompson, Frank; Walker, Edmund; Walker, Whitfield.

Confederate Monument.

The handsomest public monument in Jessamine county is that erected by the Jessamine Confederate Memorial Association, to the Confederates buried in Maple Grove cemetery, Nicholasville. This monument reflects great credit on the Confederate soldiers and friends who built it. The work was started

CONFEDERATE MONUMENT.

in 1880; the monument was dedicated on the 15th of June, 1896, and stands in the court-house yard. The platform was erected in the court-house yard as the place for the dedicatory ceremonies. Special trains were run on all the roads entering the city, and the delegation from Louisville, headed by Col. Bennett H. Young, brought the largest number of persons. The city of Nicholasville royally entertained all those who came to unite in the ceremonies. At one o'clock they began. Dr. Charles Mann, president of the association, presided. Capt. John H. Leathers and Col. Bennett H. Young, of Louisville, were the orators of the day. The monument was unvailed by Miss Josephine Mann and Master Lawson Oxley, of Cynthiana, son of Jefferson Oxley, the first president of the association. The exercises were opened with prayer by Rev. F. W. Noland, a member of the Eighth Kentucky Confederate Cavalry, and the Confederate Glee Club of Louisville, sang a beautiful and appropriate selection; the closing song, "Tread Lightly, Ye Comrades," produced a profound impression upon the audience. The history of the work of the association, in connection with the monument, was read by Prof. A. N. Gordon, its secretary and treasurer.

In 1862, Dr. Charles Mann, then a surgeon in the Confederate Army, was ordered by Gen. Kirby Smith, to gather and care for the sick and wounded who had been left about Camp Dick Robinson. About eighty of these, he brought in private conveyances to Nicholasville, where they were nursed and cared for by the ladies of the community; those who died there were buried in the Nicholasville cemetery. After the war, Dr. Mann, with the aid of James S. McKenzie and Charles Oldham, gathered other Confederate dead, including those who had been buried in the Federal cemetery at Camp Nelson, and brought them to the cemetery at Nicholasville, where a lot had been generously donated by the Cemetery Company for that purpose. .. .. ..

The original headboards, having rotted down, were replaced by Col. Bennett H. Young, and these, in turn, by beautiful granite tablets, which now mark them. ....

Jefferson Oxley, long a leading merchant in Nicholasville, and as true, brave and chivalrous a soldier as ever wore the gray, did as much as, if not more than, any one man to secure the funds necessary to construct the monument. He died when success was in sight, but before he saw the work accomplished.   His comrades, and those whose dead the monument commemorates, will long keep green his memory.

Dr. Chas. Mann, the president, was the surgeon of the Fifth Kentucky Confederate Infantry, and rendered distinguished services in the Army of Tennessee. He was frequently detailed to important positions, and returned from the war with highest commendations of his skill and efficiency as a surgeon and man, since which time he has practiced his profession in Jessamine county.

Prof. A. N. Gordon, a moving spirit in the erection of the monument, was a brave and gallant soldier in the Confederacy, for many years the brilliant leader of educational work in the county, as principal of Bethel Academy, and now principal of Allegan Academy for Boys, near Lexington.

The following is a list of the Confederate dead buried in the cemetery, in whose honor the monument was erected:

John Martin, 30th Alabama; A. L. Hale, 39th North Carolina; Henry Rice, 42d Georgia; W. H. Wallace, 6th Florida; J. E. D. Morris, 6th Florida; W. J. Hale, 40th Georgia; W. B. Carter, 9th Georgia; Peter Guin, C. S. A.; W. L. Cooley, 2d Kentucky; B. F. Kernan, 6th Kentucky; Eugene Dickson, 42d Georgia; Capt. Samuel Scott, Louisiana; C. R. Richardson, C. S. A.; W. H. Yarbrough, 1st Alabama; J. W. Washam, 17th Mississippi; W. E. Copeland, 3rd Alabama; John A. Bass, C. S. A.; S. M. Wilson, 53d Georgia; D. Campbell, 63d Virginia; J. R. Cox, 59th Georgia; J. Brock, 18th Georgia; W. M. Boge, 16th Georgia; O. W. White, 41st Alabama; L. Johnson, 6th Georgia; J. A. Bowles, 59th Georgia; J. B. Hale, 2d Georgia; E. Willoughby, 1st Georgia; Geo. W. Trabue, C. S. A.; H. Owenby, 39th North Carolina.

The peroration of Colonel Young's dedicatory address, was as follows:

"Nor can I close this address without some reference to the women of Jessamine county, who, with such patience, such industry, such zeal and such unselfishness, have labored so long to erect this monument to our beloved dead. Many who helped at the inception of the undertaking have been denied the happiness of seeing its fulfillment, but we feel the sweet presence of their spirits, though they passed over the river before success had crowned the labors of the association. If they are not here, we shall, at least, in love and gratitude, remember them and their work for this cause, and their absence alone mars the completeness of this occasion. The noblest and highest of the war's demands was to be worthy of the faith and trust of the Southern women, and it mitigated the anguish and bitterness of defeat to be able through manly tears to look down into the tear-dimmed eyes of the women of the South and tell them that in the sufferings, sacrifices and privations of all that weary struggle, there had been nothing done or left undone which rendered the men of the Confederacy unworthy of what was required by its women, and now, after the lapse of long years, we find the same gentle, loving, beautiful, brave, and unselfish women, with all the enthusiasm of their nobler nature, rearing these memorials to those of our comrades who went down amid the storms of war, and thus keeping the record of those heroes who gave their blood as a seal of their loyalty to the land of their love and of their troth. We utter benediction for such women. May the angels of blessing and peace hover over and around them in this life and at its end bring them peacefully to that place where there will be no wars, where monuments are not required, where death and sorrow never come. With reverent homage we stand by these graves of our heroes. They are hallowed in our hearts and souls, and we will honor and adore them forever. These are the men who fought with the Johnstons, Lee, Jackson, Breckinridge, Morgan and Polk, and Bragg and Hardee and Hood, and Forrest and Hill, and Cheatham and Cleburne, and hosts of immortal heroes. These are the partakers of the sublime glory of the Confederate armies, and we come in tenderness and devotion and affection to mark, beautify and bless the soil that garners their dust, and to declare by this monument, which we trust will remain forever, that the memories of the virtues, of the courage, of the chivalry, and of the bravery, of the sacrifices, of the sufferings, of the renown of our departed comrades shall be as deathless, as their deeds were illustrious.

> "By fairy hands their knell is rung, ...
> By forms unseen their dirge is sung.
> Here honor comes—a pilgrim gray—
> To bless the turf that wraps their clay.
> And Freedom doth a while repair,
> To dwell, a weeping hermit, there."

Capt. James White, a son of Elder William White, in 1862, when General Bragg invaded Kentucky, recruited a company of infantry, which was in the Fifth Kentucky Regiment Confederate Infantry, commanded by Col. Hiram Hawkins. Part of the men in this company were recruited from Grant county and were in all the great battles of the Atlanta campaign, and surrendered at Greensborough, N. C., in 1865. The following is a list of the members from Jessamine county, in Captain White's company, and in Company B, Capt. Wm. Lewis, Eighth Kentucky Cavalry, commanded by Col. Roy S. Cluke:

Adams, Thos.; Arnspiger, Geo.; Blackford, Benj.; Bowman, Sanford; Bowman, Robt.; Bowen, Harrison; Brower, Edw. A.; Brown, Samuel M.; Burch, Courtney L.; Campbell, Fernando Wood; Campbell, Peter; Campbell, Richard; Campbell, Stephen; Chrisman, Benj.; Cleveland, John; Cogar, John; Cook, John W.; Cook, T. B.; Cooley, W. L.; Corman, Geo.; Corman, Grattan; Daniel, W. H.; Davis, James; Davis, John P.; Davis, William; Deboe, Wesley; Drake, John; Elgin, Jno..S.; Elmore, Fletcher; Foster, Dr. T. W.; Funk, Henry, killed at Chickamauga; Gooch, James; Gordon, Prof. A. N.; Gregg, S. S.; Gwuyn, Edw.; Hanly, Samuel; Harris, J. W.; Hawkins, Jno. T.; Hayden, W. A.; Holloway, Dr. Jno.; Hollway, Wm.; Jones, Jonathan, at that time 62, died in '91; Jones, A. D.; Jones, James B.; Jones, O. A.; Knight, Campbell; Lampkins, Jno. B.; Lear, John T.; Lear, Jos. R.; Lear, Wm.; Lee, Melvin; Livingston, James; Lindsey, Jos.; Lowry, David; Lowry, Samuel; McAfee, Maj. Allin L.; McAfee, Capt. Jno. J.; McBrayer, Frank; McDavitt, Chas.; McKinzie, Edw. O.; McKenzie, James; McKenzie, Jno. H.; Mann, Dr. Chas.; Metcalf, Geo. W.; Musselman, Henry; Myers, W. E.; Nave, Samuel; Nave, Tilford; Noe, James; Nolan, Rev. Wm.; Patten, Wm.; Phelps, Edw.; Price, Louis S.; Reynolds, Geo.; Robinson, Jacob Creath; Roberts, Rankin; Roberts, Jas. A.; Rowland, G. T.; Rue, Allen; Rue, Frank; Sandusky, Jacob; Sandusky, L. E.; Scott, Robt., killed at Strawberry Plains; Scott, Samuel; Sparks, Moreau; Stine, Jno. G.; Soper, David; Spears, Christopher, died from wounds in Camp Douglas; Steele, Atlas; Vantries, Emanuel, killed at Chickamauga; Walls, Newbold C.; Walls, Benj. J.; Warner, Wm.; Welch, James M.; Woods, Thos. J.; Young, Bennett H.

Scenery.

Jessamine county has some remarkable natural scenery. The Hudson and the Rhine have nothing so beautiful, majestic or grand as the cliffs along the Kentucky and Dix rivers. If they had been open so as to have been accessible, they would have made Jessamine county famous; but for many years they could not be reached by railroad and only a part of them were within the limits of navigation on the Kentucky river, and the small boats and the slow time rendered the journey unattractive to the traveling public. With swift boats operated upon the river now that it is locked and dammed to the extreme limits of Jessamine county, a great tide of visitors will flow in to see these wonderful natural curiosities. The first complete American geography, written by Jedediah Morse and published in 1789 at Elizabethtown, New Jersey, gave a description of the scenery. It says:

"The banks or rather the precipices of the Kentucky and Dix rivers are to be reckoned among the natural curiosities of this county. Here the astonished eye beholds three or four hundred feet of solid perpendicular rocks, in some parts of the limestone kind and in others of fine white marble curiously checked with strata of astonishing regularity. These rivers have the appearance of deep, artificial canals. Their high, rocky banks are covered with red cedar groves. The accounts of the fertility of the soil have in some instances exceeded belief and probably been exaggerated. The high grounds of Kentucky are remarkably good. The lands of the first rate are too rich for wheat, but will produce fifty to sixty, and in some instances one hundred, bushels and even more of good corn an acre. In common the land will produce thirty bushels of wheat or rye to the acre. Barley, oats, cotton, hemp, flax, and vegetables of all kinds common in this climate yield abundantly. The old Virginia planters say, if the climate does not prove too moist, few soils known will yield more or better tobacco."

Dr. Christopher Graham prepared for Collins' History a description of some of these curiosities in Jessamine county, and described them in a most effective and attractive way. He says:

"After much vexation and annoyance, occasioned by the difficulties of the road, we arrived near the object of our visit, and

METHODIST CHURCH, SOUTH.

quitting our horses, proceeded on foot. Upon approaching the break of the precipice, under the direction of our guide, we suddenly found ourselves standing on the verge of a yawning chasm, and immediately beyond, bottomed in darkness, the Devil's Pulpit was seen rearing its black, gigantic form, from amid the obscurity of the deep and silent valley. The background to this gloomy object presented a scene of unrelieved desolation. Cliff rose on cliff and crag surmounted crag, sweeping off on either hand in huge semicircles, until the wearied eye became unable to follow the countless and billowy-like mazes of that strange and awful scene. The prevailing character of the whole was that of savage grandeur and gloom. A profound silence broods over the place, broken only by the muffled rushing of the stream far down in its narrow passage, cleaving its way to its home in the ocean. Descending by a zigzag path to the shore of the river, while our companions were making preparations to cross, I strayed through the valley. The air was cool, refreshing and fragrant, and vocal with the voices of many birds. The bending trees, the winding stream with its clear and crystal waters, the flowering shrubs, and clustering vines walled in by these adamantine ramparts—which seem to tower to the skies—make this a place of rare and picturesque beauty. The dew drops still hung glittering on the leaves, the whispering winds played with soft music through the rustling foliage, and the sunbeams struggling through the overhanging forest kissed the opening flowers, and all combined made up a scene of rural loveliness and romance, which excited emotions of unmingled delight. The boat having arrived, the river was crossed without difficulty, and we commenced the ascent, and after measuring up two hundred and seventy feet, arrived at the base of the 'Pulpit.'   Fifty paces from this point, and parallel with it, in the solid ledge of the cliff, is a cave of considerable extent. At its termination there passes out like the neck of a funnel, an opening, not larger than a hogshead. Upon pitching rocks into this cave, a rumbling was heard at an immense distance below the earth. Some are of the opinion that this cave contains a bottomless pit. We now ascended the cliffs some fifty feet further, clambering up through a fissure in the rocks, having the Pulpit on our right, and a range of cliffs on our left. To look up here makes the head dizzy. Huge and dark masses roll up above you,

10

upon whose giddy heights vast crags jut out and overhang the valley, threatening destruction to all below. The floating clouds give these crags the appearance of swimming in mid air. The ascent of these rocks, though somewhat laborious, is perfectly safe, being protected by natural walls on either side, and forming a perfect stairway, with steps from eight to ten feet thick. At the head of this passage, there is a hole through the river side of the wall, large enough to admit the body, and through which one may crawl, and look down upon the rushing stream below. At the foot of the stairway stands the Pulpit, rising from the very brink of the main ledge, at more than two hundred feet of an elevation above the river, but separated from the portion which towers up to the extreme heights. The space is twelve feet at bottom, and as the cliff retreats slightly at this point, the gap is perhaps thirty feet at the top. The best idea that can be formed of this rock is to suppose it to be a single column, standing in front of the continuous wall of some vast building, or ruin, the shaft standing as colonnades are frequently built upon an elevated platform. From the platform to the capital of the shaft is not less than one hundred feet, making the whole elevation of the 'Devil's Pulpit' three hundred feet. It is called by some the inverted candlestick, to which it has a striking resemblance. There are two swells, which form the base moulding and occupy about forty feet of the shaft. It then narrows to an oblong of about three feet by six, at which point there are fifteen distinct projections. This narrow neck continues with some irregularity for eight or ten feet, winding off at an angle of more than one degree from the line of gravity. Then commences the increased swell, and craggy offsets, first overhanging one side, and then the other, till they reach the top or cap rock, which is not so wide as the one below it, but is still fifteen feet across."

Miss Jessamine Woodson, a descendant of distinguished Jessamine ancestors, and who was named for the county, prepared for the Acme Club a history of the county, and some of her descriptions are so vivid and so exquisitely penned that they deserve preservation, in more permanent form than newspaper columns; and the author can not refrain from inserting two paragraphs:

Beautiful and highly favored for situation, and beautiful and symmetrical in form, bounded on three sides by the Kentucky river, making a horseshoe, which is for luck as well as beauty, we behold beautiful and highly improved farms, well watered and drained by three pretty creeks and intersected by 130 miles of smooth, well-kept turnpikes made of the blue limestone, which can not be found of the same hard quality anywhere else in the world, and these roads, with the thoroughbred horses, the product of the bluegrass and limestone water, is the most attractive feature of this region. Jessamine is better supplied with these roads than her neighbors. We also see her important railways crossing each other in the center of the county and diverging to the four points of the compass, fifteen or more churches and schools, sixteen postoffices and country stores, seven railway stations, three or four villages, besides the county seat, and many a neat, comfortable farm house, and a number of large and elegant country seats, some of them dating back to ante-bellum days. We see waving fields of grain, hemp and tobacco and woodland pastures, carpeted with green, velvety grass, and trees that are tall and straight and of great variety and of wondrous beauty, and under these and in the meadows are groups of fat sheep, Jerseys and Shorthorns, thoroughbred horses, Berkshire pigs and Southdown sheep. Thrifty fruit orchards we see, too, and green hedges of osage orange, and stone fences and barn-yards with all sorts of pretty domestic fowls.

Our bluegrass pasture lands are our special pride. Grass as soft as velvet, and with blades often a yard long, and as fine as a siken cord, without a weed, growing close to the very trunks of the tall, wide-spreading elms, walnut, oak and maple trees. Here is the home of the dryads and wood nymphs, and here the poet must have been inspired to write, "The Groves were God's First Temples," and these actually were to the noble army of pioneers who first set up "The Banner of the Cross" while building their log cabins with rifles in their hands. The country is gently undulating, with hill and dale, meadow and wood, giving variety and sparing the eye from monotony until you approach the river, when it becomes more rugged, but always grander and more wonderful in beauty and sublimity. It is well and beautifully watered, everywhere unfailing springs of clear, cool water, gushing out from rocky ledges or bubbling out of a mysterious cave, overtopped with waving elm, beach or sugar maple trees. A most welcome sight these were to the pioneers who knew nothing of cisterns and microbes, and they invariably decided the site of the homestead. Near many of these are still to be seen the old, moss-covered spring-house, so suggestive of cool, rich cream and firm, golden butter, and of primitive arcadian life. Such a spring is Jessamine, the source of the creek of the same name, and of Hickman and Sinking creek, which Mr. Collins tells us is a remarkable natural curiosity. It rises near the Fayette line, about a mile north of Providence church, runs west through the beautiful Lafon, Blackford and Sandusky farms, and unites with a smaller, Sinking creek, from the north in Woodford, forming Clear creek. It sinks four times, running under ground from one quarter to a mile each time. At times in the winter and spring, when the water can not sink as fast as it falls, it is fifty feet deep and a mile wide. There are many wonders and curiosities under ground besides these streams.

Jessamine Creek.

Jessamine creek rises in the northern part of Jessamine county and flows in a southern direction emptying into the Kentucky river a few miles above High Bridge. It rises about two and a half miles above Keene, on the farm now belonging to Mr. Pleasant Cook, which was early settled by the Singletons and Chownings. There are two large springs from which the water comes up, but both of these have been very much changed in later years.

One of the recent owners of the land on which is the creek head, finding the sources of the stream practically bottomless, and that his stock would sometimes fall in between the ledges, which created a sort of chasm from which the water rose, hauled four or five hundred loads of loose stones and threw them into this opening, thus endeavoring to make it safe, so that stock might walk over it. The result has been that when heavy rains fall, the water boils up on both sides within twenty or thirty feet of the spring itself. It has never been known to go dry. It comes out of the side of the hill, the rocks of which overhang the spring about ten feet high. Two large oak trees grow immediately over the spring, and rise out of the cliff overhanging it. While the stream has never gone dry within the memory of the young men, the current of water has very much decreased in the last fifty years.

The headwaters of Jessamine creek are in the midst of one of the most fertile portions of Jessamine county. The Singletons, the Cokers, the Sanduskys, the Chownings, and the Barclays settled in this neighborhood. Jeremiah Singleton, one of the earliest settlers on Jessamine creek, built a mill about half a mile below the mouth of the creek. It was used both as a saw and a grist mill. The dam was built first of stone, and afterwards lined with brick laid in cement. The mill itself was built of stone. Steam with its accommodating powers, which could be located on roads or in cities, superseded these old mills, and, about fifteen years ago, the mill was torn down and the bricks in the dam removed and used for other purposes.

Beginning at its very mouth, the creek passes through some of the finest land in Kentucky, which is admirably adapted for corn, but principally for hemp. Beautiful farms with elegant and tasteful residences are seen on every side, and the great fall which it is necessary for the stream to make in order to reach down to the bottom of the tremendous cliffs on the Kentucky river, furnishes magnificent mill sites, and there were no less than six mills along this stream. That part of the stream called the "Narrows," near Glass' mill, has some most beautiful and picturesque scenery.

The creek makes a horseshoe bend, the points of the shoe being very close together. Between these the earth rises several hundred feet high, and, standing on either side, you can look far down below upon the stream winding its way in silence and grandeur to its resting place in the bosom of the Kentucky River. High up on the cliffs on the west side of the stream near the "Narrows" is the famous Chrisman Cave. This cave extends a great distance back from the entrance, running in a northwestern course, and it is a neighborhood wonder and attracts many visitors from all parts of the country.

A short distance below Spark's Ford is a natural curiosity, known as the "Little Mountain." It is a mound standing out separate and single and having no connection with the cliffs. There by the action of the water, or by some upheaval of nature, it has cut loose from all surroundings, and stands out alone and independent.

JESSAMINE FEMALE INSTITUTE.

The creek was given its name prior to 1774, and prior to that time it had been mentioned at Harrodsburg. There are two branches of the creek known as "Main Jessamine" and "East Jessamine." The East Jessamine rises about three-fourths of a mile above Nicholasville, between the Cincinnati Southern and the R. N. I. & B. R. R., on what is known as the Horine Place. It passes through the town of Nicholasville, and, keeping to the east of the Danville Turnpike, enters the main branch about three miles below Nicholasville.

The stone mill, known now as "Glass' Mill," three miles from the Kentucky river, is certainly over one hundred and ten (110) years old. It is supposed to have been laid out as a mill-site as early as 1782. It was subsequently turned into a paper mill which was operated as late as 1849. The rag-house and office still stand in a perfect state of preservation. Subsequently it was turned into a distillery, run by a gentleman named Bryan, and is now owned by Mr. Henry Glass. It has water power sufficient to operate the mill seven months in the year, and yields 72-horse power. It is a most admirable site, and is as picturesque and beautiful as it is useful.

Jessamine creek is about thirty miles in length.

Hickman Creek.

Hickman creek rises in Fayette county not far from Lexington, and after running through Fayette and the eastern half of Jessamine county, empties into the Kentucky river near what is known as "Boone's Knob." It is a larger stream than Jessamine creek, and was named for Rev. John Hickman, a pioneer Baptist preacher. It has an east and west branch, and each of these has numerous tributaries, which pass through high cliffs and ridges, rivaling at times the cliffs on the Kentucky river itself. The country between the two branches of Hickman creek is one of the most fertile in Jessamine county. The section drained by Hickman creek is well timbered, and has still a superb growth of oak, hackberry, ash, and hickory, with a sprinkling of maple. Along this creek the earliest settlements of Jessamine county were made, and some of the best citizens who ever came to Jessamine, made their homes in this locality. Mr. Philip Swigert, who was born September 27, 1798, came from this neighborhood. When quite a young man he became a deputy in the Woodford Circuit Court Clerk's office, under John McKinney, who formerly resided in Jessamine. He afterwards removed to Frankfort and died in 1871, in the 74th year of his age. He was one of the most distinguished Masons in the state, a self-made man, and by his native force, great good sense, and indomitable perseverance, acquired a large fortune and also secured a high standing with the best men of the state. He was born on the old farm near Marble Creek schoolhouse, once the property of A. P. Davis.

Jas. Rutherford, Sr., was another of the early settlers. He was a man of native force, strong friendships, great will, and a large number of his descendants still live in that portion of the county.

Abram Vince, who was born in Pennsylvania, in 1784, and died January 17, 1874, was also one of the settlers in this district. He came to Jessamine in 1803; he was a descendant of the Swiss emigrants who settled in Bucks county, Pennsylvania, the first half of the eighteenth century. He was a man of high character, great industry, and has left for himself and those who bore his name a goodly heritage.

Harrison Daniel also owned property in this section, and long bore honorable and honored part in the government of Jessamine county. He was sheriff of Jessamine county under the Constitution of 1799, as also a Justice of the Peace. He was a man of good education and strong mind. He was a member of the legislature in 1836 and '37.

The Bridge at the Mouth of Hickman.

The bridge at the mouth of Hickman was long considered one of the engineering wonders of Kentucky. It was part of the structure of the turnpike between Lexington, Nicholasville and Lancaster. It was projected when the state was interested in internal improvements, and was lending its credit and its money to the construction of railroads, canals and turnpikes. It cost $30,000. The length of a span was 270 feet, which was unusual for a wooden bridge. Garrard county paid a part of the cost of the structure. It required six months to build it, and about eighteen workmen were employed upon it—a large proportion of these were unskilled and received a dollar a day. It was erected in 1838 by Lewis B. Wernwag, a native of Pennsylvania; he died in Lexington, Mo., in 1874, aged seventy-six years. For the time and with the materials at hand, it is a wonderful structure. It has now remained intact for more than sixty years; it has carried all the traffic required on a great thoroughfare, and during the war it was considered so important that a regiment was stationed on either side to protect it from destruction. It is not only a unique piece of engineering, but, in view of the advances in engineering since that time, was a signal triumph; and, while it has long been one of the curiosities of Jessamine, it also stands as a monument to the engineering skill, enterprise and courage of its constructors. It was built some distance above the site and floated down the river on rafts in sections, and when put together in position it was so accurately constructed that not even a hammer was required to adjust its parts.

High Bridge.

One of the most noted of the engineering feats in the past thirty years, is the celebrated High Bridge, across the Kentucky river, at the mouth of Dick's river. It was built in 1876. The railway approaches the span from either direction along a ledge of rocks several hundred feet above the river, and the perpendicular cliffs run from the track to the water's edge for a mile on either side. Where the bridge crosses the Kentucky river it has an elevation of 276 feet above the river bed. At one time it was the highest bridge on the continent, and at the period of its construction was a marvel of ingenuity. A great many distinguished engineers of the country pronounced the work an impossibility. It was necessary to build the structure without trestling, and for that reason the cantilever principle was introduced. By this principle one span is erected, and from the end of this span is built out into space part of another span. The length to which such spans may be extended out into the air without support is fixed by the weight of the span from which it is built, and these spans from which the cantilevers are extended are generally weighted so that they carry tremendous burdens. Many distinguished engineers of America pronounced the plan of C. Shaler Smith, who constructed this bridge, visionary, and decided that it was not feasible in this way to construct a bridge at this point; but Mr. Smith was a skilled, learned and practical bridge engineer.

At this point the Kentucky river with its channel had cut down through the stone cliffs to a depth of about 290 feet. It was necessary to construct the bridge without trestles, and this Mr. Smith undertook to do. He assumed the responsibility of the construction personally, and in the end his designs and his calculations were found to be correct. The great cantilever arms stretched out from the piers on either side, reaching the middle of the channel, and when the last bolt, which was to hold them in place, was driven, it was said that they did not vary 1-100 of an inch from the calculations which this man had made one day in his office in Baltimore. He immediately sprang into prominence as one of the great bridge engineers of the world, and since then others have followed his ideas and adopted his plans.

The bridge known as Young's High Bridge, named in honor of Col. Bennett H. Young, over the Kentucky river at Tyrone, has a span 200 feet longer than the one constructed at the mouth of Dick's river. It is built upon the same principle, and thus over the Kentucky river are two of the great cantilever bridges of America.

At the time the Lexington & Danville Railroad was to be built, a suspension bridge was designed to cross this chasm, but the railway company failed after the piers had been erected, and these towers stand as a monument to the genius of John A. Roebling, who had the contract from the president of the Lexington & Danville Railroad, Gen. Leslie Combs, to build a suspension bridge, and about $100,000 were spent in the erection of the towers and anchorage for the construction of the suspension bridge which it became necessary to abandon because of the lack of financial support. On one of the towers is this inscription: "Gen. Leslie Combs, born in Clark county, Kentucky, November 28, 1793."

The old Cincinnati Railroad from Cincinnati to the South, was at first proposed as an outlet from the Ohio Valley to the southeastern seaboard. The enormous cost of constructing the railroad through the mountains of Kentucky and Tennessee, deterred private means from undertaking such a task, and the city of Cincinnati, after full investigation, in the summer of 1869, undertook to build a trunk line of railroad from Cincinnati to Chattanooga, in order to give Cincinnati proper connections with all the southern railway systems which centered at Chattanooga, and also to open up to the Cincinnati markets portions of Tennessee and Kentucky.

This line passes through Jessamine county for 17 miles, and is now one of the great American railway thoroughfares. To build it, Cincinnati paid out $20,000,000, but it has proven a good investment, and though it will pass from under the control of the city which built it the cost has been amply returned in the benefits it has bestowed.

Kentucky River Improvements.

The Kentucky river flows through Jessamine county for nearly twenty-five miles. It bounds the county on almost one-half of its border lines. The state undertook to improve the Kentucky river, but it abandoned the work, and the locks never reached farther than Frankfort.

In 1865 the Kentucky River Navigation Company was incorporated by the Legislature, for the purpose of building new locks and dams, and extending the navigation of the river through Jessamine county. At the September term of the Jessamine County Court, in 1865, John S. Bronaugh was appointed a commission to subscribe for $35,000 of stock in the Kentucky River Navigation Company, and in November, 1867, he was further directed to subscribe for $65,000 additional stock in the company. The company failed and its creditors attached these subscriptions. Their validity was attacked. The courts relieved Mercer and Garrard counties of their subscriptions, but Jessamine county was held for a large proportion of hers and compelled to pay it.

The river has been ceded to the United States .The old locks have been enlarged and repaired and new ones built. Navigation is now assured to the mouth of Hickman all the year round.

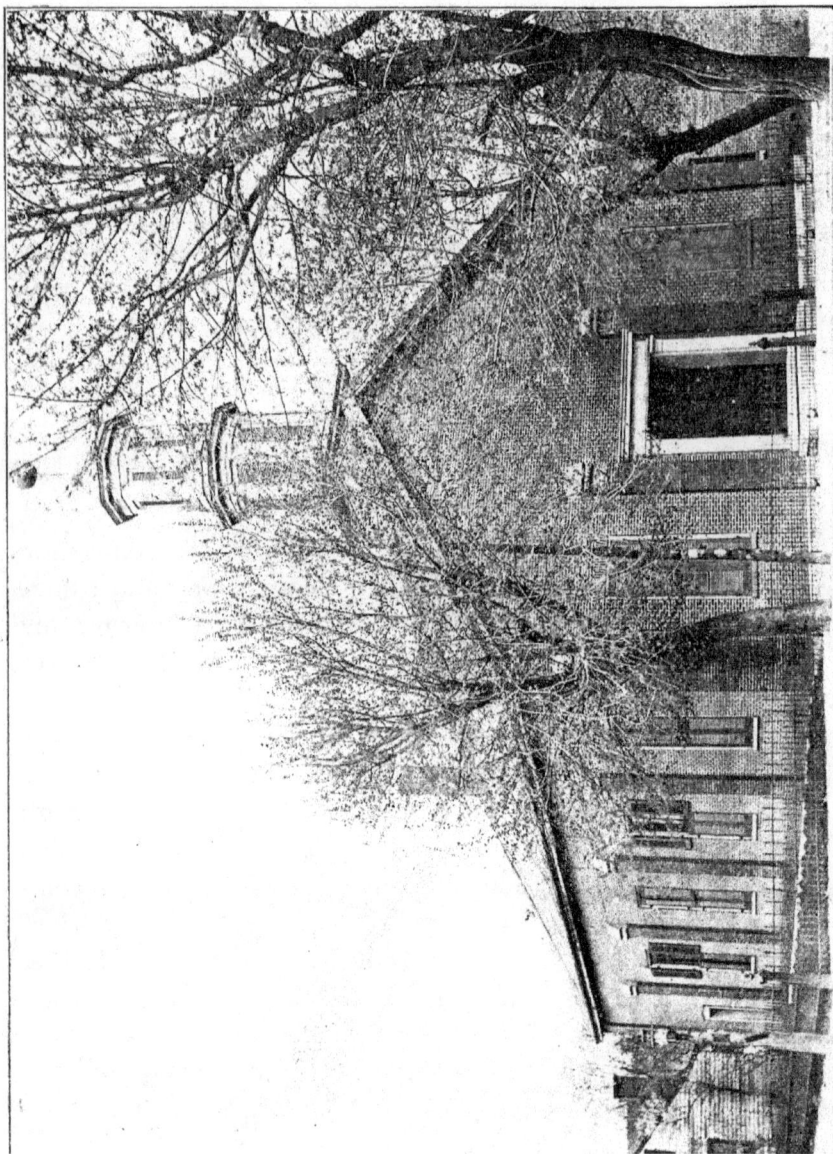

NICHOLASVILLE BAPTIST CHURCH

Another lock in process of construction will give navigation throughout the entire river border of the county and in a few years the system of locks will reach the coal fields on the North Fork of the Kentucky and secure to Jessamine county the advantage of river transit for the entire year from the coal fields to the mouth of the river at Carrollton.

Turnpikes.

Few counties in the state are better supplied with turnpikes than Jessamine. They are built partly by private subscriptions and partly by county aid. There are about 175 miles of turnpike in the county, and when it is remembered that it only has 158 square miles, it will be seen that the county is most thoroughly supplied with first-class roadways. At this time there are not ten miles of leading roads in the county that are not macadamized. The county has bought the turnpikes and hereafter they will be free.

Ferries.

Two of the earliest ferries established in Kentucky were within the limits of Jessamine county.

The first ferry in Kentucky was across the Kentucky river at Boonesboro, authorized in October, 1779, by the Legislature of Virginia, on the farm of Col. Richard Calloway; while the second ferry established by legislative authority in Kentucky was at the mouth of Hickman creek in 1785. The act was as follows:

"Be it enacted by the General Assembly, that public ferries shall be constantly kept at the following places and the rates for passing the same be as followeth, that is to say: from the land of James Hogan in the county of Lincoln across the Kentucky river at the mouth of Hickman's creek to his land on the opposite shore in the county of Fayette, for a man four pence, and for a horse the same."

Up to 1786, only five ferries had been established in Kentucky; two across the Ohio river and three across the Kentucky river. In 1786, two more were established, one of which was the ferry at the mouth of Dick's river, the legislative act for which was as follows:

"Section I.   Whereas, it has been represented to this present
General Assembly that it would be of public utility to establish
a warehouse for the reception and inspection of tobacco on the
land of John Curd in the county of Mercer;

"Sec. II.   Be it therefore enacted that an inspection of tobacco shall be and same is hereby established on the land of John
Curd lying at the mouth of Dick's river in the county of Mercer,
to be called and known by the name of Curd's warehouse.

"Sec. V.   Be it further enacted that a public ferry shall be constantly kept at the following places and the rates for passing the
same as followeth, that is to say: Upon the land of the said John
Curd in the county of Mercer across the Kentucky river to the
opposite shore, for a man four pence, and for a horse the same,
and for the transportation of wheeled carriages, tobacco, cattle
and other beasts at the place aforesaid, the ferry keeper may demand and take the same rates as are by law allowed at other ferries.   If the ferry keeper shall demand or keep from any person
or persons whatsoever any greater rates than are hereby allowed,
he shall for every offense forfeit and pay to the party aggrieved
the ferriage demanded or received and ten shillings, to be awarded
with costs before the justice of the peace of the county where the
offense shall be committed."

The Largest Corn Crop.

Jessamine county, it is claimed, has produced the largest yield
of corn ever known.

In 1840, Gen. James Shelby, of Fayette county, received from
the Agricultural Society a premium for the most productive five
acres of corn.   The five acres yielded 550 bushels, or 110 bushels
per acre; but in the same year Walter C. Young, of Jessamine
county, who then lived in the eastern part of it, gathered, by dis-
interested parties, from two acres of a field of corn, the enormous
yield of 195 and 198 1-2 bushels, respectively, which stands, so
far as known, as the largest yield ever obtained from a similar
area.

Hemp Manufacture.

The manufacture of hemp begun in Kentucky as early as 1796,
and was introduced by Nathan Burrows, of Lexington, who after-

wards produced Burrows' mustard, which received the premium
for excellence at the World's Fair in England in 1851.

The growth of hemp commenced with the earliest days of the
settlement of Kentucky. It came with the corn and flax, among
the first products of the state. The soil of Jessamine county
has always been extremely favorable to the production of this
plant. The black loam, so general throughout many parts of

GEORGE BROWN.

the county, produces hemp of very heavy and excellent fibre, and
Jessamine county stands among the greatest hemp-producing
counties of Kentucky. Per acre, no county in the state produces
a larger yield.

Melanchthon Young, who resides about a mile from Nicholasville, on the Harrodsburg pike, has been one of the great hemp

growers of the county and in the last quarter of a century has rarely failed to secure fine crops. The introduction of Chinese hemp seed thirty years ago stimulated hemp product. As showing the extreme fertility of Jessamine county soil, the land upon which Mr. Young has been growing his hemp, a portion of it at least, has been in cultivation for more than one hundred years,

MELANCHTHON YOUNG.

and the yield, after a century of use, of the ground is greater than when the crop was first planted in the virgin soil.

Jessamine county has always been one of the great hemp counties of the state. Clark, Fayette, Scott, Bourbon, Woodford and Jessamine; grow the bulk of the hemp crop raised in Kentucky, and in the earlier period of manufacture in the state this staple produced great profits and brought large gains to those who were engaged in it. Among the pioneer manufacturers of bagging and rope were George I. Brown, Moreau Brown, George Brown, Henry Metcalf, William Scott and Col. Oliver Anderson. Mr. Cleveland, in Keene, also manufactured rope and bagging. Most of the people engaged in this business amassed large fortunes. The bagging was used at that time in baling cotton throughout the Southern States, and there was no other substitute, prior to the fifties, for the Kentucky bagging.

This bagging was generally carried to the Kentucky river and shipped by steamboat to Louisville, and thence distributed throughout the South. Very few white men were ever employed in this manufacture. Most of those who operated the factories, owned in large part the negroes necessary to carry on the business, and where they did not have sufficient hands, they hired them from the surrounding farmers, by the year.

The hacking of the hemp was done in open sheds, and the dust, which has, in close factories, been so detrimental to health, was not considered injurious by those engaged in the manufacture in Jessamine county.

The hemp crop in Jessamine was not sufficient to supply all the factories operated, and much of the staple was purchased and bought in parts of Garrard, Mercer and Woodford and hauled to Nicholasville and there manufactured. Geo. I. Brown was probably the pioneer of hemp manufacture in Jessamine. He was a man of fine personality and a strong intellect. He represented Jessamine county in the Senate in 1829 and 1834, and in the House of Representatives in 1829 and 1832.

Robert Crockett, a son of Col. Joseph Crockett, built what is now known as the Union Mills, five miles northeast from Nicholasville on Hickman creek. The buildings were constructed about 1803, and comprised a grist mill, a saw mill and a powder mill. This mill has continued in operation down to the present day. The old stone house near it, which was erected at the same time, is still one of the most substantial houses in the county.

Nicholasville Beginnings.

Maj. Anderson Miller, in 1805, made up a large lot of gunpowder, at his father's residence in the northern part of Jessa-

11

NICHOLASVILLE PRESBYTERIAN CHURCH.

mine; he hauled it by wagons to Louisville, bought flatboats and shipped it to New Orleans. The venture was largely remunerative.

In July, 1824, a capillary steam engine, invented by Dr. Joseph Buchanan, was used in working Jackson's cotton factory in Nicholasville.

In early days cotton was grown quite extensively in Kentucky, in sufficient quantity to meet all the wants for family use.

Dr. Joseph Buchanan was a professor in Transylvania University, and this engine was a remarkable piece of work. It was claimed for it that it was perfectly safe and that one cord of wood would sustain a seven-horse power for twenty-four hours. Inducements were offered to owners of steamboats to avail themselves of this capillary arrangement, because of its great power in proportion to its weight, to enable boats to outrun all competitors by changing the boiler for a generator, thus converting the boilers then in use into capillary engines.

The first shoemakers in Nicholasville were Samuel Peake, Thomas Dunbar and a colored man named Martin. Also James Lusk, who carried on the business until 1837.

The first saddle and harness-maker in Nicholasville came in 1812, and was named Edmund Phipps. David Majors was another person, who carried on a saddlery and harness business three-quarters of a century ago.

Early in the twenties Edmund Emanuel Hart established a cabinet-making shop and his son, Joseph Hart, settled in Nicholasville as a cabinet-maker in 1834.

The first hat-makers were Thomas Foley and Stephen Guy, and they made wool hats in a house on the lot now occupied by the hemp factory of E. R. Sparks, and on the corner lot of Dr. Talbert, John Fritzlen carried on the making of silk and fur hats. It was with him that Robert Young learned this business of manufacturing silk and fur hats and opened a factory in Nicholasville, in 1825.

John La Fevers, of French Huguenot extraction, had a pottery establishment on the lot of the late Mrs. Eve. His daughter, Nancy La Fevers, was the first person to open a school in Nicholasville, in 1802.

Miles Greenwood, of Cincinnati, who was a day laborer on the

Lexington and Danville turnpike in 1831 and '32, helped to dig the land down on a level with the pike where the court house now stands.   He worked with James Gooch, who had undertaken to build a section of the pike running through Nicholasville, two miles each way from the town.   Mr. Greenwood afterwards became one of the most distinguished men in the business world at Cincinnati.

Postmasters of Nicholasville.

The postmasters of Nicholasville have, some of them, held unusually long terms.   Benjamin Netherland held the office from 1801 to 1822; Dr. Archibald Young from 1822 to 1826, and Wm. Rainey, from 1826 to 1835.   He was succeeded by Jas. Lusk; he by James A. Welch, he by David P. Watson, and he by Jas. A. Welch.   In 1848 D. P. Watson was again appointed postmaster, and was succeeded by R. A. Gibney, who held the office until 1856, when he was succeeded by Joseph Fritzeen.   After him, Thos. Payton held the office for eight years, then H. C. Rodenbaugh, who remained postmaster for eight years.   Then followed W. J. Denman; he was succeeded by Samuel M. Anderson who held the office for eight years, and was succeeded by John B. Smithers, who held it for four years, and he gave place to W. L. Buford, who now holds the place.

Court House in Nicholasville.

The first court house erected in Nicholasville was built in 1823. In earliest times the quarter session judges who represented the Circuit Court held their sessions in sheds or stables, or in parlors of their private homes.   Judge William Shreve, the last of the quarter session judges, often held court in a shed attached to a large stable on the ground where the Jessamine Female Institute is now built.   The court house of 1823 was a brick building and was used until 1878.   It had thus served the people fifty-five years.   It was erected by Thompson Howard, who removed to Missouri, and died there in 1836.   It was inconvenient and uncomfortable, but it served well in its day, and the men of the present generation have many delightful and pleasing memories connected with the old red brick edifice in which they have often listened to the great men who made Kentucky history, for the half-century following 1820.

The first work on the present court house was done September 5, 1878. The new building cost $38,385, and is a superb structure of modern style. The magistrates composing the County Court, when the question of either repairing the old court house or putting up a new one was first advocated by Hon. W. H. Phillips, the present County Judge, were: Dudley Portwood, John J. Cobbman, E. J. Young, Charles McDavitt, Mordecai Crutchfield, Richmond Hunter, George T. Nave, R. J. Scott, Isaac Bourne and Edmund E. Horine. A commission had been appointed, consisting of G. B. Bryant, J. L. Logan and W. G. Woods, to examine the old court house. They reported that it could not be repaired. Thereupon the construction of a new court house was undertaken. It may stand for a hundred years as a monument to the public spirit and wisdom of the officers who laid before the people the necessity and the advantages of a new structure, which in all its appointments is creditable to a great county.

It has all modern appliances and conveniences. It was provided for by taxation and the obligations of the county have long since been paid off. It was opened for the public in 1878. The ministers resident of the town of Nicholasville, were invited by County Judge Phillips to dedicate the structure with religious ceremonies, which occurred at nine o'clock on Monday morning. The following ministers were present: Rev. A. D. Rash, Baptist; W. F. Taylor, Methodist Episcopal, South; T. F. Farrell, Methodist Episcopal; Rev. Russell Cecil, Presbyterian; also the venerable John T. Hendricks, of Paducah, who died only a few months since in Texas.

Judge Phillips first spoke in the new building. He announced the purpose of the meeting. After the reading of scripture, Dr. Hendricks took the ten commandments as the basis of his address on "The Law Which Should Govern Men and States." The members of the bar at the opening of the court house in 1878 were: George S. Shanklin, Benj. P. Campbell, J. S. Bronaugh, H. A. Anderson, T. U. Wood, M. T. Lowry, A. L. McAfee, W. S. Holloway, George R. Pryor, L. D. Baldwin, J. C. Wickliffe, W.

NICHOLASVILLE CATHOLIC CHURCH.

H. Crow, G. B. Letcher, Benjamin A. Crutcher. On the same day Circuit Court met. Honorable Joseph D. Hunt, Judge of the court, arrived at noon and at one o'clock opened court, with Charles J. Bronston, Commonwealth Attorney, who had been recently elected to that position.

Of the sixteen grand jurors who were then empaneled only five remain: Lee Reynolds, G. W. Goode, W. J. Dennan and G. S. Moseley.

Hotels.

Nicholasville in its earliest days had distinguished men as proprietors of its hotels. In those times keeping hotel was a much more important business than in later years. Immediately after the cessation of the Indian raids in Kentucky, there was such a tremendous influx of travelers that almost every gentleman took out tavern license. The prices were not very extravagant, but it was more to accommodate friends and to show hospitality than to make profits. The uniform price was, for each meal of victuals, 25 cents; for lodging and a bed at night, 12 1-2 cents; horse, 12 1-2 cents; horse with corn and fodder at night, 18 3-4 cents. Whisky and brandy were plentiful, as the prices show at this time. The price was, for whisky or peach brandy, 18 3-4 cents per pint, apple brandy and cherry bounce, 4 pence a drink.

Joshua Brown was a soldier in the Revolutionary war. He married Margaret Mansel. He was in the siege of Yorktown, and served for six months under the immediate supervision of General Washington. He came from Baltimore, Maryland, and landed in Lexington, Kentucky, in 1789. He had four sons: Col. Washington Brown, Preston Brown, Samuel Brown, and Col. Thomas Jefferson Brown. The two latter were both graduates of the Transylvania University. Washington studied and practiced law. He married Gen. Hugh Chrisman's daughter Matilda; General Chrisman then lived on Hickman creek, at the old stone house, the last building erected by Gov. Thomas Metcalf in the county. Col. Geo. W. Brown settled in Nicholasville in 1825. He twice represented the county in the legislature. He was an enterprising citizen and a successful manufacturer of hemp. He left Kentucky in 1837 and moved to Charleston, South Carolina, where he died in 1862. Alexander Campbell said of him that he was the most perfect and courtly gentleman that he had ever met. The names of these two sons, Washington and Thomas Jefferson, evinced a high degree of patriotism; one being named for George Washington and the other for Thomas Jefferson.

Thomas Jefferson Brown came to Nicholasville and took charge of the hotel in 1836. He was a man of splendid appearance, six feet two inches in height, and on county militia days, in his fine uniform, and on his thoroughbred horse, in a suit of blue, with a red silk sash and golden epaulets, he impressed all who saw him with his superb physique. He studied medicine, but did not practice. He married Miss Mary J. Wallace, of Jessamine, and settled in Nicholasville, taking charge of the Central Hotel, where he died in 1849. He was reckoned as one of the most courteous men of the county. His kindly heart prompted him to many generous deeds and his helpfulness to the struggling and deserving left him many grateful and sincere mourners. He first urged the necessity of a public cemetery in Nicholasville, helped to lay off Maple Grove cemetery, and was the first person buried there. He and his wife dispensed kindly hospitality. They were charitable and humane, and created pleasing impressions on all who visited Nicholasville. They left a family who have always been prominent in county affairs. Miss Henrietta Brown, Mrs. Virginia Noland, and Mrs. Victoria Mitchell were daughters of Col. Brown.

Public Well.

The Public Well on the corner of Main and Maincross streets in Nicholasville is one of the most remarkable in Kentucky. Twice during the Civil War and in very dry seasons it had its capacity tested to the fullest extent. The Ninth Army Corps, commanded by General Burnside, encamped for three weeks around the town and the entire division used the water from this well night and day. Several thousand of General Bragg's army also encamped near Nicholasville and used water from the well in September, 1862, and even these were unable to reduce the strength and power of its flow. This well is 180 feet deep and was bored by John W. Charlotter, a blind man. The well was put down in the year 1846, and after blasting down to the unusual depth of 180 feet a stream of water was struck. It gushed up ten feet high and from that time to this has furnished all who demanded of it, clear, cool, refreshing drink. No drouth and no call upon its resources has ever lessened its flow, and after more than half a century of usefulness it is yet the pride and comfort of the citizens of the town.

Bethel Academy.

The Legislature of Virginia in 1780 set apart 8,000 acres of land for the establishment of schools in Kentucky. The Kentucky Methodists early took measures to secure part of the land appropriated to this purpose. Bishops Coke and Asbury attended a conference held at McKnight's, on the Yadkin river, North Carolina, in 1789. Here the Kentucky Methodists, by letter and messenger, requested direction. The response to this petition was that during the next year Bishop Asbury would visit Kentucky, and if the petitioners could secure a grant of 5,000 acres of land from the state or individuals, a college should be completed within ten years. Early the next spring Bishop Asbury, accompanied by his friend, Richard Whatcoat, who was himself afterwards made a Bishop, came through from Virginia on horseback to Kentucky. They stopped on their way in Southwestern Virginia, and there waited for an escort from the friends in Kentucky. The Kentucky guards did not appear as soon as had been expected, but on a certain Monday morning Bishop Asbury related to Mr. Whatcoat that the night before in a dream he had seen the friends for whom they had been waiting. After breakfast they retired to the banks of a small stream nearby for prayer and meditation. While engaged in these services he saw approaching over the hills two men. He felt at once that these were the Kentuckians coming for him. This proved to be the fact. These men were Peter Massie, afterwards known in Kentucky as the "Weeping Prophet," and John Clark. They delivered the Bishops their credentials and told them that they had left a guard of eight men in the valley below, ready to start for Kentucky, as

MT. PLEASANT BAPTIST CHURCH.

soon as was his pleasure to begin the journey. The following is the entry that Bishop Asbury made in his journal:

"After reading the letters and asking counsel of God, I concluded to go with them."

They left Southwestern Virginia early in May, 1790, with sixteen men and thirteen guns. They were to make a journey of more than 200 miles through a wilderness constantly waylaid with savages. Three times a day they halted to feed and refresh themselves, and each time they sought God's protection and guidance in prayer. The first day they rode 35 miles, the second 45 and the third 50. This rapid travel proved a little inconvenient to the Bishop, who complained that he could neither sleep nor eat. He says: "While in camp some were on guard, while others rested." They frequently passed the graves of those who had been slain by the savages. In one camp he saw 24 graves.

They arrived in Lexington on the 12th of May. On that day the Bishop preached and then held a conference in the house of Richard Masterson. Constant services were held; ministers were ordained. Francis Poythress, the Bishop declared, was much alive to God, and they arranged for a school to be known as Bethel Academy.

They rode to the land of Thomas Lewis, at the bend of the Kentucky river, near High Bridge, and Mr. Lewis there offered the Bishop a hundred acres of land as a site for Bethel Academy. The Bishop remained in the vicinity nearly two weeks, preaching every day, making acquaintances and many friends for the projected scheme.

His principal asistants in establishing Bethel Academy were Rev. Francis Poythress and Rev. John Metcalf. A brief sketch of Mr. Poythress will not be out of place.

He belonged to an old and distinguished family of Virginia. He sought the instructions of a minister of the church of England, and in 1773 he was led to the Saviour and connected himself with the Methodist church.

In North Carolina, Maryland, Tennessee and Virginia he did splendid work for the church to which he had made his allegiance. Whenever there was danger he was always ready to go where duty called. Whenever there was a difficult commission he would say: "Here am I, send me." He traveled over a large part of these states, preaching under the trees and in cabins, enduring all the hardships of the settlers in their wilderness homes. A man of some scholarship, he was easily enlisted in the work of building Bethel Academy, in which he was not altogether successful and was unjustly censured. His health failed and his mind gave way. He removed from Kentucky afterwards to North Carolina. He never entirely recovered either his spirits or his health or his energy. He returned to Kentucky in 1801, but no work was assigned to him. He made his home in Nicholasville. In 1810 Bishop Asbury saw him and was deeply distressed at his condition.

In 1792 Bishop Asbury made his second visit to Kentucky and he entered in his journal: "I wrote an address on behalf of Bethel School," and later on he says, "I find it necessary to change the plan of the house to make it more comfortable for the scholars." Rev. Thomas Hinde, a contemporary of Bishop Asbury, makes this entry: "Bethel Academy. Our conference for 1797 was held at Bethel School, a large three-story building erected by Mr. Poythress on the bank of the Kentucky river, in Jessamine county."

The work of building had progressed so that in the year 1794 a school was opened. The following letter from Rev. Jno. Metcalf, will be interesting:

Nicholasville, Jessamine Co., Ky.
June 13, 1794.

Hon. George Nicholas:

I have lately received from you two of your kind letters and would have answered them before now, but I have taken charge of Bethel Academy and I have been so confined for the last two weeks in fitting up suitable places of abode for some of my pupils that I have greatly neglected my private affairs, especially that portion of it which you are attending to in Lexington.

Your friend,

JOHN METCALF.

The Kentucky conference of the Methodist church in 1797 met in Bethel Academy. The Rev. Mr. Metcalf was principal until 1803. For a while Bethel School was a competitor of

Transylvania Academy, at Lexington, then under control of Presbyterians. The original site of Bethel Academy was chosen for
its wonderful beauty and for its adaptability for a village. The
lines of travel and lines of settlement could not then be determined. It ought naturally to have been the county seat of the
county.

In 1799 Rev. Valentine Cook took charge of the literary department with Rev. Francis Poythress as assistant. Mr. Cook
was a man of scholarly attainments and was a distinguished graduate of Cokesburg College, at Abbington, Md. He remained
with the school one year. His anti-slavery views induced his removal.

In 1803 Rev. John Metcalf moved to Nicholasville and opened in his own house a school which he called Bethel Academy,
Mr. Harris maintaining Bethel School on the Kentucky river as
a neighborhood school until 1805. In 1798 Mr. Metcalf purchased several lots in the village of Nicholasville and erected a
good log house, which still stands and is the property of his
grandson, John Metcalf. At this house Bethel Academy was
continued until 1820, when a new brick building was built and the
school was continued in it under the name of Bethel Academy.

About this time Mr. Metcalf died, in the sixty-third year of
his age.

In 1798 the Legislature of Kentucky passed an act incorporat-
ing Bethel Academy. The first section of the act is as follows:

CHAP. XXXI.

An Act Establishing Bethel Academy, and Incorporating the Trustees Thereof.

Approved Feb. 10, 1798.

1. Be it enacted by the General Assembly, that the Reverend Francis Poythress, John Knobler, Nathaniel Harris, John
Metcalf, Barnabas McHenry, James Crutcher, James Hord and
Richard Masterson, shall be, and they are hereby, constituted a
body politic and corporate, to be known by the name of trustees
of Bethel Academy, and by that name shall have perpetual suc-
cession, and a common seal, with power to change the same at

NORTHERN METHODIST CHURCH.

pleasure; and as such shall be authorized to execute all powers and privileges that are enjoyed by trustees, governors or visitors of any college or university within this state, not herein limited or otherwise directed.

Section 6 provides as follows:

"The President of said academy shall be a man of most approved ability in literature."

For five years from 1841 Professor A. R. Northup, A. M., a graduate of the Wesleyan University, was at its head. He was succeeded by Charles F. Smith. In the early part of the century a grant of 6,000 acres of land was made by the state of Kentucky to Bethel Academy. In 1876 Professor A. M. Gordon was elected principal. He was the ablest teacher ever in charge of the school. In 1877 the property of the academy was leased to Professor Gordon for ten years, Professor Gordon introducing the condition that five indigent, sprightly boys should attend the academy each year free of charge for tuition.

Under the direction of Professor Gordon Bethel Academy attained high rank as a school. The buildings as modernized are in the middle of five acres of ground, and they are large and elegant, and were erected in 1878 at a cost of $7,000. After the abandonment of the site on the Kentucky river the one hundred acres of land given by Mr. Lewis reverted to his estate, but portions of the material of the building were taken to Nicholasville and used in erecting a school building there. At the end of 105 years Bethel Academy has been turned over to Nicholasville, and is now a graded school. It is used for the public benefit. It has lost its denominational control, and is part of the great system of the general education of the masses in the State of Kentucky.

The first site of Bethel Academy is still easily found. On the splendid eminence overlooking the mighty banks of the Kentucky, one can stand on the ruins of the ancient building, in which was begun the life of this school, and for miles around can see what a hundred years of cultivation and growth have wrought. The school is gone. The structure, then palatial as an educational home, has crumbled and decayed, but as the eye takes in the picturesque and charming landscape, covering parts of Garrard, Jessamine, Woodford and Mercer counties, with fertile farms, happy homes, large families, loyal and true citizens, all

contented in their abiding places and all busy and satisfied with
their places in life, the saddening memories of the old school, are
hushed by admiration for the prosperity, peace and industry
which rise up to tell that the work of a century is not lost, but
that the grandsons and great-grandsons of these educational pioneers are not unworthy of the founders of this ancient school, in
which were centered the hopes and aims of the brave and liberal
men who gave it a name and being in the wilds of a wilderness.

Jessamine Female Institute.

One of the most important and successful of all the enterprises
in the county has been Jessamine Female Institute.   In 1854 an
act of the Legislature was passed allowing the organization of a
company for the purpose of conducting a female school of a high
character; such as would attract patronage from abroad, as well
as give the highest facility for education in the town.   The capital
stock was fixed at $2,500 in shares of $100 each.   The articles of
incorporation under this act were signed by Alexander Lyle,
Thos. E. West, L. H. Chrisman, J. D. Hill, R. E. Woodson, Hervey Scott, Robt. Young, D. B. Price, J. A. Scrogin, J. P. Letcher,
W. C. Letcher, M. T. Lowry, G. M. Barkley, Isaac Barkley, J.
F. Barkley, C. F. Smith, A. L. McAfee, M. T. Young, Samuel
McDowell, Wm. McDowell, Jas. H. McCampbell.

After this, in 1855, the school was reorganized, and Rev. M.
Branch Price, a Presbyterian minister, was elected principal.
After some years of successful administration he was removed by
death, and was succeeded by Mrs. Jacob Price, wife of the Rev.
Jacob Price, a Presbyterian minister.   In 1857 she was succeeded
by Rev. Mr. Frazee, a Presbyterian divine, and he in turn, by
Mrs. Browning, who presided one year.

In 1860 Rev. Joseph McDowell Matthews, of Hillsboro, Ohio,
rented the ground and building and conducted the school under
the name of the Jessamine Female College.   The incorporators
of this collge were J. C. Wilmore, Henry M. Chrisman, J. B.
Cook, T. J. Cassell, Moreau Brown, S. S. Mizner, J. S. Bronaugh,
J. W. Olds, R. M. Messick, John McMurtry, P. H. Smith, W. R.
Welch, Wm. Brown, Thos. B. Crutcher and J. S. Mitchell.

At the end of the term of 1862 Dr. Matthews returned to Ohio.

In 1863-64 Rev. J. E. Spilman, then pastor of the Presbyterian church, conducted the school for several years.

In February, 1866, the Legislature of Kentucky granted a charter for the Jessamine County Female Institute, with the following incorporators: Robert Young, George Brown, Dr. Joseph P. Letcher, T. B. Crutcher and J. S. Bronaugh. Under this charter the school was to be non-sectarian. In 1881 the school was closed for want of patronage and in September of that year Miss M. F. Hewitt took charge of it as principal. Under her management it was highly successful for twelve years. In the very beginning of her administration the number of pupils was largely increased, and it became necessary to erect new and more commodious buildings.

In 1881 the Board of Trustees determined to erect the present building, at a cost of $20,000. This money was almost altogether subscribed by the citizens of the town and county.

There have been a large number of graduates from the school; several hundred, all of whom occupy either as teachers or in society, most prominent and distinguished positions.

Miss Hewitt was compelled to resign her position as principal by reason of declining health, and in 1893 Mrs. B. W. Vineyard, the present principal, assumed control of the institution. Under her conduct the reputation of the school has not declined and the condition of the buildings has been greatly improved. It now stands as one of the leading institutions in the state, has a large patronage from all parts of Kentucky and the South. The curriculum is wide enough and broad enough for all purposes and the patronage has met the expectations of all connected with the management and control of the institution.

Newspapers.

There are two newspapers published in Jessamine county; the Jessamine Journal and the Nicholasville Democrat. The Jessamine Journal was founded by J. M. Parish, who came from Mt. Sterling in 1872, and was its editor and owner. For several years it was printed on a Washington hand-press and had a hard struggle for its existence. It changed owners seven or eight times, and the office was destroyed by fire in 1886. At the time of

COLORED METHODIST CHURCH.

this fire it was well equipped with a large power press and a first-class outfit of type. J. M. Kerr, who purchased the plant from C. W. Metcalf after the fire, ran it on a small scale for a short time and in 1887 sold it to Col. H. M. McCarty, who was one of the most successful and distinguished journalists in Kentucky. He was secretary of state under Governor Knott, and held other

LOUIS PILCHER.

positions of distinction. Harry McCarty, one of the editors, was the junior member of the company.

At this time its editorials were quoted very largely throughout the state. At the death of Col. McCarty in 1891 his interest was sold to T. H. Morris, who was connected with the paper until 1894, when he disposed of his interest to J. B. Stears.

The paper is now edited by Mr. Harry McCarty and Mr. Stears. It has a wide circulation, democratic in its politics.

The Nicholasville Democrat, an eight column folio, was established in June, 1888. At that time it was the property of Louis Pilcher, the present editor and proprietor, and his brother Thomas Fielding Pilcher. After a short time a job printing plant was established. For eight years its office was in the old historic building erected by Judge Wake.

Thomas F. Pilcher and his brother, Louis Pilcher, assumed the management of the paper. The former assisted in establishing the Lexington Argonaut. He did his first newspaper work on the Lyceum Debater, afterward on the Central Courier, and was for five years the correspondent of the Cincinnati and Louisville dailies. He was one of the promoters of the Lexington Advertiser. Later he edited the Nicholasville Star. In 1895 he established "The Coming Nation," which absorbed the Illustrated Kentuckian, and these two were merged into the Argonaut. He afterward founded the Blue Grass World and then returned to his present position as editor and proprietor of the Nicholasville Democrat.

Mr. Pilcher has had a wide experience as a newspaper man. In the Cleveland campaign, he did work on the Louisville Courier-Journal, paragraphing and producing comic articles with Donald Padman. He was born in Nicholasville, July 11, 1855, opposite where the newspaper office now stands.

The first paper published in Nicholasville of political character was the Nicholasville Democrat, in 1857 to 1860. It was strongly anti-slavery, and the office was raided and the type pied and dumped in the streets. Samuel Leffingwell and the late Dr. Jno. C. Welch were its editors. For a while, from 1871 to 1875, Nicholasville was without a paper. The Central Courier was established by Samuel Owens in 1875 and subsequently consolidated with the Jessamine Journal, and was known as the Journal-Courier. In 1875 the late L. D. Baldwin purchased a plant in Frankfort and edited a paper for one week. He sold it to W. T. Jones, who never printed an issue. At this time Col. McCarty came to Nicholasville and secured the necessary means to establish the Jessamine Journal.

In 1895 the third paper was started, with M. E. Wilhoit as editor. It was printed in Lexington. This paper passed into the hands of J. T. Farrow and shortly afterward suspended. The

Nicholasville News was published in 1878 by A. W. Huggins for a brief period. The first paper ever published in Nicholasville was a religious publication under Presbyterian auspices and was founded in early years, it is said. Others deny the whole story.

Sulphur Well.

Sulphur Well, about five miles from Nicholasville in the southeastern part of the county, was for many years a prosperous village. The discovery of a well of sulphur water gave this town its name. For a long time many persons frequented the place to have the benefit of the waters, which were supposed to have medicinal value. It is on the main road from Nicholasville to Hickman creek. The first settler in the village was John Walters, a Baptist minister, and he succeeded in having a Baptist church built there in 1813. Mr. Walters and Robert Ashurst preached to the church for several years.

Of late years, the village has had its name changed to Ambrose. It is improved very much, and the buildings in the village are neat and tasteful, and the people kind and hospitable.

Wilmore.

The following history of the ambitious and thriving city of Wilmore was prepared by Wm. G. Wilhite, and it is inserted as written by him:

The village of Wilmore, the second in population in Jessamine county, is situated on the Cincinnati Southern railway, five miles southwest of Nicholasville and about the same distance north of the celebrated High Bridge, where the railway crosses the Kentucky river, 276 feet above the water. Although but eight years old, it contains a population of about 600, and is probably growing more rapidly than any little town in Central Kentucky. A steady and constant increase, without any inflation or boom methods, has made a stable population of healthy growth. There is not a vacant house in the town today, and as fast as built a house is occupied. Its existence practically began with the foundation of Asbury College, which started September 2, 1890, in four rooms, with two teachers and eleven pupils. Its growth has been, to a large extent, coexistent with the growth of this college, both in building and increase of faculty and students.

In the first year there were enrolled 70 pupils. In the second year, 120. The highest number enrolled in any year was 160. In the eight years of its existence there have been over 1,000 students enrolled and 25 graduates. Sixty ministers of the gospel have also been sent out from this school to various parts of the country in this time. Students from 20 states and from Canada, England, Japan and Persia have attended here, and its influence has been widespread and is growing.

Organized just 100 years after the founding of Bethel Academy, the second chartered institution of American Methodism, and within four miles of the original site; it has renewed the work of its venerable predecessor with vigor and grown into a power.

There are now six buildings, with the president's house, and a large chapel, on six acres of campus. The college has a capacity for teaching 300 students and boarding 100, with a faculty of eight teachers.

This remarkable growth is due in a large measure to the energy, ability, and foresight of Rev. J. W. Hughes, the founder and president since its organization, whose constant labors have made Asbury College a strong and worthy monument to himself, and a power for good in the community and abroad. * *

BUSINESS.

Its nine business houses, carrying almost everything in stock that is needed or used, draw a trade far beyond its limits, and from three counties. Two drug stores and three doctors, insure the continuance of a healthy community; three blacksmith and carriage repair shops, find profitable employment; one leather and harness shop is kept busy supplying everything in its line, from a buckle to a buggy top; two butcher shops, and three large stores of clothing, dry goods, general merchandise and hardware supply the general needs of the outer and inner man.

The Glass Milling Company was established here on July 1, 1891. Its mill, which ground 60,000 bushels of wheat last year, with a capacity of sixty barrels of flour per day, is one mile from the railway station. Its offices and warehouses, in Wilmore, were built February, 1897, and since then all its business has been transacted from this point. This company also deals in coal and lumber, and since its establishment, in the town, has handled over 2,000 tons of coal.

The Saegerser Mill Company has a grist mill in the town, run by a gasoline engine, and does general grinding, and deals in meal, feed-stuffs, etc.

A good livery stable, well-patronized, is one of the conveniences.

Wilmore is an important shipping point on the railway, as evidenced by the amount of freight received and forwarded. The receipts to the railway companies amount to about $25,000 per annum for freight and about $3,000 for passengers. Large amounts of grain, cattle, hogs, produce, etc., are both shipped from and received here, in addition to merchandise, coal, lumber and articles of domestic consumption.

It is essentially a moral and religious community, and the influence of its churches and missionary work is felt widely beyond the limits of Jessamine county.

The Presbyterian church, with a handsome place of worship, and a membership of 150, presided over by Rev. Dr. E. O. Guer-rant, himself a noted preacher and evangelist, in addition to hand-somely supporting itself and him, keeps at its own expense, five missionary ministers in the mountains of Kentucky, a record not equalled by any church in Central Kentucky. In addition it has educated two young men for the ministry, keeps up a perma-nent contribution to an orphan asylum in South Carolina, and gives largely to charity and foreign and home missions. Its record for liberality and quick response to worthy appeals is noted in its presbytery. Its pastor is a man celebrated throughout the South and East as a powerful and successful evangelist, both in the large cities and in the most remote mountains.

The Methodist church adjoins Asbury College. It is also a commodious and handsome building. Its history and work is almost coexistent with that of Asbury, and much that has been said of the college in a former paragraph, applies also to the church. It was founded fifteen years ago, and is the oldest and also the largest congregation in Wilmore, with a membership of 225. This church is also in connection with Asbury College, noted for its evangelistic work and spreads its influence through and beyond the state. The Rev. E. S. Savage, who has lately succeeded Rev. J. A. Sawyer, is the regular pastor, whose hands are worthily upheld by his congregation.

The Christian church, though the youngest (founded in 1888), is second in membership, having 150 communicants. The church has probably the handsomest interior of all. Rev. Mr. Robinson, lately appointed minister, is popular with his congregation.

A colored church, with forty members, completes the list of houses of worship in the town, though two miles east is the thriving and steady Mt. Freedom Baptist church. It is the oldest of the churches in the immediate neighborhood and numbers its members a generation back.

With a well-conducted public school of seventy-five pupils, in a new and commodious schoolhouse; with handsome, modern dwellings,, and with social and educational advantages unexcelled anywhere in the state, it is not necessary to "boom" Wilmore, as a desirable place to reside or do business in, and we can, therefore, rest on the statement on which the Declaration of Independence was founded: "Let facts be submitted to a candid world."

Church Land.

Judge Tucker Woodson's place was for a long time known as "Church Land," and the origin of the name was interesting. An English gentleman of finished education and culture, of scientific tastes and talents, was a guest at Chaumiere, and became in time almost a part of the household. His name was Church. He had been with Robert Fulton experimenting with steam, and came from Pittsburgh down the Ohio river to Maysville on the first steamboat that ever ran on the river. From Maysville he came to Lexington, and thence to Maysville, and made many experiments in his endeavors to perfect this wonderful invention and its application to the movement of vessels. He finally returned to England, married and brought his wife to Jessamine county to be near Colonel Meade and family. He was a man of independent means and built a quaint English cottage on the Woodson estate in the place now occupied by Mr. Jesse Bryan and lived there some years, and from this circumstance the place was always called Church Land. After some years Mr. Church removed to Lexington and died there.

Camp Nelson.

Camp Nelson has become quite an important village in the last few years. It is at the mouth of Hickman creek, near the wooden bridge, that spans the Kentucky river, on the line of the Lexington and Danville turnpike. It was established in 1863, and was the principal point for the concentration of Federal forces and munitions of war on the line of the Cumberland river. It was named in honor of Gen. William Nelson, who was born in Mason county, was a distinguished soldier, and was killed in Louisville by Gen. Jefferson C. Davis, whom he had grossly insulted.

It remained a military camp until the close of the war, and has a fortified circumference of about ten miles formed, in large part, by the high hills and cliffs of the Kentucky river, and partly by breastworks thrown up, that yet remain. On the land has been established a United States military cemetery, in which are interred over 5,000 Federal soldiers. The population of the village is, at this time, about 200, mostly colored people, who have settled on the cliffs and hills near the Kentucky river.

Ariel College is located at Camp Nelson. This is an institution for the education of colored men and women. It is officered by white teachers, and has been the source of great good and help to the colored people.

Rev. John C. Randolph was the first native Kentuckian who enlisted negro soldiers in Jessamine county. A copy of the following letter written by him to Gen. Burbridge is interesting, historically:

Nicholasville, Ky., June 9, 1864.
Gen. S. G. Burbridge,
        Commander, Department of Kentucky:

Sir—There is a slave in the county jail here, confined for no civil crime, but because his master feared he would run off. The boy has told me he wishes to volunteer as a soldier. Have

COLORED BAPTIST CHURCH.

I the right to take him from the county jail and let him come into the army in the state? Most respectfully,

J. C. RANDOLPH.

Deputy Marshal and Superintendent of Colored Enlistment at Camp Nelson.

Another letter written about this time from Nicholasville will prove interesting. It was sent to the postmaster at Keene, and is as follows:

Office Provost Marshal,
Nicholasville, Ky., July 18, 1863. '

To the Postmaster of Keene, Ky.:

I am informed that the Cincinnati Enquirer is distributed at your office. Military authorities forbid its circulation at your office. You will stop it at once, or you will be arrested by the military authorities.

JOHN PENDLETON,
Captain and Provost Marshal.

Keene.

This village is about six miles northwest from Nicholasville, on the Versailles turnpike. It was laid out in 1813 and called North Liberty, but its name was changed to "Keene," in 1848, through the influence of Thomas Jones, a hatter, who came and settled in the village about the year 1845. His native town in New Hampshire was Keene, and through his influence North Liberty was blotted out, and Keene was established. About the time of the change of the name, in boring for a well a fine stream of sulphur water was found. In those days, sulphur water, wherever found, was supposed to have valuable medicinal properties, and, during the prevalence of cholera, in Lexington, about this time, a large number of people came to Keene and lived during the panic, occasioned by this disease in Lexington and surrounding towns. Keene had several stores and a very nice hotel; and its stores do a first-class local business. It is within sight of the Mt. Pleasant Baptist church.

The neighborhood surrounding Keene was settled by some of the best men who in early times came to Jessamine county.

There is an old stone-mill at Keene, which was built in 1794. In the last few years it has fallen into decay. This mill was provided with a combination of horse and water power, and was erected by Manoah Singleton.

The Singletons were among the best people who came to Jessamine, and were good farmers and enterprising men, and they built this stone mill, which was a fine structure in its day. It has been operated until within the last twenty years. It relied for its water power upon a large spring, which was located about a mile and a half away, upon a place formerly owned by Mr. Robert Young, and sold by him to Mr. Andrew Hampton. This spring rises up in the valley, and runs down into a large cave, which was a habitation for the Indians before the advent of the white man in this section of Kentucky. This spring reappears some distance from Keene, and this and the water that flowed from other small streams in the neighborhood, supplied the power for the operation of the mill at Keene.

In the early days, when steam was unknown, mill-sites were very valuable. When the hunters and pioneers first came to Kentucky, in crossing streams they would mark mill-sites, and in their notes state that at such and such a place was a good mill-site, and the lands that were contiguous to such sites were always considered of great value, and were promptly taken up by the settlers, or by their representatives.

Surveyors in these days would laugh at the preservation of the water and its use in the operation of these mills, but in the days of our forefathers, it was either water power or horse power, and horse power was extremely slow and ineffectual, and, as it sometimes required a mill-race to run a mile and a half to get the proper fall, opportunities were promptly and energetically seized wherever a proper fall of water could be secured by dams to operate these country mills.

Mt. Pleasant Baptist Church.

One of the oldest churches in Jessamine county is Mt. Pleasant Baptist church, near Keene. It is located in a fine neighborhood, in the midst of rich lands, which were settled about 1790 by some of the most enterprising and best-educated people who came to Jessamine county at that period of its history. From time to time there had been preaching in this locality by the Baptists who were connected with the South Elkhorn church, which was over the Fayette line, but in 1801 at the request of one hundred members of the South Elkhorn church who were living in the neighborhood of Mt. Pleasant, application was made to organize a new congregation, and Rev. John Shackleford, Absalom Bainbridge, and John Kellar were authorized to investigate and constitute a church at this point. The South Elkhorn church still exists, but is not so prosperous as its daughter, Mt. Pleasant.

The rules of the church which were adopted at this time were very peculiar, and were headed, "Rules of the Church While Sitting on Business":

1st.   It is agreed that no motion be attended to without the person making such motion addresses the Moderator standing, and this proposition be seconded.

2nd.   That no member speak while the church is on business except to the Moderator, and then in a mild and Christian manner.

3rd.   That no member speak in church meeting to the same matter more than twice without leave of the Moderator.

4th.   That no member leave his seat in time of business.

5th.   The Moderator shall call to order, whenever these rules are violated. Any member called to order has a right to a voice of the church, if he chooses.

Among the first members were the Williamses, the Woods, the Hugheses, the Smiths, the Singletons, the Haydons, the Hamptons, the Sales, the Mosbys, the Barclays, the Holloways and the Proctors.

From its commencement Mt. Pleasant has always been one of the most prosperous of the Baptist churches in the Bluegrass section. The neighborhood, settled by Baptists, has been dominated and controlled by Baptists from the time of the organization of this church down to the present. It is an evidence of the persistence of the religious denomination in any community where once fairly planted.

The first pastor was Rev. George Stokes Smith. He was a man of strong individuality, great talent, and was a member of the convention which framed the Constitution of 1792, and represented Fayette county in that body. He was prominent and influential, and was pastor of the church from 1803 down to 1810. In that year Edmund Waller, a nephew of Rev. G. S. Smith, was called as pastor of the church, and remained with it until June, 1843. He was a man of great power, great earnestness, and great consecration, and built up a very large congregation. The church book shows that the deacons in memory of Mr. Waller draped the pulpit in mourning for him who had been the true and faithful pastor of the church for thirty-two years, and the first Sabbath of July in that year was directed to be set apart as a day of fasting and prayer. Edmund Waller, who was the father of John L. Waller, was born at Spottsylvania Court House, Va., in 1775. He was the son of Wm. E. Waller and brother of Wm. Smith Waller, the Lexington banker. His mother was a sister of George Stokes Smith.

He was buried a few miles from Mt. Pleasant in one direction, while his uncle Smith is buried three miles south. He served the church longer than any other pastor. The church has had twenty-one pastors, the minister being the Rev. E. W. Argabrite, and under his ministration the church bids fair to have many years of continued usefulness.

Nicholasville Presbyterian Church.

The Nicholasville Presbyterian church was organized June 12, 1820, by Rev. John Lyle. Alex. McFeeters, Samuel Rice and James Ewing were chosen the Elders. Previous to this the Presbyterian preaching place had been established about one and a half miles from Nicholasville on the farm of Samuel McDowell, which is now owned by his son, William McDowell.

The first member to connect herself with the church was Mrs. Jane Meaux. She was always one of its most faithful and liberal supporters. She donated to the church the ground on which the present church edifice and parsonage are situated. Rev. John F. Coons supplied the church from 1839 to 1852.

The first church was erected when Rev. John Hudson was pastor. It was on the corner diagonally opposite the Jessamine Female Institute, occupied quite a large space, and had in connection with it, a burying-ground. The building was completed in 1825, but not dedicated until October 7, 1827. At this time a protracted meeting was held, and the church received a great out-pouring, and more than sixty persons were added to the membership.

This church has sent into the ministry an unusually large number of men, among whom may be mentioned Rev. John T. Hendrick, Rev. Wm. G. Rice, Rev. Charles Sturtevant, Rev. M. B. Price, Rev. Thomas R. Welch, D. D., Rev. Daniel P. Young, Rev. Chas. W. Price, Rev. J. E. Spilman, Rev. Robert Mann and Rev. Jas. Priest, who was a slave of Mrs. Meaux, and who, after his emigration to Liberia, was vice-president of that republic, having gone there as a missionary.

The present church building was dedicated on the 3rd of January, 1851, by Rev. R. J. Breckinridge, D. D. The present pastor is Rev. R. E. Douglass. The gentlemen who have served as its elders have been among the most prominent citizens of Jessamine during the past seventy-five years, in addition to those already named, Ephraim Tanner, Dr. Archibald Young, Maj. Daniel B. Price, Reuben B. Berry, Wm. H. Rainey, Oliver Anderson, Jas. Clement, Jas. McKee, John L. Price, Otho Roberts, Thos. E. West, Jas. Anderson, Wm. S. Scott, Chas. F. Smith, John A. Scroggan, Wm. M. Todd, Robt. Young, John A. Willis, Wm. Clark, W. D. Young, Harvey Scott, W. G. Woods, S. D. Young, A. N. Gordon, Thomas Butler and John Steele.

Maj. D. B. Price was Clerk of the Session for thirty-two years, while John A. Willis has acted in the same capacity for thirty-eight years.

This church is regarded as one of the most liberal of the Presbyterian churches in Kentucky. Its donations to Center College, Central University, Danville Theological Seminary, and to all the causes of the church have been extremely generous, and give the church a high standing among all Presbyterians. This church is the mother of the church at Wilmore, the church there having been supported and maintained by the Nicholasville church until it became self-supporting.

COLORED CHRISTIAN CHURCH.

Clear Creek Presbyterian Church.

One of the most interesting of the ancient structures in Jessamine county, is Clear Creek Presbyterian church. It was erected about 1829, and was organized by Rev. Nathan H. Hall. Among the names of the founders are those of Dr. Archibald Young, James Carrothers, Ephraim Carter, David McKee, and Archibald Logan. This old church is about a mile and a half from Wilmore on the Nicholasville turnpike. It was abandoned some years since, and sold to the colored people, who now use it as a house of worship. At one time it was a very important congregation, and a large and prosperous church. Its first pastor was Rev. Simeon H. Crane, who served the church for one-third of his time for $150 per annum.

It was built entirely of stone, and the old seats and floors and pulpit are still intact.

In a little cemetery across the road sleeps the dust of many pious members, whose faith found expression in song and prayer in this old church.

St. Luke's Catholic Church.

The only Catholic church in Jessamine county is that of St. Luke, in Nicholasville, Ky. It was erected in 1866 on ground deeded for that purpose by Moreau Brown. It was dedicated to the service of God in 1866 by Rev. Father Willie, and in this the Centennial year of Nicholasville has 156 members.

Bethany Christian Church.

One of the most interesting churches in Jessamine county is Bethany Christian church. It was organized on the first of February, 1845, through the ministration of Jacob Creath, Samuel J. Pinkerton and James Simms. For a long time it was one of the most prosperous and successful of the churches of that denomination in the county, but has recently been reduced. It had such members as Dr. James J. Burch, Samuel Muir, George S. Bryant, Benjamin Robinson, Dr. John Bryant, William H.

13

Daniel, Benj. J. Mitchell, and other responsible and prominent citizens.

The Northern Methodist Church

Was erected in Nicholasville in 1875. It is one of the handsome church edifices of the town, and was built almost altogether through the efforts of Moreau Brown, Esq., who was so long a resident of Nicholasville, and one of its most successful and prominent members, and who died in 1886.

The present pastor of this church is the Rev. V. T. Willis.

The Nicholasville Christian Church

Was organized in the spring of 1828 by Elder George W. Elley. Mr. Elley had a religious debate with George W. Sturtivant, a young Presbyterian minister and was engaged in the boot and shoe business in Nicholasville in 1826, removing from there to Lexington in 1829, where for 20 years he was engaged in business and was a leading member of the Christian church.

The records of this church have been burned, and it is impossible to get all the data concerning its organization. Elder Jacob Creath, in a letter written some years ago, says: "Brother Campbell and myself went to Kentucky from Guyandotte, Western Virginia, which was in 1828. In January, 1829, I was invited by my deceased uncle, J. E. Creath, Sr., to hold a meeting in Nicholasville with Brother William Morton. We held the meeting in the Presbyterian meeting house which was located in the west end of the town. During the meeting it rained very hard all day. I preached from John xx, 30 and 31. 'Many other signs truly did Jesus in the presence of his disciples, which are not written in this book.'"

The first church building of this congregation was erected in 1830. William Shreve and John Wallace were chosen elders and James Simms and James Sale deacons. William White, James Simms and Moses Hawkins were long leading and faithful members of the church. The present handsome edifice was erected in 1874 and is one of the most comfortable and convenient church structures in the city. The congregation has a numerous membership and has a most influential position in the county.

First Baptist Church.

This church was organized on the 10th of February, 1849, by a commission composed of Rev. R. T. Dillard, Joseph R. Barbee and E. Darnaby. There were only seventeen members then present. Stephen P. Waller was chosen clerk and Jonathan Baker and E. A. Waller were chosen the first deacons. Its first pastor was Rev. Thomas J. Drane. It has had a line of distinguished ministers through the fifty years of its existence, and, while not a very large congregation, has always been an extremely faithful and earnest one. The present pastor is Rev. William D. Nowlin. The edifice in which the congregation worships was built in the year 1852.

Ebenezer Church.

Ebenezer Presbyterian church was organized by the Rev. Adam Rankin, somewhere between 1785 and 1790. He came to Kentucky from Virginia in October, 1784. This church is on Clear creek close to the town of Troy. Change of roads and lines of travel have rendered the location unsuitable. The first church was built of logs, and the stone church, which was abandoned in 1876, was begun in 1805, and was used continuously for nearly a century by the descendants of the people who organized this congregation. Among the first members were Wm. Evans and wife, Thos. Woods and wife, Wm. Garrard and wife, Robt. Gwin and wife, Ephraim Tanner and wife, Thos. Read and wife, Robt. Black and wife, Jas. Black and wife, Hugh Garrett, Robt. Lowrey, Mrs. Nancy Drake, and the Lambkins, Beattys, Longs, Scanlands, Reamers, Hedges, Phillipses and Logans.

The descendants of many of these godly people remain in the neighborhood and still support the church of their fathers. One of the most useful and honored of all the ministers of Ebenezer church was Rev. Neal Gordon, who came from Georgia and supplied the church for thirty years. He was a most zealous and self-denying servant of Christ. His grave is close by the door of the old stone church. In this old building are the straight benches and the white painted pulpit which were used for more than fifty years. Around its deserted walls rests the dust of its faithful supporters for one hundred years; in silence and solitude these graves still speak of the faithfulness and consecration of the people of this church.

The members of the Ebenezer and the Clear Creek churches united in 1870 and formed the Troy Presbyterian church, and while Troy church is just over the Woodford line, quite a large proportion of its membership resides in Jessamine. Rev. E. O. Guerrant, D. D., was called as pastor of the Troy church in 1886. He infused new life and energy into the organization. He has since resigned the pastorate and taken charge of the church at Wilmore, which by a large increase in membership demands the whole time of the pastor.

Methodist Episcopal Church, South.

The first church building erected in Nicholasville was by the members of the Methodist Episcopal church in 1799. The frame church which stood on the same lot some twenty steps from the present fine building was erected through the labors of the Rev. John Metcalf and the Rev. Nathaniel Harris. The house was 56 x 36 and had a room for the colored people 30 x 15.

One of the ablest ministers who preached in this church was the Rev. Chas. Watson; he was a successful and distinguished evangelist. Oftentimes at meetings he took occasion to show his brethren his ordination certificate which bore the autograph of Bishop Asbury. These were considered most valuable mementoes among the early Methodist people.

Bishop Asbury laid the foundation of the Methodist church in America, and his piety, learning and consecration did much to widely spread the doctrines of this denomination. The house was dedicated by the Rev. Charles Chenowerth.

The following letter conveyed the invitation:

Jessamine county, Kentucky, Sept. 9, 1799.

Rev. Charles Chenowerth:

Dear Brother: Our meeting house is completed, and I invite you to be with us the second Sunday in October to preach the first sermon in the new house. I have written several others to assist in holding the revival, and am still living on the bank of the Kentucky river, and preach every Sunday.

Yours truly,

JOHN METCALF.

To which the following response was written:

Near Harrodsburg, Ky., Sept. 26, 1799.

Dear Bro. Metcalf: I was handed your letter to-day by Bro. Rule, and will inform you that I will come if no unforeseen occasion prevents me from doing so.

Truly yours in the Gospel of Peace,

CHAS. CHENOWERTH.

Rev. John Metcalf was the first minister. He had preached in Nicholasville for years before the erection of the church building. His preaching was often at the house of Elijah Wallace who then lived where Judge Phillips now resides.

In 1789 Rev. Thomas Williamson succeeded Mr. Metcalf, but Mr. Metcalf returned in 1804. In 1805 Mr. Metcalf moved his family to Nicholasville, as also Bethel Academy, which was then carried on, on the banks of the Kentucky river.

In 1821 the distinguished Methodist, H. H. Kavanaugh, afterward bishop, filled the pulpit. In 1846 the old frame church was torn down after standing forty-six years, and a new brick house was erected, and a few years since the present beautiful and elegant structure was erected on the same ground. Rev. T. W. Watts is the minister now in charge. The congregation has always been considered one full of faith and good works, and has done efficient service for the cause of God.

In 1843, there was a great revival in the Methodist church at Nicholasville, which was under the conduct of Rev. Rice Harris. The following preachers were in attendance: Jonathan Stampers, Benjamin Crouch, Richard Deering, Charles Watson, B. H. McCown, Thos. N. Rawlston, Rev. Mr. Kelly.

The following letter written by David Crozer, who was the owner of and was operating Crozer's Mill on Jessamine creek, to the Hon. Tucker Woodson, gives an account of this meeting:

"Jessamine county, Ky.

"Four miles east of Nicholasville, Feb. 13, 1843.

"Hon. Tucker Woodson:

"Dear Sir: Your esteemed favor of 10th is received, and having a little leisure I hasten to answer it. I was not aware of the fact stated by you, that the roads I named to you were under the control of the local boards. I knew that there was a law of last session, authorizing the state board to take the management of all the roads, and had understood that they had generally done so. On the subject of the proposed bank, I am greatly at a loss to give you my opinion, and can not exactly see and appreciate your present position on this, only I know that you were elected as opposed to relief measures. I am greatly astonished at the news this morning from Nicholasville. There is a great revival going on at the Methodist church; more than thirty have been added to the church. Among the converts are Thomas H. Ballard, Stephen Spragens, Moreau Brown, Mrs. Keene, Mrs. Wilmore (wife of T. D. Wilmore), Jacob Wilmore, Jr., Sandy Wake, James Buskett and Wm. B. Payne. The Rev. Rice Harris was greatly assisted in this meeting by his brethren from other circuits.

"We must ourselves watch and avoid the careless side of life.

"Your friend,

"D. Crozer."

Mr. Crozer was mistaken as to Judge Wake. He never joined the Methodist church.

African Methodist Episcopal Church.

This church is situated on East street in Nicholasville, and was organized September 15, 1845, by Rev. Samuel Miller, who then erected the first house of worship that this congregation ever had. The present beautiful structure was built through the labors of Rev. James Turner. This church has a very active membership and a large, successful Sunday-school, which exerts a fine influence throughout the members of the church. The minutes show that it is one of the most liberal of the colored churches, and that in thirty years it has contributed to benevolent objects about $18,000. Its membership includes a very large list of names. It present pastor is Rev. P. A. Nicholas, a native of Harrison county, Ky.

Colored Christian Church.

One of the handsomest colored churches in the county or state, is the Colored Christian Church, Nicholasville, which was erected in 1843 and for several years used as a house of worship, being then known as the Union Church, where all the colored people from time to time held their services. It was not until the year 1867 that the officers of the church bought the Union Church and became a separate organization. The present pastor. the Rev. W. H. Dickinson, came to the congregation on the first of September, 1896. He is a native of Virginia. The church building now in use was erected in 1890. It has a large membership and is one of the most prosperous of the colored churches in Central Kentucky.

Colored Baptist Church.

The first colored Baptist church in Nicholasville was organized in 1846. Few of its records have been preserved. Rev. Robert Irvin was the first pastor, who remained in the church four years. The present membership is 356. It has been prosperous and particularly so under the ministrations of its present pastor. Rev. John William Clark.

Biographical Sketches of Prominent Citizens of Jessamine County.

James Irvin.

The last Revolutionary soldier to die in Jessamine county was James Irvin. He was born in Mecklenburg county, Va., in 1754, and died in Jessamine county in 1851, at ninety-seven years. He served seven years in the Revolutionary war and was badly wounded at the Battle of Guilford Court House, March 15, 1781. He was shot in the left hip. He came to Jessamine county in 1793 and raised a large family of daughters who all lived to be over eighty-seven years of age.

He is the only Revolutionary soldier who very many of the people in Jessamine county ever saw. When Gen. William O. Butler was a Democratic candidate for Governor of Kentucky in 1844, James Irvin and four other Revolutionary veterans rode in the carriage with General Butler from the place of Mr. John Butler, on Jessamine creek, on the Danville pike, to Nicholasville, where General Butler was to speak, in the field adjoining the colored cemetery, close to the line of the R., N., I. & B. R. R.

When Irvin was wounded in battle he was left at the house of the father of William A. Graham, the distinguished politician of North Carolina, and Secretary of the Navy under Millard Fillmore. While sick he cut his initials on a stone and the date of his wounding and brought this stone with him to Kentucky when he emigrated to the state. He lived on the place now owned by Mr. Dean, near Sulphur Well, and was buried in the Hickman neighborhood.

Frederick Zimmerman.

One of the strong characters in the early history of Jessamine county was Frederick Zimmerman, its first surveyor. His ancestors came from Salzwedel, Germany. His forefathers emigrated to New York. After a passage of six weeks over the Atlantic they settled on the Hudson river, at the village of Rheinbeck, in Dutchess county. Remaining in New York four months two brothers settled in Culpeper county, Virginia, where was born Frederick Zimmerman. He moved to Jessamine county prior to 1792, and lived in the Marble creek district. He married Judith Bourne, daughter of Henry Bourne. His work in the surveys of Jessamine county shows that he was a competent and faithful official. His sons and daughters have been industrious, upright citizens and have performed well the duties devolved upon them. John Zimmerman, Daniel Zimmerman, Augustus Zimmerman and Morton Zimmerman, long and favorably known in the county, were sons of Frederick Zimmerman. A numerous posterity still reside in the county which their ancestor helped to redeem from the savages, and in the earlier history of which he was a strong and influential factor.

Francis Phipps

Was born on the 21st of October, 1751, and was for a long time a resident of Jessamine county. He was engaged in surveying the Lexington and Danville pike, by Col. W. R. McKee in 1829-30. He resided at Mr. Thos. Scott's house for several years, at which place the letter, copied below, was found. References are made to Rev. John Price, who, afterwards, came to Jessamine county, and was long a Baptist minister in this locality, and the letter is otherwise full of interesting matter:

In Mess, No. 10, Colonel Hamilton's Regiment, Little York, 12
    miles from Williamsburg, Oct. 21st, 1781.

My Dear Parents: I have only time to inform you that the British army, under old Cornwallis, surrendered to General Washington on the 19th. Capt. Charles Johnston, who will leave for Mecklenburg to-morrow, will give you full particulars of this great and glorious achievement.

On the 25th of September our army, led by the beloved Washington, reached the headquarters of General La Fayette, at Williamsburg, and on the 30th, our army marched in a body to attack York and Gloucester. On the 7th of October, Washington opened the attack on Cornwallis with 100 pieces of cannon. It

was a most beautiful sight to see our bomb-shells bursting in the
midst of the enemy, tearing down whole companies of our enemies—as we could see them from the high ground near the river.
During the siege, which lasted 17 days, two strong redoubts were
stormed by our regiment, led by Col. Hamilton. We were assisted in the charge by the French. When within a few yards of
the redoubt, Col. Hamilton rode up to the regiment, and said in
a voice like the bursting of a shell: "Charge those men, my brave
comrades, who wish to make slaves of our people." We rushed
at them with a loud shout, and captured over two hundred—killing and wounding about fifty. We lost about seventy-five of as
brave men as ever pulled a trigger at an enemy of our liberty.
Our French soldiers lost as many as we did. It would have done
the heart of every lover of liberty good to have seen the red-coated
rascals surrender to our army on the 19th—old Cornwallis and his
army—numbering 8,000 muskets; I counted fifty brass and one
hundred and sixty iron cannon.

At about 12 o'clock our army was drawn up in two lines, extending more than a mile in length. Our French fellow-soldiers
were placed on our left and headed by their General. At the head
of our ragged, but brave soldiers, I saw the noble Washington, on
his horse, looking calm and cool as he was when crossing the
Delaware river a few years before. Many of the rustic people
of this part of Virginia, consisting of old men, women and children, assembled in numbers equal to the military, to witness the
surrender of the old murderer, Cornwallis. Every face beamed
with joy and gladness—but a profound silence prevailed; no talking, no noise of any kind, save the slow, measured step of our
enemies, was heard. General Tarleton's troops at Gloucester
surrendered at the same time to our French soldiers. Everything
was done in a quiet manner.

After the surrender, I saw our beloved Washington and Colonel Hamilton talking with all the British officers. Old Cornwallis and Tarleton were very polite to our officers, and it was a
surprise to see old Cornwallis treating our beloved commander
and Colonel Hamilton with so much consideration. Cornwallis
is a large man, with dark brown hair, a ruddy face, good nose and
has the appearance of a man of kind heart and good intentions.
General Tarleton is also a large man, but not so big as old Corn-

wallis. His countenance is hard and tyrannical; and his mean, dark eyes are full of cruelty. Some few of the Carolinians saw him after the surrender was over, and cursed him as he passed up the road on his way to the ship that was to take the British to New York. When the boys cursed him he never made any reply, but rode away, showing no high temper, that he was known to have by some Carolinians who remembered his cruelties in South Carolina.

The Rev. John Price preached for the soldiers on Sunday last. His sermon was listened to by many officers, such as General Lincoln, Cols. Henry Lee, Hamilton and Woodford. My health is good, and my wound in the arm is well. I can not tell you where to send me a letter, as I have no means of knowing where our regiment is ordered to. Some say we are to go to New York, and the rumor is that we are to remain in Virginia, or at the town of Trenton, in "the Jersies." Present my love to my youngest sister, also to Mr. Watkins and family, and tell Mr. Watkins his son is truly a self-denying soldier, one who loves his country and is willing, if need be, to die in her defense. Pray for me that I may be spared to see you once more alive.

Your loving son,

Francis Phipps.

Gen. Henry M. Chrisman.

General Chrisman, who received his title from the militia service, was the youngest son of Hugh Chrisman and was born in the old stone house on the Hickman creek in 1800, and died in Nicholasville, in 1876. His mother was a McKinney, and his grandmother was a sister of Jas. McDowell who was in a company of Colonel Dudley's regiment in the war of 1812.

One of the most pleasant traits of General Chrisman's character was his hospitality clothed with kindness and benevolence. He was fond of company and his house was thronged with young and old friends, and they made that part of Jessamine happy by their constant courtesies to their neighbors. His wife died in 1852, he in 1876, and they are buried on the cliffs near the old stone building. This house was put up by Thomas Metcalf, who was known as "the old stone hammer" governor, for which position he offered himself twenty-eight years afterward, when he was elected, defeating Maj. Wm. T. Barry by a majority of only 709. It is related of Governor Metcalf that at one time, when working at Chaumiere, he was invited to take dinner with David Meade, but he declined upon the ground that Mr. Meade had not asked his hands to dine with him. Colonel Meade then predicted that the stone mason would become governor of Kentucky, and he lived long enough to see this prophecy verified.

Peter Simpson

Was born in Washington county, Pennsylvania, in 1758. He served two years in the Revolutionary war under General Wayne, was in several battles and skirmishes in New York and New Jersey, and at the battle of Monmouth was slightly wounded. He was visiting Jessamine county in 1794, and was present at Colonel Price's Fourth of July celebration that year. He returned to Virginia, and in 1802 removed from the valley in Virginia and settled in the Marble creek neighborhood, where he lived until his death in 1835.

Col. John McKinney

Was one of South Carolina's contributions to Jessamine county. He was born on the Pedee river, South Carolina, in 1756, and served in the Revolutionary war, first under General Patterson, and also under Gen. Francis Marion, Colonel Sumter, and Gen. Harry Lee.

He first settled on what is known as the Butler farm, in 1790, and that year he erected a log house on that place which was only torn down a few years ago, and in this house most of his children were born. His daughter, Mrs. Sallie Cloke, who died in Versailles some years ago, at an advanced age, was born on this farm in 1794, while Mrs. Catherine Brown, wife of George I., was born in 1802.

Colonel McKinney was a gentleman of the old school, an enterprising farmer and a patriotic citizen. He removed to Woodford county, where he spent the remaining years of his life, and died at an advanced age.

Col. John Mosely.

This gentleman was born in Buckingham county, Virginia, in 1760, and settled in Jessamine in 1793. He served in the Revolutionary war, and was a gallant soldier. He enjoyed the distinction of having reared the largest family every known in Jessamine—he had three daughters and eighteen sons. He was extremely popular in his neighborhood, and his descendants in Jessamine are very numerous and still live in the immediate neighborhood where their brave and prolific ancestor settled.

Com. Daniel Boone Ridgeley.

Com. D. B. Ridgeley, who served with distinction in the United States navy, was born in Jessamine county on the 30th of August, 1813, and died in Philadelphia, May 5, 1868.

He entered the navy as midshipman April 1, 1828. He participated in the bombardment and capture of Vera Cruz and other Mexican ports, and was connected with the Naval Observatory at Washington in 1850-52. He commanded the steamer "Atlanta" in the Paraguayan expedition. He volunteered for active service in the Civil war, and commanded the steamer "Santiago de Cuba." He commanded a steamer in the North Atlantic squadron, and assisted in the bombardment of Fort Fisher, North Carolina. He was a member of the Board of Naval Examiners at Philadelphia, in 1868, at the time of his death. His mother was a daughter of Col. John Price, who was chiefly instrumental in organizing Jessamine county, and was born on the farm of his grandfather in the Hickman neighborhood. He purchased the McKinney farm in Jessamine in 1850, and passed his vacations there. He always spoke with great pride of his native county, and held the old home place as a sentimental investment.

John Speed Smith

Was born on the Caspar Harbaugh place, Jessamine county, July 31, 1792. He esrved with distinction in the War of 1812—was at the battle of Tippecanoe, and was Aide to General Harrison at the battle of the Thames.

He removed to Madison county in his early manhood, where he became a distinguished lawyer. He represented Madison county in the legislature in 1819, '27, '30, '39, '41, and '45, and the Senate in 1846 and '50. He was speaker of the House of Representatives in 1827. He was a member of Congress in 1821-23, and was Secretary to the Legation of the United States Commissioners sent to the South American colonies. Jackson appointed him United States District Attorney for Kentucky. In 1839 he was made joint Commissioner with Gov. Jas. T. Morehead to visit the Ohio legislature to secure the passage of laws to prevent the enticement of slaves and to provide a more efficient means of returning slaves who had escaped; the Commissioners were successful in this work.

For several years prior to his death he was State Superintendent of Public Works, and through his life was one of the most prominent and popular men in Kentucky.

William T. Barry

Was one of the most brilliant and eloquent men who made Kentucky so famous in the first thirty years of its existence. He was in his childhood a resident of Jessamine county. Born in Virginia in 1783, he came, with his father, when a child to Kentucky, and lived for a short while in Fayette, and then moved to Jessamine county, where he lived several years, when the family returned to Lexington. After attending school at the Woodford Academy he graduated at Transylvania University and commenced the practice of law when twenty-one years of age, in Lexington.

From 1805 to 1835, his life was a wonderful series of successes. Fortune appeared to lavish upon him all of its choicest blessings.

He was, very early in his professional career, appointed Attorney for the Commonwealth in Fayette county. His learning, eloquence and industry at once gave him both popularity and prominence. He was elected to fill a vacancy in the Legislature from Fayette in 1807. He was again elected in 1809; chosen to represent the Ashland district in Congress in 1810, he was again elected representative in the Legislature in 1814. In the discussion of the matters which led up to the War of 1812, no man was more eloquent, earnest or wise, and by his brilliant, patriotic speeches he won the admiration and confidence of all parties. In the war he exhibited a high degree of courage and gallantry while serving on the staff of Governor Shelby, who, disregarding precedents, took the field as the Commander-in-Chief of the Kentucky forces. He was in the battle of the Thames, which added such splendid lustre and renown to Kentucky and her soldiers.

He became Speaker of the Kentucky House of Representatives in 1814, and was elected to the United States Senate while holding that place. He represented Kentucky in the Senate for two sessions, and then resigned to accept the Circuit Judgeship upon a meager salary. In 1817, he was forced to stand as a candidate for the State Senate, and it was his magnetic power and influence which enabled him while in the Kentucky Senate, to secure large aid to Transylvania University and afterwards he became a lecturer in the Law Department. His name gave the Law School prestige and magnificent success. In 1820 he was elected Lieutenant Governor by an overwhelming majority of 11,000 votes in a total of 55,000, and at this time was unquestionably the most popular man in Kentucky.

Henry Clay, in 1825, accepted the place of Secretary of State and identified himself with the Adams administration. This cost Mr. Clay many friends in Kentucky, where the recollection of New England's opposition to the admission of Kentucky into the Union, had left great prejudice against it. Barry sided with those opposed to Mr. Clay.

Mr. Barry was appointed Chief Justice of "The New Court" in January, 1825, and held the place until a repeal of the New Court Act, in 1826. He was a candidate for Governor in 1828, and was defeated by only 709 votes, but his wonderful canvass and superb eloquence caused the state in the following year to cast its vote for Andrew Jackson, by a majority of 7,934. Mr. Barry was appointed Postmaster General by Jackson, and held the office until declining health forced him to surrender it.

In the hope that a change in location and a milder climate might restore his health, the President nominated Mr. Barry to be Minister to Spain. He sailed for his post, but died at Liverpool, England, in 1835.

Nineteen years later (1854), by an act of the Legislature, the remains of Mr. Barry were disinterred, brought to Kentucky and buried in the state lot, at Frankfort. His friends erected a monument to his memory in the court house yard in Lexington.

Theodore O'Hara, the brilliant poet, delivered an oration upon this occasion (Nov. 8, 1854), concluding with these thrilling words :

"Let the marble like a minstrel rise to sing to the future generations of the Commonwealth, the inspiring lay of his high genius and lofty deeds. Let the autumn wind harp on the dropping leaves, her softest requiem over him. Let the winter's purest snow rest spotless on his grave. Let spring entwine her brightest garland for his tomb, and summer gild it with her mildest sunshine, and let him sleep embalmed in glory till the last trump shall reveal him to us, all radiant with the halo of his life."

Jessamine, as the scene of his earliest youth, claims a part in the history of this child of most auspicious fate, whose career, for splendid achievement, superb eloquence, courageous contest, unvarying success, unchanging popularity, and wondrous influence has no equal in the past of Kentucky and will have none in its future.

Rev. John Metcalf.

To Rev. John Metcalf belongs the honor of laying off the county seat of Jessamine, and also of naming the town. He was a native of Southampton county, Virginia, and came to Kentucky in the spring of 1790, bringing with him not only his credentials as a minister, but also a heart full of love to God. Bethel Academy was established in 1790, and was opened for the reception of pupils in January, 1794. It was the second institution of learning ever established by the Methodist church in the United States, the one at Cokesburg being the first. The labors of Mr. Metcalf were confined largely to Jessamine county. He traveled a few circuits in Fayette and Mercer, but his life work was connected with Jessamine. He took charge of Bethel Academy at the request of Bishop Asbury. He began his work as founder and continued his labors there as the principal of this school in the "wilderness." He infused his own earnest and enthusiastic spirit into the institution. He labored under tremendous disadvantages in his work, but he overcame most of them, and brought success where other men would have had only failure.

He was the first Methodist minister who ever preached a sermon in Lexington. Pastoral work in those days was done under great difficulties, traveling on horseback through the traces with no well-defined roads, and hunting up the pioneers in their cabins, and far removed from neighbors in their loneliness and their surrounding dangers, this man of God was ever ready to discharge his duties. He was compelled to ride through the canebrakes and woods and pathless forests, but he had the spirit of his Master, and he never faltered in the work which the Head of the Church had given him to do. In his studies, in his pastoral work and at the head of the school, he found enough in those days to occupy the heart and hands of any man. Plain, practical and earnest, he attracted attention and won hearts, and he generally drew large crowds of people, who were glad to hear him. He was largely instrumental in building up the Methodist church in Jessamine county. He was born in 1758 and died at his home in Nicholasville, in 1820, having reached his 61st year. It was through his labors that the white frame Methodist church, was first erected in Nicholasville, in 1799.

Rev. Nathaniel Harris.

Few men have ever been better known in Jessamine county than Rev. Nathaniel Harris. He was born in Powhattan county, Va., in 1759, of Presbyterian parentage. Being an only son, he was indulged in many things, which in the end proved hurtful. His intercourse with what were then known as the gentlemen of the day, caused him to become both profane and wicked.

Shortly after his father removed from the old home place he became a volunteer in the American army, and was in the battle of Guilford Courthouse, North Carolina.

He was converted in August, 1783, and joined the Methodist church, and the conviction forced itself upon his mind that he was called to preach. He settled in Jessamine county in 1790, and he was principal of the English department in the Bethel Academy.

He preached in the various towns in Central Kentucky, and in administering to the afflicted and the sick none ever excelled him.

14

At marriages and funerals his presence was always sought, because of his tender sympathy and because of the love and confidence manifested towards him. He founded several Methodist churches in Jessamine county.

The last years of his life were spent in Versailles, where he purchased a home for himself and his two maiden daughters. He died on the 12th day of August, 1849, lacking only a few days of ninety years of age. He had been in the Methodist ministry for more than sixty years. On the 26th of August, 1843, he entered in his journal, "I am this day eighty-four years old. I stand to my engagement to be holy for the Lord."

The records which contain the certificates of the earlier marriages in Jessamine county, show that his services for these ceremonies were largely in demand. On the 14th of March, 1799, he married Jesse Hughes and Nancy Nicholson, and a very large proportion of the early marriages celebrated in the county were solemnized by him. He was a faithful, earnest, devout man of God. Some might call his sphere humble, but his influence on the religious and moral condition of Jessamine county will long be felt, and in it he has a monument, which should be both to his church and to those of his name, a cause of unfailing pride.

Samuel H. Woodson.

Samuel H. Woodson was a step-son of Col. Joseph Crockett. While in the military service in Albemarle county, Virginia, and guarding prisoners which had been surrendered by Burgoyne. Colonel Crockett protected the property of Mr. and Mrs. Tucker Woodson. There resulted from this circumstance a warm attachment between Mr. Woodson and Mrs. Woodson and the young officer. Shortly after Colonel Crockett had been ordered to come west and serve under George Rogers Clark, in command of the Illinois or Crockett Regiment, which had been dispatched by the state of Virginia to assist Clark in his contest with the Indians, Tucker Woodson died, and after Colonel Crockett returned from the West he fell in love with the handsome young widow and married her.

After this marriage, in 1783, Colonel Crocket came to Kentucky and soon brought his family here, in 1784, and with him came out Samuel H. Woodson, his step-son. Colonel Crockett gave him a father's love, affection and attention. He was prepared for the law and had every advantage the educational facilities of Kentucky then could offer.

He entered for his step-son about a thousand acres of land, part of which is that now owned by Mr. Jesse Bryant, on the pike between Nicholasville and Lexington.

He read law with Col. George Nicholas and named one of his sons for Judge Nicholas. At the time of the formation of Jessamine county he was chosen clerk for the county. As he held his office for life, it was considered a distinguished place. He built the house on the Sheeley place, about one mile from Nicholasville on the Danville turnpike, and kept his office as clerk there. There were no county buildings in those days and the judges and clerks used their residences for the discharge of their official duties. He married Annie Randolph Meade, a daughter of Col. David Meade, of Chaumiere.

He resigned the clerkship in 1819 and was succeeded by Daniel B. Price. He was elected to congress from the district, and moved to Frankfort in 1826. He came, in 1827, to attend circuit court in Nicholasville and rode, in very warm weather, on horseback from Frankfort to Nicholasville. During the term of court he went out to Chaumiere, was taken suddenly ill and died, in the forty-seventh year of his age. He was a man of great culture, superb integrity, much learning, and in his day was one of the distinguished men of Kentucky. He left a large family, and the people, not only of his district but of Jessamine and Franklin, his adopted home, mourned his early death. He represented Jessamine county in the legislature from 1819 to 1825.

Maj. Daniel B. Price.

Maj. Daniel B. Price was born in Powhattan county, Virginia, the 11th day of May, 1789. His father, John Price, removed to Kentucky in 1794, taking with him Daniel, his only son, and purchased 1,200 acres of land in Bourbon county. The title proving defective, he afterwards removed to Clark county, where he lived to the extreme old age of ninety years.

When a boy, Major Price came to Nicholasville and was appointed deputy clerk for Samuel H. Woodson, and when Mr. Woodson resigned, in 1816, he succeeded him and held the office, giving entire satisfaction until 1851, a period of thirty-five years, which is the longest period any one office was ever held by the same man in the county.

In 1813 he married Eliza Crockett, the fourth child of Col. Joseph Crockett, who died during a cholera epidemic in 1832. He subsequently married Miss Stuart, daughter of Rev. Robert Stuart.

He was a member of the Presbyterian church in Nicholasville and for half a century a ruling elder. He was also a trustee of Center College and one of the directors of the Theological Seminary at Danville. Dr. Robert J. Breckinridge said of him: "Probably no citizen of Jessamine county was ever more generally and favorably known, and certainly no one was ever more thoroughly respected. A man resolute for God's saving truth in proportion as his meek and gentle spirit, he lived upon it as his life and soul."

He won and retained the respect and confidence of the entire

community. He was looked up to as a man of splendid judgment and unswerving integrity. Noble memories of his life and character survive after a lapse of nearly forty years.

Tucker Woodson.

At Chaumiere, in Jessamine county, in 1804, Tucker Woodson was born. It is a remarkable fact that he and his wife were born in the same house and in the same room. His wife was Evelyn Byrd, and she was a daughter of Sarah Meade, daughter of David Meade. He and his wife were both possessed of ample fortune.

They received the best education that Kentucky could give. He
chose the law as his profession but spent most of his life in care
of his landed estates. He was a born politician, a man of the
highest refinement of feeling, of the strictest integrity, the kindest
heart and charming manners. He was a great Whig and a fol-
lower of Mr. Clay. He represented Jessamine county in the
legislature in 1835, '36, '37 and '40. Was also in the senate in
1842-46 and 1853-7.

He was always popular among his neighbors and friends and
even his political opponents loved him. Of distinguished lineage,
he was always the friend of the humbler people. He owned land
in what was then known as the Plaquemine District which included Sulphur Well, now Ambrose. This was considered in
early days the roughest district in the county, but it was there
that Mr. Woodson had his warmest friends.

In the great race for Congress between John C. Breckinridge
and Robert P. Letcher, in 1853, in which Breckinridge was
elected by 526 majority, Mr. Woodson had charge of the Plaquemine District, and for a long time it was remembered in Jessamine county how shrewdly and beautifully he played his opponents. A leading Democrat had been sent by Major Breckinridge to handle the money and control the votes in the Plaquemine District. In those days pecuniary inducements paid to
voters were not looked upon in the same light in which they are
now regarded. The idea that all things were fair in politics and
war pervaded the public mind and the purchase of votes was
carried on with a good deal of publicity and without any reproach
or disapproval on the part of political opponents.

The Democratic manager had been provided with a large
number of new bills issued by the Northern Bank of Kentucky.
They were fives and tens, for even in those days good prices were
paid for votes, and especially in this election, which called forth
the highest enthusiasm and the greatest devotion of the rank and
file on both sides. Mr. Woodson saw with dismay the large
amount of new notes which were being circulated by his political
opponents, and he turned over in his mind a plan by which the
effect of this new money could be avoided. Taking one of the
men aside whom he knew very well, and who had received already one of these new bills, he asked him if he was sure that it

was good; saying, what was true, that there had been circulated a large number of counterfeit bills lately and that if he and his friends were taking money from the Democratic manager, Mr. Scott, they had better be very careful as to its genuineness. At the same time he pulled from his own pocket a roll of well-worn and old-time bills and placing the new and old bills side by side, commented upon some differences. The news spread like wild-fire that the new bills were counterfeit and the floaters refused to receive them and turned in disgust from the Democratic manager, who only had new bills, and would receive nothing but the old time Whig money, which Mr. Woodson and his friends were ready, under proper conditions, to distribute.

A strong pro-slavery man, he sided with the government in the Civil war, but it was conceded on all hands that he acted from conviction, and few men of his prominence and of his activity escaped with so small a number of enemies.

In 1872 he was elected county judge on the Republican ticket and died in 1874. Hospitable, courteous, cultivated, honest, patriotic and true, he left behind him a large array of friends who mourned his death.

His home was always open to friends and strangers alike. Gifted in conversation, a capable raconteur, and full of the purest and gentlest kindness, he won the hearts of all who came under his roof. His wife, one of the housekeepers of those times which made Kentucky housekeeping renowned in all the civilized world, sympathized with the hospitable instincts of her husband, and united with him to make his home always pleasing and attractive. Some of the rich treasures of Chaumiere had descended to them and these, enlarged by contributions from other relatives and ancestors, gave their home a charm which will never be forgotten by those who entered its portals. For thirty years Judge Woodson and his family entertained more and more delightfully than any citizen of Jessamine county, and no couple ever left more delightful memories of real Kentucky home life than they.

Chaumiere.

In 1796 there was established in Jessamine county one of the most beautiful and attractive country homes in America. It was founded by David Meade, who was born in Virginia on the 29th of July, 1743. At seven years of age he was sent to England with the hope that change of climate might improve his health and also for the purpose of furnishing better means of education than were then in existence in America.

Here he remained until 1761, when he returned to his native land. He had acquired only a general knowledge of mathematics, geography, French, grammar and drawing, but he had cultivated science and the elegant arts.

He had two brothers, younger than himself, both of whom afterwards became distinguished in the American army. Richard Kidder, an aid de camp to General Washington, and who had charge of the details of the execution of Major Andre, and Everard, who was an aid de camp to General Lincoln, and he himself was subsequently raised to the rank of General.

In his twenty-fourth year he married Sarah Waters, a daughter of Mr. William Waters, of Williamsburg, Virginia, and in 1769 he was elected to represent Nansemond county in the House of Burgesses. This was his first and only political experience. This assembly was dissolved by the representative of the crown on account of certain resolutions which it had passed upon the subject of the disagreement between England and the colonies.

Prior to 1796 David Meade, a son of the founder of Chaumiere, came to Kentucky. He was attracted by the splendid climate, fertile soil, wonderful forests and charming surroundings, and induced his father to leave a beautiful home in Virginia. on the James river, and come to the wilds of Kentucky. He was captivated by the glowing description of the new land given by his son, and, though accustomed to all that wealth and culture could give, he was willing to abandon the comforts and the associations of his Virginia home and build him a new one amid the forests of Kentucky.

David Meade was a man of large fortune. Under the laws of primogeniture, then prevailing in Virginia, he inherited the major share of his father's estate, and his wife also brought him no inconsiderable dowry. He came to Kentucky in 1796 and debated for some time whether he would settle on the forks of Elkhorn, in Franklin county, or in Jessamine county, but through his personal regard for Col. Joseph Crockett, who had come to Kentucky in

1784, and settled in Jessamine county, in 1787, he was induced to choose Jessamine as his future home.

He purchased about three hundred acres of land from the Crocketts and Woodsons. This land is four miles from Nicholasville, on the turnpike which connects the Lexington and Danville, and the Harrodsburg and Lexington turnpikes, and is now owned in large part by Mr. John Steel. The beautiful forest trees attracted his admiration and won his affections. Sugar trees, poplar, ash, oak, hackberry and walnut, all growing in most superb profusion, determined his choice of residence. He had large tracts of land in other parts of Kentucky.

He founded at this locality a home, called Chaumiere des Prairies, but it was familiarly known throughout the country as Chaumiere, which is the French for Indian Village. On this small place David Meade lavished vast sums of money. He had all the tastes of an educated and refined Englishman. Whatever could have induced such a man with such a fortune to have come down the Ohio river in a flatboat, and land at Maysville and suffer the inconvenience of travel and transportation from Nicholasville to Jessamine county, and to live in such a remote and unimproved district, is almost impossible to understand.

He laid out a hundred acres of Chaumiere into a beautiful garden. He imported rare and exquisite plants. He made lakes, constructed water falls, shaped islands, built summer houses and porters' lodges, and in this backwoods wilderness created an ideal Englishman's home. He had a large retinue of liveried servants, splendid coaches, magnificent furniture, service largely of silver, and maintained in every way the style of a feudal lord.

The house was one-story, built of various materials, stone, brick and wood, but all erected for comfort and for convenience. Here David Meade lived from 1796 to 1832. During his thirty-six years of residence in Jessamine county he made no change in his method or manner of living. His service, his carriages, his liveries, fashion of entertainment, his own personal dress and that of his wife, always elegant, were still maintained in true English style. Different from everybody else in Kentucky in his style of living, he never excited the envy of his less wealthy or less cultured neighbors. The hospitality and elegance of his home were the boast of Kentucky. No distinguished man ever came to the state who did not express a desire to see this wonderful place, and none were ever disappointed in receiving a cordial invitation for the enjoyment of its hospitality.

No other home in Kentucky ever entertained so many Presidents, for at various times the roof of Chaumiere covered Monroe, General Jackson, General Charles Scott, and General Taylor. All the distinguished families of Kentucky were invited and always welcomed within its borders. Henry Clay was a constant visitor at this delightful residence, and a very funny story is told of the politeness of Mr. Clay and Mr. Meade. Mr. Clay had come to spend the night at Chaumiere. Mr. Meade was too polite to suggest to Mr. Clay that it was time to retire, and Mr. Clay was too polite to tell Mr. Meade that he desired to retire, and so they sat up and talked all night.

Aaron Burr often visited Chaumiere. He was there again and again with Blennerhasset, and there is in possession of a member of the family a mirror before which Aaron Burr sat and had his hair powdered. After the arrest of Aaron Burr he was permitted to remain in custody at Chaumiere, and Col. Meade's son acted as chief of the guard during his stay.

Mrs. Meade was as elegant, refined and cultured as her husband. They died within six months of each other.

The costly furniture, cut glass and china, with which one hundred guests could at one time be served, have been scattered throughout the country. The lovely and beautiful bric-a-brac can be found in many homes, and there is still in Chillicothe, Ohio, a piano upon which Mrs. Meade, when three-score and ten, played, and it was the first instrument of its kind ever brought into the state of Kentucky.

The eldest son had died young and unmarried. At Colonel Meade's death, none were able to maintain or to hold Chaumiere, and so it went under the hammer on the block and was bought by a plain, practical farmer. This surprised and distressed the citizens of Jessamine county, who had taken a just pride in this strange and beautiful home, and in a little while after the new owner of the place had been announced, there was placarded in large letters on the houses over the grounds the words "Paradise Lost." This caused the purchaser to become indignant, and in less than a week the beautiful flower gardens were filled with horses, cattle and hogs. The glorious forest trees were felled, lodges torn down, parks destroyed, and lakes drained. A portion of the house was pulled down, and in the rooms which were once the resort of fashion and made memorable by the presence of the most distinguished people in the land, were stored wheat and corn. Only three rooms now remain of this once magnificent home.

On a hill overlooking Chaumiere in a neglected burying-ground, sleeps the dust of David Meade and his wife and a few of his family, but the memories of Chaumiere will long live in Jessamine county and in the West.

Nothwithstanding its difference from the other homes in Jessamine county, and notwithstanding the difference between him and his neighbors, there was no jealousy. He did not interfere with his fellow-countrymen. He entertained their guests if they were refined and reputable, and he sought no political preferment, asked for no honors, only desiring to be permitted to live in his own way and to exhibit his own taste in his own home.

It was arranged that General La Fayette should be entertained at Chaumiere, and for this purpose Colonel Meade constructed a beautiful octagonal room. This, with two other small rooms off of the octagonal room, are all that remains as a monument to the beauty and to the charming associations connected with this marvelous home in the wilderness.

John Cawbey.

John Cawbey was a resident of Independence, Mo. In September, 1884, he wrote to S. M. Duncan a letter which contains many interesting facts in regard to some of the olden time people in Jessamine, and also some reminiscences in regard to Dr. Trisler, the first physician in Jessamine, and which indicates that Dr. Trisler was something of a medium and fortune teller and practiced these arts in addition to medicine. For many years, traditions have been floating among the people of pristine Jessamine, in regard to the marvelous power of Dr. Trisler and his possession of mysterious powers in locating disease, finding lost property, and in early days there were many who accredited the good, old doctor with the highest order of supernatural vision.

Mr. Cawbey says: "My mother died at Franklin, Ind., in her 70th year; my father died in his 47th year; my grandfather, John Cawbey, lived to the age of 87 years. His wife, my grandmother, lived to the age of 105 years, and died in Mercer county, Ky. My grandfather was born in Lincoln county, Kentucky, and settled in Jessamine county in 1808, where he spent all his life, and was buried at old West Union church lot, better known as the "Hoover graveyard." In this old lot lie my first wife, her brother, father, and grandfather, Conrad Earthenhouse, the father of the late venerable Elizabeth Bowman, who lived to reach the great age of 108. She died in 1886. I have in my keeping Dr. Peter Trisler's German medical works, printed in Wittenberg, Germany, in 1442, which makes 442 years since they were printed. (Printing was invented in 1440.) I have also the Bible of Dr. Trisler, which is 400 years old and a commentary over 300 years old, in the German language. The first of his medical books contains 1,180 pages, the second book, 1,342 pages. I send you this information for the purpose of giving you a correct account, and the dates that I found concerning the first settlers on Jessamine creek, among my papers which I sent to Missouri several months before I left Jessamine county. When I have more time it will afford me pleasure to give you many more interesting facts concerning the old settlers along Jessamine creek and their occupation. Beginning on the west side of Hickman road, running down Jessamine creek, there was the home of Joseph Wallace, who was a farmer and tanner. Next was John Carroll, farmer and auctioneer; Peter Funk, farmer and distiller; Michael Ritter, farmer and vender of crockery ware, etc.; Samuel Walls, farmer; Thos. Reynolds, father of Barney Reynolds, farmer and distiller, and spent much of his life fishing; Jacob Myers, father of the late W. B. Myers, was a manufacturer of gun powder on the farm where Wm. Mathews now lives; Richard West was a gunsmith and farmer, and owned the farm where Wm. Bourne is now living; Christopher Arnspiger lived on the other side of the creek, was a farmer and cooper; next came the old Howser mill property, owned by Abraham Howser and George Mason. Both had an equal share in the mill, and each one had his part of the farm, and both carried on a distillery of their own; next was the Bennett farm— this old Mr. Bennett fell down from his barn loft and killed himself. He was an old bachelor, and would often hide himself when ladies passed his house; Conrad Earthenhouse was a farmer and weaver, and also had a distillery; George Smith, the grandfather of Willis B. Smith, lived on the farm now occupied by Willis; he was a farmer and distiller. On that old farm in his grandfather's lifetime, I ground corn for the said distillery in the year 1827. At old Thomas Haydon's mills, now owned by James Lewallen, formerly by Frank Grow, there was a distillery attached to this property. It has passed through many hands since I first knew the place; the next farm on the creek was the old Crozier mill and cotton factory. This property, like many others in those days, had a distillery on it. It was here on this farm that the first steam engine was ever used in Jessamine county. Mr. Crozier and James Hill ran it for nineteen years. The next place was that owned by Mr. Womack and Thos. Bryan, who owned the old paper mill and grist mill built by old John Lewis. This mill was the first one erected in Jessamine county, and had the first French buhr stones brought to Jessamine county, which cost Mr. Lewis $1,200. The old mill is now owned by John H. Glass.

"Before closing this long letter I will relate some of Dr. Trisler's strange performances. He would sometimes invite his neighbors to see him. He would then disappear in the very presence of the company, and none could tell what had become of him. He could stop the flow of blood from any wound by giving the initials of the proper name of any man or women—this was all that was required. He could tell where stolen property was concealed. He could light a candle in a large room by rubbing his hands together. He could tell the exact number of pigs a sow would have at a litter. These are matters of fact and have been tested and are well known as facts, among the early settlers of Jessamine county. I remember, myself, there lived a man on the farm of Thomas Gordon, about one mile south of Nicholasville, who had a horse stolen. He came to see Dr. Trisler, three times before he would tell him where the horse was. On the third day Dr. Trisler met the owner of the stolen horse and told him to go to the town of Lancaster, in Garrard county, and near the county jail he would find the horse hitched to a fence; he added: "But the man that took the horse from your stable has been killed in a drunken frolic." This may appear unreasonable, but I know it to be true.   Very truly, your friend,

JOHN CAWBEY.

Alexander Wake.

Alexander Wake was the first County Judge of Jessamine county under the Constitution of 1850. He was born in Fauquier county, Virginia, in 1797, and died in Nicholasville in 1867. Through his maternal and paternal ancestors, he inherited the love of liberty, for both took part in the war for independence. In the beginning of the present century, Judge Wake's father removed to Woodford county. He brought with him from Virginia, a large number of slaves. Judge Wake commenced the study of law and was admitted to the practice of his profession in 1820. In 1851, when he was elected County Judge, he refused to grant license to sell liquor. Judge James Letcher, of Garrard county, was the first judge who refused to grant such license, and he was immediately followed by Judge Wake, of Jessamine. He was a fearless man in the discharge of his official duty; he knew neither friend or foe on the bench; he followed the dictates of his conscience and his judgment, and commanded the respect and confidence of his fellow-citizens.

John B. Cook.

In 1810 Dawson Cook, who was a native of King and Queen county, Virginia, removed to Nicholasville, bringing with him his son, John B. Cook, then four years of age. Early in life Mr. Cook entered business in Nicholasville, became a member of the Methodist church, and in all the relations of life acted well his part. He was kind, generous, thoughtful and courteous to his friends and neighbors. One characteristic of his life was his devotion to his church. For fifty-two years he was an earnest supporter of the Nicholasville Methodist church, and was rarely, if ever, absent from his seat in the sanctuary. He died in 1886, in the seventy-third year of his age.

One of his sons, Rev. T. B. Cook, was adjutant of the Fifth Kentucky Confederate infantry, and later a distinguished Methodist divine. His sons, John, Edward, and Bush L. Cook, the latter proprietor of the Hotel Nicholas, and one daughter survive him. His piety and his patriotism combined with his kind and genial manners render him one of the best remembered citizens of Jessamine county.

Capt. John Wallace

Was born in Bucks county, Pennsylvania, Dec. 18, 1748. His father had come from Ireland in 1737. Captain Wallace served in the Revolutionary armies under General Washington. He had three brothers in his company. He was with Washington when he crossed the Delaware, and fought the battle of Trenton. Colonel Rahl, the commander of the Hessians, in that battle, was killed by one of the sharpshooters in Captain Wallace's company. There Captain Wallace took from one of the Hessian officers a sword, which was kept in the family for eighty years, and was taken by Federal soldiers from the house of the Rev. Joseph Wallace, in Independence, Missouri, during the late war. After his marriage to Jane Finley, in 1777, he removed to Virginia, but shortly after came to Fayette county, Ky., accompanied by several members of his family. His son, Joseph Wallace, married Sarah Barr, January 24, 1829, and shortly after this Captain Wallace settled in Jessamine county, where the East Fork and main Jessamine Creek unite, and carried on for more than forty years an extensive tannery. He was a most efficient business man, kindly and considerate in all the relations of life, and was one of the best citizens that ever lived in Jessamine. He died at his place, a few miles south of Nicholasville, Dec. 19, 1855, in the 76th year of his age. Mrs. T. J. Brown was one of his daughters. Scattered throughout Kentucky and Missouri are his descendants. They carry with them as their inheritance the manly, patriotic, intelligent and Christian instincts which marked their ancestors.

A Romantic Story.

On the first day of January, 1841, a young man about thirty years of age, made his appearance in Nicholasville, which then had a population of only 550 inhabitants. His name was Ross

Hughes, and he was a stage driver, a native of Ireland and a man of pluck and energy. He obtained employment, and rented an old house then belonging to Albert Young. He and his wife constituted the family. He drove the stage from Nicholasville to Harrodsburg, over rough roads in winter. After he quit driving the stage, he one day told his wife that he must visit Louisville and New Orleans. He remained away from home for a long time and the gossips of the town made the young wife unhappy by their disagreeable insinuations. After an absence of four months the husband returned, but within a week he received a budget of letters, and told his wife that he must go at once to St. Louis, and in a few hours, he took his departure for the last time from Nicholasville, and gossip again turned its hateful tongue to the disturbance of the life and heart of the young wife. The public felt that she was deserted. Shortly after she became a mother, and for eighteen months lived on in silence, hoping and trusting. At the end of this time she received a letter from her husband directing her to come at once with her child, which she did, after disposing of her little household effects. Upon reaching St. Louis she found that her husband was the owner of a splendidly furnished house with every convenience for her comfort, and with colored servants ready to obey her wishes. In due time the little girl born in the little log house on the 27th of January, 1841, became a lady in fashionable society in St. Louis, and later the wife of an English Lord, and the mistress of a superb mansion in London society. She died Lady Stirling, on the 6th day of September, 1889, in London. Her first husband was a distinguished Major General, in the Federal army. The old log house in which Lady Stirling was born is still standing, and is the property of Mr. Corrington. It has been altered and weatherboarded anew, and is still one of the most comfortable residences in the town. It was erected in 1804, and is on the corner lot in the rear of Joseph Lear's livery stable.

Prolific of Statesmen.

In one corner of Jessamine county there were six neighborhood boys, living almost in sight of each other, all of whom played together and attended the same school. Four of these—George

S. Shanklin, Otho R. Singleton, Sam'l H. Woodson and A. G. Talbott—became members of Congress; the fifth—Jos. B. Crockett—became one of the most distinguished state judges in America, and was for many years Chief Justice of California; while the sixth—Richard K. Call—was elected to Congress from Florida, in 1823. He was Governor of Florida from 1836 to 1839, and again from 1841 to 1844. Such a record of distinguished services from one neighborhood is certainly rare in this or any other county.

George S. Shanklin.

Hon. G. S. Shanklin was the youngest son of John Shanklin, who was one of the early pioneers, emigrating from Pennsylvania

to Kentucky. He settled in Jessamine county in 1785. He early attended the celebrated school of Joshua Fry. He was not a

15

politician or time-server. He was a man of a high sense of integrity, modesty, courtesy and of retiring disposition. He was an able and successful practitioner of law, a man of most incorruptible honor. He was elected to Congress in 1865, and represented Jessamine county in the lower house in 1838, and was Presidential Elector in 1864. The latter years of his life were spent upon his farm, about three miles from Nicholasville, on the Versailles turnpike. He died April 1st, 1883, seventy-five years of age.

Otho R. Singleton.

One of the distinguished sons of Jessamine was Otho R. Singleton. He was born near Keene, in 1816. In 1842 he settled in the state of Mississippi. He was a gifted man, of superb presence, fine courage and attractive address, and in his adopted state became very prominent. He was the son of Lewis Singleton, and nephew of Elijah Singleton. He attended Bardstown College in his early life, and immediately after going to Mississippi was elected and served two years in the legislature. He afterwards served six years in the Mississippi State Senate, and in 1852 was the presidental elector from Mississippi. He was chosen as a member of the 33d, 35th and 36th Congresses. He entered the Civil War with a Mississippi regiment, and acquitted himself with great gallantry. At the battle of Leesburg a Federal officer from Boston—a Captain Watson—demanded his surrender. At that time Mr. Singleton was a captain in the Second Mississippi regiment. His response to the Federal officer was a shot which killed him instantly. After the war Mr. Singleton was elected a member of the 44th Congress, and served in 1875 as a member of that body. His father was an extensive hemp manufacturer, and maintained his factory near Keene. He died a few years since at Jackson, Miss.

Rev. John T. Hendricks, D. D.

Mr. Hendricks was one of the most useful and also one of the most distinguished men educated in Jessamine. Having united with the Nicholasville Presbyterian church, the officers of the congregation discovered that he was a man of fine mind and deep religious convictions. The church undertook his education for the ministry, and amply did he repay it for the services rendered by it to him in his youth.

He was born in Barren county in 1810. His father came from Virginia and settled in Kentucky in 1805, and died in Jessamine county in 1839, two miles east of Nicholasville. His wife who was Mary Tilman, died at the same place in February, 1838. His ancestors were staunch Protestants and served under William, Prince of Orange, in the war waged by Philip II. of Spain against the Protestants of Holland, about the middle of the Sixteenth century.

While preparing for the ministry, he undertook the work of colporteur in Jessamine county, and his report of his labors is still in existence. He distributed 31 Bibles free, sold 15, donated 25 Testaments, and sold 5. His report closes with these words: "'I have been engaged five days, finding my own horse, "at one dollar per day, which I have received.

"March 6, 1830."

He visited in all 148 families in the territory bounded as follows: From Nicholasville with the Shaker road to Jessamine creek, with the same to the river, up the river to the Paint Lick road, to the beginning.

Dr. Hendricks died only a few months ago in the 88th year of his age. His services at Clarksville, Paducah and other portions of the Presbyterian church in the Southern states, have given him wide distinction as a man of great earnestness, and great faithfulness in his Master's cause.

John Corman.

John Corman, a member of Captain Price's company, was a native of Wayne county, Pa. He was born in 1792. He removed to Kentucky in very early life, and when the call was made for volunteers, in 1812, he promptly offered his services. He was the first man in Captain Price's command to fire a gun in the battle of Raisin. He killed an Indian and a British soldier early in the morning.

He long lived in the western part of Jessamine county as one of its best and worthiest citizens and died in 1876, in his eighty-second year. He was brave, honest and patriotic.

Capt. Thomas T. Cogar.

Nature was generous to Capt. Thos. T. Cogar, and gave him as his portion in life, fourscore-and-six years.

His father, Michael Cogar, settled in Jessamine in 1790 at the head of Jessamine creek, and there his son Thomas was born in 1796.

Captain Cogar was a man of strong mind and the kindest impulses. His devotion to friends knew no limitations. He married Miss Ruth Ewing in 1822, and in 1847 removed to the Kentucky river, at Cogar's Landing, sometimes called Brooklyn. Here he carried on a large trade and managed the shipping business on the Kentucky river, from that point.

He became a distinguished Mason; and commanded, for many years, one of the crack military companies of the county. He managed to secure a large pork-packing establishment at his landing and by his energy and popularity built up a remunerative trade for such a locality.

He represented Jessamine county for two terms, in the legislature of 1867-71, and died in Nicholasville in 1882. He was an honorable man, a patriotic citizen, a loyal friend, and an intelligent and faithful legislator.

John Barkley.

In the earlier history of Jessamine county that portion of it lying in the general neighborhood of Keene produced an unusual number of very enterprising as well as very gifted men. Among these was John Barkley, who held large landed interests in Jessamine county prior to 1834. At that time Mr. Barkley removed to Boyle county, and established the first hemp manufactory south of the Kentucky river. He was largely engaged in merchandise and was also one of the leading men in the development of the state. He was born in Jessamine county in 1809.

He was the first President of the proposed railroad from Lexington to Danville from the South. Railroad building at that period presented almost insurmountable difficulties. Mr. Barkley went to New York and engaged a civil engineer to examine the prospects for the construction of the road. The mighty chasms of the Kentucky river stood in the way. Cantilever and suspension bridges for railways had not then been used or even invented, The construction of a railway was practically impossible without a bridge which would span the Kentucky river. Mr. Adams, the engineer, surveying the road from Lexington to Danville, proposed to span the Kentucky at the point where the Cincinnati Southern now crosses.

The engineering and financial difficulties would have defeated most men, but they only aroused Mr. Barkley to higher effort. He was a man of great pluck, high order of talent, sparkling wit and a fine conversationalist. He had received the best educational advantages and had followed these with wide reading, especially in English literature.

He represented Boyle county in the legislature in 1845, and was a leader in all movements for the prosperity and development of the county.

Prior to his death he had purchased one of the finest farms in Boyle county, near Danville, and was residing there at the time he undertook the construction of the Lexington & Danville Railroad. While on his way from Danville to Nicholasville, in company with Mr. Adams, the engineer, to arrange some matters in connection with the enterprise, the horse, which he was driving, became frightened on the cliffs of the Kentucky river, and ran away, striking the vehicle against a rock on the side of the road. He was thrown out and instantly killed. This occurred on the 21st day of January, 1853.

Few men at that time would have been a greater loss to Kentucky. Mr. Barkley was one of the master spirits of enterprise in that period when Kentucky, above all others, needed men to lead, promote and advance internal improvements.

He left the work which he had inaugurated for others to complete, but the boldness of his plans and the wisdom of his designs have been vindicated in later years and that great thoroughfare, the Cincinnati Southern Railway, is the consummation of that which Mr. Barkley had devised at a time when other men would have dismissed such a project from their minds as utterly impossible.

Joseph B. Crockett.

In 1808, Joseph B. Crockett was born at Union Mills, on Hickman creek, A short while after, his father removed to Logan county, and there the son attended a classical school. In 1827 he entered the University of Tennessee, at Nashville, but in consequence of the straitened pecuniary condition of his father, he was compelled to leave the University after one year. He studied law at Hopkinsville with Governor Morehead. In 1830 he formed a partnership with Gustavus A. Henry, which, after two years, was dissolved. In 1833, he was elected to the legislature, where, at once, his talents and his industry gave him a high stand. He was again elected to the legislature in 1836, to fill a vacancy, and shortly after this he was appointed Commonwealth's Attorney by Governor Clark. His career as a prosecutor was brilliant and able, but the duties of the office were uncongenial; his talents led him to prefer the defense rather than the prosecution, and he soon established a reputation for being one of the ablest criminal lawyers ever known in Kentucky.

In 1840, he removed to St. Louis, Mo., where a most brilliant success crowned his career, but, his health giving way, in 1852 he settled in California, and in a little while found himself in the very front rank of the bar in that state.

His kindness of heart and his generous courtesy secured for him the highest popularity. Upon the death of Judge Shapter, of the Supreme Court of California, Mr. Crockett was appointed to fill the unexpired term. He held the place of Chief Justice for twelve years and retired in 1880—the result of infirmity produced by advanced years. He was regarded by the people of California as one of the most brilliant, able and distinguished judges who ever sat on the bench of the Supreme Court.

David Bowman.

One of the unique characters in the early history of Jessamine county was David Bowman. He was born in Bucks county, Pa., in 1784, and settled in Jessamine county, on Jessamine creek, in

1800. His forefathers in Pennsylvania were members of the Church of the United Brethren. Mr. Bowman united with the Presbyterian church in Nicholasville in 1825, and was for more than sixty-five years a faithful and devoted attendant. At the time of his death in 1879, he was the oldest member of the church and was the last of the old men born in the eighteenth century.

When a young man he became addicted to the use of liquor; resolving to rid himself of this habit, he went to Lexington and after a three days' walk in the mud, reached that city. There he received the help of a gentleman, who aided him to go to New Orleans on a flatboat, and there he took service on a ship, which plied between New Orleans and Havana, and followed the sea for twelve years, and accumulated quite a fortune. He returned to Jessamine county, married, and on twelve acres of land always had corn and wheat, and money to spare.

For many years he attended church in Nicholasville, coming on horseback, with his wife behind him. He insisted to the time of his death upon wearing a blue, spade-tail coat.

John Butler.

John Butler was the son of Thomas Butler, one of the old sheriffs of Jessamine county, under the Constitution of 1779. He was born in Jefferson county, Va., in July, 1813, and was only six years old when his father settled in Jessamine county. He was a kind, honest and upright man, and commanded the respect and confidence of his fellow-citizens. He was deputy sheriff two terms, and died March 1, 1870. He was one of the substantial and enterprising men of Jessamine county.

James R. Davis.

James R. Davis was born near Nicholasville in 1809. He was the third son of James Davis, and nephew of William Davis, two brothers, who came from Culpeper Court House, Va , and settled in Jessamine county in 1798. James Davis was the son of Henry Davis, of Culpeper county, Va., who served in the Revolutionary War, under General Washington, and General Wayne. He died in Fayette county in 1794.

James R. Davis lived in the Sulphur Wells neighborhood for fifty years. He was a good and worthy man, noted for his hospitality. He died in 1886.

Samuel Woodson Price.

Samuel Woodson Price, son of Maj. D. B. Price and Eliza Crockett, was born on the 5th of August, 1828, in Nicholasville, Ky. He early exhibited a marvelous talent for drawing, and he

could draw the capital letters before he knew his alphabet. All his holidays and Saturdays were spent in sketching on paper and modeling in clay. When quite a boy he was sitting in the court house at a famous trial. Thomas F. Marshall was addressing the jury for the prisoner. During this speech the attention of the young artist was drawn to an old and prominent farmer who was listening, with eager attention to the eloquent words which were being uttered. His head was resting on his hands, his fingers along the side of his face, while his mouth was wide open. In a little while the sketch was completed. He handed it to the sheriff, who laughed aloud and in turn handed it to the judge, who also was not able to suppress his mirth. It was passed from neighbor to neighbor, and everybody laughed, and the speaker was compelled to pause for a few minutes.

After attending the Nicholasville Academy he was sent to the Kentucky Institute to complete his education. This was in the fall of 1846. He was at once made Professor of Drawing, with the rank of First Lieutenant. In 1847 the University suspended and he went at once to Lexington to pursue his studies with the renowned painter, Oliver Frazier. There he attained splendid success. His painting, "Old King Solomon," is one of the most noted ever produced in Kentucky. His portrait of Chief Justice George Robertson, and the painting of Dr. J. J. Bullock and his family, rank among the masterpieces of the state. The Government purchased from him a portrait of Major-General Thomas, which is now in the National Gallery, at Washington.

At the beginning of the war he commanded an independent company at Lexington, known as the Old Infantry. Most of this company entered the Federal service. He was afterwards appointed Colonel of the Twenty-first Kentucky Infantry. He brought this regiment to a high state of efficiency, and the service it afterward performed in the Civil war, from '61 to '65, was in considerable measure induced by his splendid training. At the battle of Stone River he made a heroic stand and was opposed to the Kentucky Confederate troops under Breckinridge.

General Price was badly wounded at Kenesaw Mountain and taken from the field. This incapacitated him for further active service. He was appointed commandant of the post at Lexington, and was such at the close of the war. He was breveted Brigadier-General for his gallant conduct at Kennesaw, and afterwards was Postmaster at Lexington, which place he held for two terms. He moved to Louisville after his retirement from the position of Postmaster, to pursue his profession, portrait painting, but the loss of his eyesight prevented him from further work, and he is now totally blind. He is a writer of vigor and a member of the Filson Club, for which he frequently prepares sketches, which are greatly appreciated and highly valued. Several of his paintings take high rank, and one, "Caught Napping," is a masterpiece of its kind. The closing of his professional life by the destruction of his sight, was a great loss, not only to Kentucky but to all lovers of art.

William T. Willis.

Captain Willis was born on the 10th of June, 1794, in Culpeper county, Va., and was killed at the battle of Buena Vista, February 23rd, 1847. He married first Hetty E. Howe, daughter of a Presbyterian minister. He had been educated at a seminary taught by his father-in-law. He was elected to represent Green county in the Legislature several times, and also represented Green and Hart in the Senate in 1833 and 1838. He made the race for Congress in that district in 1839, with a majority of 2,000 against him, which he reduced to 200. At that time he was believed to be on his death-bed, and this seriously affected his vote. After his marriage he began merchandising, and shipped large quantities of tobacco by flat-boat, and drove horses through the country to New Orleans. The partner, who he sent on one of these expeditions, was taken sick after selling the horses and tobacco, and died, and before Captain Willis could reach the place of his demise, the proceeds of the sale had disappeared. Being involved, he returned at once, sold out his stock, and commenced studying law and practiced in Green and adjoining counties. Notwithstanding that he had a large debt and a family of eight children, and at that time was compelled to meet such men as Samuel Brent, Ben Hardin, Judge Underwood and Judge Buckner, he succeeded admirably in his profession. In 1840 he removed to Harrodsburg, remained there three years, and then came to Jessamine county. He was a man of singular energy and great ability. He had built up a large practice, and was regarded throughout Kentucky as one of its most promising statesmen. Although fifty years of age at the breaking out of the Mexican war, he at once organized a company for service and his ardent patriotism is best attested by the fact that with him, three of his sons volunteered as privates; the youngest of whom was barely fifteen years of age.

The following is a list of his men:

Roll of Company "F," Second Regiment, Kentucky Foot Volunteers—Mexican War:

Wm. T. Willis, 1st captain, killed at Buena Vista.

Captain—James O. Hervy. First Lieutenant—William R. Keene. Second Lieutenant—Thos. J. Proctor. Second Lieutenant—Wm. C. Lowry. Sergeants—William L. Smith 1st, Andrew J. Nave, 2d, Jno. C. Winter 3d, William Cox 4th; Corporals—Edward P. Green 1st, Dudley Portwood 2d, John A. Willis 3d, Chas. C. Hagan 4th. Drummer—Cortney L. Burch.

Privates—Allen, Jno. H.; Brown, Geo. W.; Burchell, Daniel; Burton, Theodric; Bruner, Thos. J.; Beymer, Saml.; Castle, Augustus B.; Crane, Asa C.; Crane, Jno. P.; Collins, William; Daniel, Wm. H.; Dickerson, Woodson; Day, Wm.; Duman, James; Easby, Andrew L.; Easby, Josiah; England, Jas. S.; Fain, John; Ford, Joshua G.; Ford, Edward D.; Garison, John A.; Graves, Living; Gibony, William; Grant, Geo. W.; Howard, Robt. S.; Hamilton, William; Hunter, John; Hayden, Isah P.; Hill, Greensbury; Harvey, Trotter; Hawkins, James; Jackman, Jos.; Masters, Irvine; Marvin, Wm. F.; Masters, Jackson; Marks, Geo. I.; Martin, Robert; Moore, Andrew B.; McCampbell, Jno. G.; McConnel, Jas. A.; McMurtry, John; Nooe, Albert K.; O'Brien, William; Overstreet, Saml. R.; Page, Thos. C.; Patterson, Wm.; Roberson, Jacob C.; Roberts, Andrew J.; Rash, John; Saunders, Jno. A.; Saunders, Geo. W.; Sacre, John; Sharp, Ezekiel K.; Sweitzer, John; Tutt, Wm.; Thompson, Jno. T.; White, Jas. N.; Wilson, John; Willis, Edmond C.; Willis, Jas. H.

Jacob Kreath Robinson, in the official list spelled Robertson, was one of the youngest men in this company. He was born in 1829. The oldest man in the company, John Hunter, was born in 1804, and was the son of John Hunter, the first settler. He was severely wounded in the leg at the battle of Buena Vista and died in 1881. Robinson was also a soldier in the late war, passed through all its hardships and dangers, endured its privations, and now resides at Harrodsburg, Ky.

This company was ordered to report at Louisville to be mustered into service. They assembled at Mundy's Landing on the

Kentucky river; some came on horseback, some in carriages, and they were ordered there to meet the steamboat Blue Wing. When the company reached the river the steamboat was at Brooklyn, and while coming down to Mundy's Landing ran into a sandbar and stuck. Capt. Philip Thomson's company from Mercer county, was also on the way to Louisville. With ropes the soldiers pulled the steamer from off the sandbar twice, and, after it had stuck the third time, Capt. Thomson went to Salvisa and obtained wagons and drove through to Louisville, while Captain Willis's company took coalboats at Mundy's Landing, rowed themselves down to Frankfort, and arrived there the next day. After taking breakfast in Frankfort, the steamer arrived at the landing and they took passage and reached Louisville, and were mustered in by Col. George Croghan. From Louisville they were transported to New Orleans by steamers, and after remaining there a few days, they crossed the Gulf of Mexico in some old British sailing vessels, and arrived at Brazos on the Rio Grande river. A part of the regiment was engaged in the battle of Monterey. Shortly after this the regiment was ordered to the city of Saltillo, and from thence, marching with General Taylor, they engaged in the battle of Buena Vista. This was one of the most brilliant battles that crowned American arms, and it was the only battle in which the entire regiment, with which Captain Willis' company was connected, was engaged. This regiment was commanded by Col. William R. McKee, from Lancaster; Henry Clay, Jr., was Lieutenant-Colonel, and Cary H. Fry, Major. The company was enrolled on the 21st of May, 1846, in Nicholasville, and was mustered in at Louisville June 9, 1846, and was mustered out at New Orleans June 9, 1847.

The story of this battle has always reflected great credit and renown on Kentucky courage. The second Kentucky Regiment was on the right flank of the army and held it throughout the battle, defeating the enemy opposite to them, which was twice their number. At this time the left flank gave way, and its retreat was only stopped by General Taylor and Jefferson Davis and the cavalry, who drove them back to face the enemy. It was then that Colonel Hardin, of the First Illinois, and Colonel McKee, of the Second, made a disastrous charge against an overwhelming force. This charge was made against the earnest protest of Colonel Mc-

Kee and Captain Willis, but Hardin insisted upon making it, and Lieutenant-Colonel Clay urged it, and the Kentucky boys, fearing that the Illinois men would get the glory, McKee then united in the charge and was killed. Col. Henry Clay, Jr., was wounded, and Captain Willis, with the high courage and noble generosity which marked his whole career, was urging his men to take the Lieutenant-Colonel from the field, when the Mexican Lancers came rapidly down and killed both Colonel Clay and Captain Willis. Harvey Trotter, a soldier from Jessamine, was killed at the same time. James O. Hervey succeeded Captain Willis, and only four of the men who were engaged in the battle of Buena Vista in this company, now remain in Jessamine: John A. Willis, William C. Lowrey, William Hamilton and David Switzer. Captain Willis' remains, as well as those of Trotter, were removed by the State of Kentucky, and reinterred in the state ground in Frankfort cemetery. It was upon the occasion of the reinterment of these soldiers that Theodore O'Hara wrote his immortal poem of " The Bivouac of the Dead," commencing as follows:

"The muffled drum's sad roll has beat
   The soldier's last tattoo;
No more on Life's parade shall meet
   That brave and fallen few.
On Fame's eternal camping-ground
   Their silent tents are spread,
And glory guards, with solemn round,
   The bivouac of the dead."

Robert Young.

Robert Young, a resident of Jessamine county for more than sixty-four years, was born in Fayette county, on Elkhorn creek, not far from the Jessamine line, in 1803. His father, John Young, was a Revolutionary soldier and served three years under General Greene. At the breaking out of the war he was only sixteen years of age. He was engaged in the battles of Eutaw Springs, Monk's Corner, Guilford Court House, and at Yorktown. Robert Young was the son of John Young by his second wife, Cynthia McCullough.

ROBERT YOUNG.

JOSEPHINE YOUNG.

He learned hat manufacturing with his brother-in-law, Mr. Fritzlen, at Versailles, and in 1825 established himself in Nicholasville. He accumulated a moderate fortune and in 1848 purchased a farm and retired from business as a manufacturer.

He married Josephine Henderson, a granddaughter of Col. Joseph Crockett, and reared a large family. His oldest son, Rev. Daniel P. Young, was one of the leading Presbyterian ministers of Kentucky; his two sons, Robert and Melanchthon, two of the county's most substantial and successful farmers and most respected and loved citizens, while his other son, Col. Bennett H. Young, resides in Louisville and is the author of this book. His eldest daughter married Dr. Charles Mann and his youngest daughter, Josephine, now resides in Nicholasville.

Robert Young was a man of high integrity and possessed all the best and noblest qualities of citizenship. His word was better than his bond. Just, generous and conscientious in all his dealings, he commanded, as he deserved, the respect and confidence of his friends and acquaintances. He was an earnest, faithful member and officer of the Presbyterian church and was an honored member in many of its councils. No one ever questioned the reality of his religion; he carried it into all the dealings of his life. He died November 29th, 1889, beloved and deeply mourned by the entire community. He never failed to help those who were in want and the grateful remembrance of those who had received of his liberality and kindness is a rich legacy for any man.

Albert Gallatin Talbot

Was born in Jessamine county, in the Keene neighborhood, where his father at that time resided. He subsequently removed to Boyle county, and represented that county in the Legislature in 1869-73, and in 1850 he was a member of the Thirty-fourth and Thirty-fifth Congresses, and of the Constitutional Convention of 1849.

He was a man of idomitable energy, agreeable manners, and was a successful politician.

David Crozier.

David Crozier was a native of Pennsylvania, born in 1795, and came to Jessamine county when he was quite a young man. He built what is known as Crozier's Mill, which is half stone and half wood, on Jessamine creek. In 1845 he carried on a cotton factory at his mill. He worked about forty hands, mostly boys and girls, and manufactured cotton cloth and jeans. With the introduction of railroads, and with the difficulty in getting materials (for by this time Jessamine county had ceased to grow cotton, and the supply of wool was never large enough to run the mill), this mill was closed. Thereafter Mr. Crozier became associated with Dr. A. K. Marshall in carrying the mails from Lexington to Bean Station, Tenn.

He was energetic and enterprising and did much to foster and maintain the earlier manufacturing establishments of the county.

Dr. Francis Marion Jasper.

Dr. Francis Marion Jasper, who died at Cincinnati on the 22nd of June, 1892, while not a native of Jessamine county, was long one of its most successful physicians, and his descent entitles him to more than passing notice. His Revolutionary ancestors came from Wales. His great-grandfather, Abraham - Jasper, was born in Wales in 1728 and settled in Georgetown, South Carolina. From there he moved to a residence on Cooper river, near Charleston. His oldest son became a prominent Tory, while his other sons, Nicholas Jasper, John Jasper and William Jasper, were brave and devoted soldiers in the cause of their country during the Revolutionary war, having served under General Sumter in North and South Carolina.

After the Revolutionary war, Nicholas Jasper settled in Pulaski county, Ky., and became the father of a large family of brave and patriotic sons. Nicholas Jasper was born near Charleston, South Carolina, in 1752. Sergt. William Jasper was the youngest child, born in 1757. He was not quite twenty years old during the siege of Fort Moultrie, near Charleston, when the flagstaff was broken by a shot from the British. On seeing the flag thus lowered by a shot, Sergeant Jasper immediately sprang down and replaced the flag amid a tremendous fire from the British fleet, commanded by Sir Peter Parker. For his bravery on that occasion Governor Rutledge, in the presence of the regiment, took his sword from his side and presented it to Sergeant Jasper. He offered the brave soldier a commission, which he refused. He was killed in the assault on Savannah, Oct. 7, 1779, when he was not quite twenty-two years of age.

Capt. Thomas Jasper, who was the father of Dr. Francis Marion

Jasper, represented Pulaski county in the legislature of Kentucky in 1833, '34 and '35, and when the War of 1812 was declared he enlisted in the company commanded by Capt. Harry James. He was in the regiment of Colonel Simrall. He was at the battle of the Thames and fought with splendid courage on that occasion.

Dr. Jasper practiced his profession in Jessamine county more than thirty years. He answered every known call for his ser-

16

vices. He was kind, tender and gentle, and the question of remuneration affected neither the length nor the ability of his services. He was one of Jessamine's best citizens.

Henry Metcalf

Was the oldest son of Rev. John Metcalf, who surveyed Nicholasville. He was born in the year 1800, and died at his home in

Nicholasville, January 18, 1879. He passed his entire life in Nicholasville. He was a useful citizen and a manufacturer of ropes and bagging. He had a large factory which he operated for a long time successfully. He was a man of extraordinary sweetness of temper, and also of high character. He did the right as he knew it. He opened the first Sunday-school in the Southern Methodist Church in Nicholasville in the spring of

1843, and was for long years one of the stewards in that church and was liberal in the support of his church and earnest in its cause. He married a daughter of John Fishback, who settled in Kentucky in 1790, in Jessamine county, where he died in 1845. Mr. John Metcalf, who still survives and lives in Nicholasville, was his eldest son. George Metcalf, another son, now resides in Lexington, and was a gallant soldier in the Fifth Kentucky Infantry, C. S. A., while Charles Metcalf, the youngest son, is one of the leading lawyers in Tennessee, and President of the Tennessee State Bar Association. John Metcalf and James Metcalf, two of his sons, are still living, while two of his daughters, Miss Sallie and Miss Alice, now reside in Nicholasville at the old home place of their grandfather, who laid out and named the town.

Louis H. Chrisman.

Among the men of Jessamine who were prominent in the first fifty years of its existence was Louis H. Chrisman. He was born in 1813 and died in 1866, at his home two miles north of Nicholasville on the Lexington and Danville pike. He was always active in politics, was a warm partisan, and after a heated contest was elected sheriff of Jessamine county in 1858. He was the youngest son of Joseph Chrisman, brother of Gen. Hugh Chrisman. Joseph Chrisman was born in Rockingham county, Va., in 1776, and came to Kentucky with his brother and settled in Jessamine county in 1790.

Mr. Chrisman served as a volunteer aid on the staff of Gen. Wm. R. Terrell, of the Federal army, who was killed at Perryville. He was one of the leaders of the Whig party in Jessamine county and was always a delightful companion wherever he went on account his fine social qualities. He was an extraordinary whistler. He could carry the several parts while whistling a tune and this made him a welcome guest at every political meeting. He was a kind neighbor, a sincere friend, a generous opponent and a patriotic citizen. Mr. A. L. and George Chrisman, his sons, still reside on the old homestead.

Daniel P. Young.

Rev. Stuart Robinson, in speaking of Rev. D. P. Young, said:
"Mr. Young was perhaps the most successful of all the ministers of the Presbyterian church in Kentucky in winning souls to Christ. His greatness consisted in his wonderful skill in engaging the attention, alike of the converted and unconverted, in the Gospel way of salvation, and his eminent ability in expounding the Scriptures, setting forth that way, and beseeching men in Christ's stead to be reconciled to God. The secret of his success was in large part that his heart was in his work; and he was a man who had a very large heart, filled with the love of Christ and the love of souls. Nobody who knew him ever doubted the earnestness of his piety and holy zeal in the service of his Master. The many people all over Kentucky, who these twenty years after his death, grasp the hands of his children with a warmer clasp when they know who they are, and who speak their affection for him with tears in their eyes, is the greatest evidence of the warm place he held in the hearts of those who came under his influence."

Daniel P. Young was the oldest child of Robert and Josephine Henderson Young, and on the lot where Jessamine Female Institute now stands, was born on February 22d, 1833.

Under his mother's influence he early consecrated his life to Christ and resolved in his boyhood to devote himself to the gospel ministry.

After passing through the home schools he entered Hanover College, at Hanover, Indiana, and graduated in the class of 1852. After finishing his course there, he prepared to attend Transylvania University to pursue the study of law, but while on his way to Lexington he was induced by his conflicting emotions to change his mind and turned back to Danville, Ky., where he entered the Presbyterian Theological Seminary.

His first charge was at Georgetown, Ky., where under his ministry the membership of the church was largely augmented and in an unusual degree he won the love and affection of his congregation.

From there he removed to the renowned Providence church, in Mercer county, and from there he was induced by the insistence of friends to accept the charge of the Nicholasville church. In both success crowned his efforts and he was blessed in the up-building of these churches.

In 1878, he was called to the charge of the Presbyterian church at Anchorage, and in conjunction with it the principalship of Bellewood Seminary and Kentucky Presbyterian Normal School. His eminent fitness for this position was recognized on every hand, but, within a few months after he removed to Anchorage, on June 30th, 1878, he ended the labors of his earnest, useful and faithful life.

John Lafon.

The Lafons who came to American were refugees from France during the Huguenot persecution. The founders of the family settled in South Carolina and Virginia, and their descendant, Richard Lafon, married Miss Anna Maxey, removed to Kentucky and settled in Jessamine county in 1793. They came over the Wilderness Road, with their herds and household effects and slaves and settled, through a patent, a thousand acres, comprising the original Fountain House tract, being the lands now occupied by Burrier, Phillips, Bryants, and Elkins and others, about two and a half miles from Keene, toward Lexington. Richard Lafon was a man of unusual education for that period. He left a reasonable fortune, although he died a comparatively young man. He built one of the first brick dwelling houses in the county.

His son, John Lafon, was born December 4, 1800. He early had every social and literary advantage, and traveled not only in the United States but abroad. He was a man of unusual energy, great judgment, broad and comprehensive views, and was a born leader of men. As a result of his trading and manufacture he spent his winters in Cuba and New Orleans and his summers in Kentucky on his farm. At one time he leased all the hemp factories in three counties and shipped their product to the South by way of the Kentucky and Ohio rivers.

He was a close friend of Henry Clay and in many important matters his adviser. He was the moving spirit and the president of the Lexington & Harrodsburg Turnpike Company at the period of its completion. The road was commenced in 1834, by

the state, then abandoned and then leased by the state to Lewis
Singleton for twenty years. Singleton died shortly after the
acquisition of the road, and it was then taken up by John Lafon
and completed through to Perryville in 1847. The work near
the Kentucky river was done under Mr. Lafon's administration,
and required very large outlay and a high order of engineering
skill. He had tremendous difficulties, both physical and financial,

to overcome, but with his master mind he worked out a magnificent success and in the completion of this turnpike rendered
Fayette, Jessamine, Mercer and Boyle counties an incalculable
benefit.

Backed by his energy and financial ability, this great thoroughfare was built in the face of great difficulties. Such improvements in those days could only be carried on at large expenditure,
relatively much larger than now, and to undertake the construc-

tion of a graded road such as this pike, through the country on either side contiguous to the Kentucky river, demonstrates that he was a man of a high order of moral courage as well as the possessor of great sagacity and unyielding will.

. He married Mary Ann Barkley, whose grandfather had been compelled to leave Ireland, where a price had been placed on his head. And in the struggle for Irish independence he was the friend of Robert Emmett and devoted to the liberty of his country. Mrs. Lafon was also a descendant of the Higbees and they came from New Jersey. In early days they built boats on South Elkhorn and hauled them to Brooklyn and other landings on the Kentucky and launched them, from whence they were floated to New Orleans.

A man of culture himself, possessed of a large estate, inherited both from his father and his mother, he made a home in every way attractive and delightful. His hospitality was unbounded; he accumulated one of the best libraries in Kentucky, collected curios, and by his intelligence, his enterprise and his talents became associated with and was the friend of many of the leading men of the state. His home at one time almost rivaled Chaumiere. He built a beautiful house, he laid out handsome grounds, erected bath houses and spring houses, built laundries with hot and cold pipes, constructed artificial lakes, and improved charming drives. There was on his land an apparently bottomless spring from which boiled up a great volume of water. This, by a splendid circular stone basin, he changed into a most attractive fountain and called his home after it—Fountain House. With these surroundings he founded an elegant and ideal home. He secured rare flowers and adorned his yard with every variety of tree that could be grown in the locality. He died in 1848 in the very meridian of his career. His early demise was a great loss to his native county in its social, physical and educational interests.

Dr. John W. Holloway.

Dr. John W. Holloway, who represented Jessamine county in the Constitutional Convention of 1890, and who took a prominent part in the deliberations of that body, was a son of Spencer Holloway, and was born in the county on the 30th of April, 1823.

His grandfather, James Holloway, was a native of Virginia, and was a captain in the Revolutionary war, and settled in Jessamine county very early in its history. His son, Spencer Holloway, was born in 1792, and died at the advanced age of 89, in the year 1883. His son, John W. Holloway, passed his early life on a farm. At 23 years of age he went to Louisville and undertook the study of medicine under Dr. John L. Price and remained there three years, and finally graduated in 1850, from the Medical Department of the University of Louisville.

From that time on to the present he has practiced medicine at Keene. He has met with unqualified success in his profession as well as in his conduct of a large farm. He is a man of strong mental vigor, truest friendship, unflinching courage and highest integrity.

In the Constitutional Convention he earnestly advocated equal property rights for women and bitterly opposed the ballot system. While the convention did not adopt his views they all respected his sincerity, his integrity and his unusual courtesy.

Letcher Saunders.

Mr. Saunders was born in Nicholasville on October 29, 1864. His father, C. B. Saunders, died in Nicholasville in 1874. Mr.

Saunders was educated in the common schools of Nicholasville. He is one of the most expert penmen and careful clerks that have ever served the people of Jessamine. He was a pupil of Prof. A. N. Gordon, while principal of Bethel Academy, and when sixteen years of age, he entered the Circuit Court Clerk's office as deputy of Lewis D. Baldwin. Subsequently he became clerk in the general freight offices of the Louisville & Nashville R. R. Co., at Louisville. He returned to Nicholasville in 1885, and one month after his return he was nominated for Circuit Clerk at the Democratic primary, defeating his competitor by a handsome majority. His conduct of the office was such that he was nominated without opposition for a second term. As Circuit Clerk he took the front rank in Kentucky. He married the daughter of Jas. W. Glass, of Garrard county, January 1, 1887. His grandfather, Austin Smithers, during the epidemic of cholera in 1855 went through the tents visiting the sick and caring for the dead and dying. White and black alike received his attention, and he never wearied in waiting on those who needed his services during that terrible scourge. Mr. Saunders comes of an ancestry full of humane and noble characteristics, and his popularity is undoubtedly the result of these inherited qualities.

G. W. Lyne.

Few men have done more for Jessamine county than Mr. G. W. Lyne. He has been engaged in the real estate business, and his enthusiasm and energy have enabled him during that period to dispose of $2,000,000 worth of property and he has been instrumental in inducing a large number of strangers to settle in the county. Mr. Lyne is comparatively a young man, only thirty-one years of age. He is a successful auctioneer and is the only man who ever made the real estate business in Jessamine county a success.

William W. White.

William W. White, who died at his residence, in Nicholasville, on January 5, 1887, in the 80th year of his age, was one of the most earnest supporters of the doctrines of Alexander Campbell and was instrumental in building up several congregations of that faith in the county. He organized what is known as the Little Hickman church on the 27th of January, 1841. He was a son of William G. White, who came from Culpeper Court House,

Va. He became impressed with the doctrines propounded by Mr. Campbell and from the time of his uniting with that denomination until the end of his life gave his time and talents and energy to building up the church which adopted them. His membership was in the Nicholasville Christian church. However people might differ with Mr. White in his theological views, none ever doubted the earnestness and the faithfulness of his Christian service and of the unselfishness of his ministration. He was plain, simple-hearted and earnest. While engaged in other business, he preached always as occasion offered and never failed to respond to such calls as his church made upon him.

Rev. Thomas R. Welch, D. D.

Rev. Thomas R. Welch, D. D., one of the leading Presbyterian ministers of the Southern Presbyterian church, the son of John Welch and B. J. Rice, was born near Nicholasville, September 15th, 1825. Most of his ministerial life was passed in Arkansas, where he removed in 1851, and took charge of the church in Little Rock. After a course in Bethel Academy, he graduated from Center College in 1844, and in 1870, his Alma Mater conferred upon him the degree of Doctor of Divinity. Dr. Welch was singularly honored by his church. He held many positions of trust in its courts and institutions. He led a busy and successful life. Possessed of a fine presence, genial manners and ready sympathy, he found a welcome everywhere. Another has said of him:

"By long residence, abundant labors, eminent administrative ability, Dr. Welch is the Presbyterian Nestor of Arkansas, and no man in the state is held in higher esteem or wields a stronger influence."

He died a few years since, deeply regretted by the people of the great denomination to which he belonged and sincerely mourned by the members of his own congregation at Little Rock.

Mrs. Sarah Withers, an aunt of Dr. Welch, and long a resident of Bloomington, Illinois, was a most benevolent, charitable and earnest Christian woman. At her death, a few years since, she made the officers of the Nicholasville Presbyterian church her residuary legatees, and directed that the funds thus bequeathed should be used for the maintenance of a public library in Nicholasville. Quite a large sum, estimated at about $20,000, will be realized and it will be sufficient to equip and maintain a complete and efficient library in the city.

Maj. J. H. Hanly.

Maj. John Hay Hanly, born in Seville, Spain, in 1784, who settled in Jessamine county, in 1871, was the son of an officer of the British army.

On his arrival at his new home, in what was then the far west, he purchased a very large tract of land on the Kentucky river, six miles south of Nicholasville. His house, a frame cottage of liberal dimensions, located on a bluff many feet above the river, was appropriately named "Cliff Cottage." Its picturesque beauty of location excited the admiration of the distinguished painter, Healy, who visited Maj. Hanly, when sent by the king, Louis Phillippe, of France, to paint the portrait of Henry Clay. On entering the grounds, he is said to have exclaimed, "Grand and beautiful."

It was at this home of beauty that the generous proprietor and his estimable family dispensed old time Kentucky hospitality, during a period of more than half a century.

Maj. Hanly was a very positive character, highly intellectual, just in all his dealings, truthful, honest, and brave; he was, in all the elements that constitute a gentleman of the old school, a man to be admired and trusted. He was a firm believer in the Roman Catholic faith and in the democracy of Andrew Jackson. He was a fine shot, and prided himself upon the accuracy of his aim.

On one occasion, Col. David Goodloe, who had been challenged by Mr. White, M. C., of Madison county, to fight a duel, came to Maj. Hanly to practice with the major's dueling pistols. He became so expert, after considerable practice, as to hit the bull's eye repeatedly. When the duel finally came off, his antagonist stood with his back to a barn. Both gentlemen were game and fired at the word. Neither were hit, and much to their disgust,

Major Hanly, after a most diligent search, failed to find that the colonel's bullet had even struck the barn.

John A. Willis.

John A. Willis, son of Capt. W. T. Willis, while not a native of Jessamine, has resided within its borders for fifty-five years. He was born in Green county on the 5th day of August, 1820;

attended a seminary at Greensburg, and afterwards at Munfords-ville, and in 1839 attended St. Mary's College, near Lebanon. He joined the Presbyterian church in Greensburg in 1840, came with his father to Mercer county and studied law and obtained his license in 1843, and moved with his father to Nicholasville in 1844. He enlisted in his father's company, and was appointed a corporal. He followed the Second Kentucky Regiment in all its battles and marches, and was mustered out at New Orleans in 1847. While the regiment was stationed at Comargo, Mr. Willis was stricken with fever, and all thought that it was impossible for him to live. After the death of McKee and Clay and Captain Willis, the regiment were anxious to be mustered out of the service, and, at the expiration of twelve months, the time for which they were enlisted, they were brought to New Orleans and disbanded.

Mr. Willis, after taking a full course in the Commercial College, in Cincinnati, returned to Nicholasville and taught in Keene. After two years' service in the county schools, he became assistant in Bethel Academy, in Nicholasville. After this time he was appointed Master Commissioner of the Jessamine Circuit Court by Judge William C. Goodloe, upon the unanimous petition of the entire bar, embracing both Whigs and Democrats. The place was given to Mr. Willis without any solicitation on his part, and he retained it for sixteen years. After the close of the civil war he was elected twice as County Clerk, both times without opposition. A one-armed Confederate soldier was nominated against him in the last race, but withdrew.

Upon retiring from the Clerk's office in 1871 with such citizens as Mr. George Brown, Dr. Brown Young, G. S. Shanklin, Samuel Muir, Charles Farra, Hervey Scott, and William H. Hoover, he organized the First National Bank of Nicholasville, and acted as its cashier from 1871 until 1881, when he was elected president, and held this position until 1896. He was elected elder in the Nicholasville Presbyterian church at the same time with Robert Young, in the year 1859. In 1860 he was elected clerk of the session, shortly before the death of Maj. D. B. Price, and has been such clerk for thirty-two years.

Patriotic, honest, faithful, just, conservative and kindly, Mr. Willis has been a leading citizen of Jessamine county since his return from service in the Mexican War, to which he gave his father and one year of hard and trying service.

William Brown.

William Brown, the youngest son of George I. Brown, was born in Nicholasville on the 23d of May, 1839; he died June 1, 1890. He was a man of brilliant parts. He allied himself with the Republican party, and attained a high place in its councils. Senator James B. Beck said of him that he was the strongest man of his party with whom he had ever come in contact. He was a warm, personal friend of James G. Blaine, who had a great admiration for his talents and his ability. His mind was analytic, comprehensive and logical. At school he did not appear to study as other boys, but he always knew his lessons and fully understood every subject of which the text books treated. He was fearless and on many occasions eloquent. Had he devoted himself to the law, his chosen profession, rather than to have entered the domain of politics, he would have become one of the first jurists of the country.

E. R. Sparks.

No history of Jessamine county would be complete without a sketch of Hon. E. R. Sparks. His enterprise, coupled with his faith in the future of Nicholasville, and his large investments, both in manufactories and in the laying out of additions and construction of streets and houses, have been greatly instrumental in increasing the population of Nicholasville, and in widening its influence and traffic. He was born about a mile east of Nicholasville on the 31st of January, 1840, and was the son of Isaac and Mary Ann Hendricks Sparks. His mother was a sister of the late Rev. John T. Hendrick, D. D., the distinguished Presbyterian divine. Mr. Sparks' father was born in Ohio and in early life moved to Jessamine county, where he lived until his death, on Jan. 28th, 1887, in his eighty-first year. Mr. Sparks was named for a distinguished Methodist minister, Rev. Edwin Roberts. From his early manhood he has demonstrated himself to be the possessor of great sagacity, and his uniform success in all his financial transactions has given him a wide reputation for business capacity. He has held few public offices. In 1882, he was elected State

Senator and served until 1886. In the Senate he was popular, conservative, and secured the confidence and the respect of those associated with him in that body. For years he was a councilman, and was prominent in the city government of Nicholasville. He has carried on a large manufactory for hemp in the county

seat, which gives employment to a number of hands. He is in the highest degree public spirited, and is always helpful to his town and his county in every public enterprise.

John Harrison Welch.

John Harrison Welch, although comparatively a young man, has held quite a number of public offices in Jessamine county and is at present Master Commissioner of the Jessamine Circuit Court. He was born in Nicholasville. His great grandfather,

John Welch, early settled in Jessamine county, having removed from Virginia to that county in 1782. Mr. Welch was educated at Bethel Academy; was also a graduate of Kentucky Wesleyan College, at Millersburg, in 1877. He graduated from the Louisville Law School in 1881, located in Nicholasville, where he has since practiced his profession. At twenty years of age, he was elected Superintendent of common schools of Jessamine county.

He represented the county in the lower house of the General Assembly of Kentucky, in 1889 and '90, in '91, '92 and '93, and has been prominent in the county affairs since his majority.

Rev. George Stokes Smith.

Reverend George Stokes Smith was a Baptist preacher and was also a delegate to the convention, at Danville, in 1792, which framed the first Kentucky Constitution. He was the maternal grandfather of the large and numerous family of Moseleys, Wallers and Smiths, who live in the Keene neighborhood. He has over 250 descendants in Kentucky, and was one of the men who lived in the limits of Jessamine county in the earliest days of its settlement.

He was a successful Baptist preacher, and served several churches in Woodford and Mercer counties, and at the old Mount Pleasant Church, at Keene. He led a useful, honorable and distinguished life. His election to the Constitutional Convention in 1792, shows his wide popularity and his distinguished position. Fayette county had five members, and among them men of high standing, but none wielded more influence than their ministerial colleague.

CHAS. EVANS.

Hon. Thos. J. Scott.

Jessamine county is at present in a judicial district, composed of Jessamine, Madison, Estill, Clark and Powell. The Circuit Judge is Hon. Thomas J. Scott, who was born in Madison county, but his father, Dr. John Scott, was a native of Jessamine county, whence his father removed, when quite a young man, to Richmond,

Ky. His mother was a descendant of Col. Estill, one of the most celebrated pioneers of Kentucky. He was educated at Mount Pleasant College, in Missouri, from which he graduated at the age of nineteen. Immediately he returned to Richmond, where he entered the law office of Maj. Squire Turner; in 1871 he was admitted to the bar, and in 1875 was elected County Attorney, to which position he was re-elected twice without opposition. In 1886 he was elected Common Pleas Judge for the district composed of the counties of Madison, Clark, Bourbon, Bath, and Montgomery; and in 1892, he was elected Circuit Judge of the Twenty-ninth judicial district without opposition, and has been similarly re-elected for the second term. He is recognized throughout the state as one of the ablest Circuit Judges. His careful preparation, his studious habits and his sterling integrity render him a model circuit judge. Although genial and kindly in his personal relations, on the bench he knows nothing but the strictest justice, and this has won for him the respect and admiration of all the people of the district.

Rev. Stephen Noland.

This distinguished Methodist divine was born in Wayne county, Indiana, on the 13th of May, 1818. His ancestors came from Wales and settled in Virginia twenty-five years before the war of the American Revolution. In his seventh year, his mother died and he was brought to Kentucky, and made his home with his grandparents. In 1834 he entered the clerk's office in Richmond, Ky., where he remained five years. He used all his leisure moments for the study of law, and was admitted to the bar in 1839. He began the practice of his profession in Richmond, and shortly removed to Irvine, Estill county, Ky., and there he sought licensure in the Methodist ministry. In 1839 he married a sister of the late Samuel F. Miller, one of the Associate Justices of the Supreme Court of the United States. Rev. Stephen Noland, who succeeded his father in the banking business, was the second son—his other son, Samuel H. Noland, removed to Texas. Stephen Noland made the race for Commonwealth's Attorney in the district, which then embraced seven counties, against C. C. Rodgers, of Lexington, and defeated him by a majority of 800 votes. While holding the office of Commonwealth Attorney, he became a terror to evil-doers throughout the district. All sorts of influences were brought to bear to defeat Mr. Noland, but they were without avail. In 1854 he came to Nicholasville, and shortly afterwards assumed charge of the Methodist Episcopal church, South. Notwithstanding the variety of his occupations, he never gave up the preaching of the Gospel.

The first bank in Nicholasville was organized by Mr. No-

land in 1864, it was known as the Bank of Noland, Wilmore &
Co. He was a man of great sagacity and judgment in the conduct of his business; of wide benevolence and charitable impulses,
he has probably given away as much money in charity as any man
who ever lived in Jessamine. His second wife, Miss Virginia
Brown, daughter of Thos. J. Brown, who inherited the many

excellent traits of her family, survived him. He died on the 27th
of January, 1890, after a lingering illness, and deeply regretted
by the entire community, among whom he spent the last forty
years of his life.

The Duncans.

Among the earliest settlers in Jessamine county were James
Duncan and Charles Duncan. They located within the boundary
of Jessamine early in 1788. Charles Duncan was born in Culpeper county, Va., in 1761. He was the father of William Dun-

can, so long known, who died at his home immediately above Nicholasville in 1863. William Duncan's mother was Margaret Burnside, sister of the Revolutionary soldier, Robert Burnside, the great uncle of Gen. A. E. Burnside. William Duncan was born near Barclay's old mill in 1788. In 1813 he married Nancy Blackford, daughter of Benj. Blackford.

James Duncan, the grandfather of S. M. Duncan, was born in Culpeper county, Va., July 18, 1763, and was among the last white men killed by the Indians. With two companions, John Huckstep and Joseph Burnside, he went to the mouth of Paint Lick to get salt. They had made the salt and were returning home, when suddenly the report of a gun was heard and Burnside fell with a bullet through his heart. James Duncan was shot by another Indian who had climbed up on a high bluff, and the bullet entered the head of James Duncan, killing him instantly. Huckstep escaped to Crab Orchard, where Col. Whitley sent out a party in pursuit of the Indians and followed them to near Cumberland Gap. They captured the horses of the two men who had been killed, but the Indians made their escape.

Alexander C. Duncan, the father of S. M. Duncan, was the oldest child of James Duncan, who was killed in his 28th year and left three small children. When a small boy James Duncan ran away from home in company with Nathaniel Harris, the distinguished Methodist minister, and enlisted in the army of General Greene, and was at the battle of Guilford Court House and at the siege of Yorktown. James Duncan was born July 18, 1763, and was married to Mary Crockett, daughter of William Crockett, of Wythe county, in 1787. One hundred years after the death of James Duncan, there came a great rise in the creeks which enter Paint Lick. They disclosed a skeleton. On examination of this skeleton a bullet hole was found in the head and the remains were identified as those of James Duncan, who had been killed and buried at that point nearly a century before. Every bone was perfect with the exception of the right foot. The remains were removed to Nicholasville cemetery and laid to rest amid kindred dust.

The descendants of James Duncan and his brother, who thus early made their home in Jessamine county, in large numbers still reside in the county and they have always been good citizens and patriots.

S. M. Duncan.

Mr. S. M. Duncan, who has been one of the most diligent, and faithful of all the antiquarians in Kentucky, was a son of Alexander Crockett Duncan and Hannah N. Williams, the latter being à native of Mecklenburg county North Carolina. She was born March 8, 1793, and died in 1861. Mr. Duncan's father was

born in Fort Blackamore, Russell county, Virginia, and came to Jessamine county in 1788. He was an infant when his father, James Duncan, settled within the limits of Jessamine county. S. M. Duncan was born in Pulaski county, in 1830. He enjoyed limited advantages of education, but most wonderfully improved them—he only had three months' schooling. He worked for thirty years at his trade as carpenter, and learned cabinet-making, which he followed five years, but afterwards gave that up and returned to his original calling. He has gathered together an immense amount of material concerning not only the earliest history of Jessamine county and its people, but in regard to the early history of Kentucky. He has always had a passion for acquiring old letters and documents, and, but for his patience and care and labor, not only in the finding, but in the preservation, of materials, it would have been impossible for any one to write a history of Jessamine county. Mr. Duncan began this collection of material when quite a young man. He talked with men who had been in the Revolutionary War, and to those who had in their minds fresh recollections of the struggles, trials and dangers of pioneer life in Kentucky. He has written a great deal on the subject, and deserves the thanks of the people, not only of Jessamine county, but of Central Kentucky.

Andrew Hemphill.

Andrew Hemphill was one of the most scholarly men that lived in Jessamine county in its early days. He lived in the southern part of the county, settling there in 1823. He was born in Tyrone county, Ireland, in 1800. He obtained his education at Trinity College, Dublin, and came to American in 1819, landing at Philadelphia. In a very short time he was chosen as teacher of Latin in an academy in the city of Reading, in Berks county, and subsequently became principal of the academy, which position he held for two years. He settled in Jessamine county in 1823, and was married to Mildred Tapp. He came to Jessamine county through his uncle James Hemphill who had purchased a farm in that section of the county many years before. In 1823 James Hemphill died and made Andrew his heir, devising to him 250 acres of land on Hickman creek six miles east of Nicholasville. Mr. Hemphill through all his life retained his scholarship. He read Latin and Greek with great fluency. He died in 1863.

It was his custom for many years to visit the schools in which the classics were taught. These comings were always regarded by the Latin and Greek scholars with fear and trembling. While he was there he would call upon them to read selections from the Roman and Grecian authors. The scholars imagined that they could never do the thing just as Mr. Hemphill would do it; yet he was always kindly, helpful and suggestive in his examinations, and never went away from the schools without saying pleasant and agreeable words to the scholars. He was the father of a large family of children, many of whom are now residents of Jessamine county, and are among its best and most substantial citizens.

Mr. John Henry Glass.

Mr. John Henry Glass, who now owns Glass Mills, near Wilmore, was born in 1838, of German parentage, in Jessamine county. After going to school during his boyhood in Cincinnati, he learned the trade of cabinetmaker, with his father, who was one of the most skilled mechanics who ever lived in Jessamine county. In 1870 Mr. Glass erected a mill in Lancaster, Ky., which is still in successful operation. Afterwards he sold out to George Denny, the president of the national bank, and moved back to Jessamine and bought the property known as the old paper mill, on Jessamine creek, about three miles above its mouth. This mill had been operated for more than 100 years. After running it about three years he tore part of it down and erected a new building and put in new machinery, retaining, however, the water power, which had been in constant use for more than a century.

This mill is operated all the year round, has its office and switch at Wilmore, Ky., and is one of the best manufacturing enterprises in Jessamine county. It has a large trade up and down the Cincinnati Southern Railroad, and its brands of flour are considered among the very best manufactured in the West. The principal of these, "The Daniel Boone," shows Mr. Glass' patriotism. Mr. Glass has been instrumental in building ten miles of turnpike in the western part of the county and in furnishing a constant and liberal home demand for grain, which has much increased land values in that section. Blessed with a large family, he has trained them both to industry and morality, and he is one of the useful men of the community.

Benjamin A. Crutcher.

Benjamin A. Crutcher, the present Commonwealth's Attorney for the Twenty-fifth Judicial district, which includes Jessamine, Madison, Estill, Clark, and Powell counties, was born in Nicholasville, June 21, 1856. Elected County Attorney in 1884, he resigned to become a candidate for Commonwealth's Attor-

ney. He was re-elected Commonwealth's Attorney in 1897. He is a man of conservative instincts, careful preparation, unquestionable honesty and great industry. He has proven a most admirable Prosecuting Attorney, firm, faithful, yet considerate and just, he represents the commonwealth as if he were representing his own affairs, and the entire district recognizes his great efficiency and ability.

Thomas B. Crutcher.

The Hon. Thos. B. Crutcher is now Police Judge of Nicholasville. He was born in Jessamine county in 1831. He is the father of Benj. A. Crutcher, the Commonwealth's Attorney for the district. For a long time he was one of the leading merchants in

Jessamine. He is a man of the old school, upright, conscientious, always considerate to others. For five years he has been Judge of the City Court of Nicholasville, and has made a most excellent record. He is a member of the First Baptist church and is one of its most earnest and enthusiastic supporters.

John Spears Bronaugh.

John Spears Bronaugh was born in the Keene neighborhood and spent his early years on his father's farm. With a vigorous constitution as well as a vigorous mind, he improved all his educational advantages, and attended college at Transylvania University, at Lexington. He read law with Judge James Prior, near Carrollton, Ky. Faithful, studious, patient and laborious, when admitted to the bar in 1847, at Nicholasville, he was well prepared for the practice of his profession. For more than half a century he has been prominent in all the litigation which affected the people of Jessamine, and by his good judgment, his

great learning and wise counsel, he has endeared himself to the whole community, and secured a high place in the estimation of his fellow-citizens. At a time when the government of Nicholasville needed a strong hand and an economical administration, Mr. Bronaugh was called by the voice of his townsmen to assume the duties of the Mayoralty. He evolved order out of chaos, systematized all the affairs of the city government and as executive officer so conducted himself and the affairs of the town that it

was with difficulty he could avoid the solicitations of the voters
to hold the office always, and it was only his persistent refusal to
accept the office which caused the people of the town to elect another man.　He has always stood for the best interests of the
county and town, and while conservative, he had been enterprising and has been a leader in all that has brought the county to
its present prosperity and splendid development.　The county
has trusted him in many important transactions and he has always conducted them with prudence, skill and ability.

THOS. J. BROWN.

Robert Curd, Esq.,

Is one of the Magistrates of the county and resides in the neighborhood of Wilmore station. Successful in business, kindly in manner, faithful in his official life, he commands, as he de-

serves, the support and confidence of his district. Whatever is for the best interests of the whole county always has his hearty approval and assistance.

Levi Luther Todd.

The Levi Luther Todd referred to in the minutes of the town of Nicholasville, was born in Lexington, Ky., July 26, 1791. He was educated at Transylvania University, and practiced law several years. He served with distinction in the war of 1812.

He removed to Lafayette, Ind., in 1833, and there held a distinguished judicial position.

In 1867 he came to Lexington and presented to the Masonic Grand Lodge, of Kentucky, then in session there, the sword and belt of Col. Joseph Hamilton Daveiss, which were worn by Col. Daveiss when he was killed, in the battle of Tippecanoe, on the 7th of November, 1811. He died near Indianapolis, in 1867.

Dr. T. R. Welch.

On the one-hundredth anniversary of the existence of Nicholasville, Jessamine county is part of the Senatorial district in which are included Woodford and Scott counties. The Senator from this district is Thomas R. Welch, M. D., an able and successful homeopathic physician, now residing in Nicholasville, in which place he was born on the 4th of February, 1860.

He was educated at Bethel Academy under Professor Gordon, and is a graduate of the Wesleyan College. He taught in the city schools of Nicholasville and graduated from the Hahnemann College in 1885, and from that time on has practiced in Jessamine county. He is a member of the Board of Examiners for the schools of the county, of the Nicholasville Board of Education, the State Homeopathic Association and of the American Institute of Homeopathy. He is also a member of the Baptist church and of the Odd Fellows and Knights of Pythias.

He has been earnest and faithful in the discharge of his duties in his profession. In 1879 the Twenty-second Senatorial district, of which Jessamine was a part, became a political battle-ground. It was the home district of the Hon. J. C. S. Blackburn, and the Hon. Henry L. Martin was nominated on a platform antagonistic to Senator Blackburn's views. Jessamine county, by courtesy, was entitled to name the Democratic candidate, and a strong popular man was required. By a unanimous demand Dr. Welch was called to make the race for Blackburn. His majority in the district was 2,454, an extraordinary manifestation of the confidence of the people of the district. Jessamine county gave him an almost unprecedented majority of 977 votes. His conduct in the legislature justified the confidence of his district. He took a prominent part in the deliberations of that historical legislature.

Harrison Daniel.

Harrison Daniel was for many years one of the most prominent citizens of Jessamine county. He was the grandson of Col. John Price, and born in 1790. His father, John Daniel, was a native of Orange county, Virginia, and came to Kentucky in the year 1787. He was related to the Daniels in the northern neck of Virginia, and family history says that he served in the army of General Washington at Brandywine, Trenton and Monmouth. He settled on Marble creek and here his son was born. In the early history of Kentucky Mr. Daniel was a useful and important character. He was High Sheriff and represented Jessamine county in the legislature in 1826. He possessed extraordinary mathematical talents. His son, William Daniel, went to the Mexican war in the company of Captain Willis. He had a wonderful faculty for making and keeping friends, and many of his descendants still remain in Jessamine county, whose people their ancestor so faithfully served.

Dr. John C. Welch.

Dr. John C. Welch was born in Jessamine county in 1823. He practiced medicine for forty years in the county, except during his service for four years as surgeon of the Twentieth Kentucky volunteer infantry. In 1863 he was promoted to brigade surgeon. In 1877 and 1879 he represented Jessamine county in the lower house of the legislature. He was a brother of Dr. Thomas R. Welch, the distinguished Presbyterian divine.

George Brown.

George Brown was born in Nicholasville on February 28, 1819, and died October 30, 1897. He first attended school at St. Joseph's, Bardstown, Ky., afterward at Center College, Danville and finally at Transylvania University in Lexington. Upon leaving college he at once engaged in the business of the manufacture of hemp. His father had been one of the pioneers in hemp manufacture in Lexington and the son acquired a practical knowledge of the business in early life. Owning a large number of slaves, which he used in his business, he made it extremely profitable and he continued in the manufacture of hemp for many years. In the fall of 1853 he moved to a farm on Jessamine creek, about two miles from Nicholasville, and in conjunction with his farm operated a hemp manufactory. He married Ann M. Hemphill in 1843, who proved to him an affectionate, faithful and helpful wife. She was one of the model housekeepers of Jessamine county and as neighbor and friend had no superior.

Mr. Brown was a man of intense activity; domestic in his taste, he loved his home and added to it those things which made it attractive. He was a model husband and father. When twenty-two years of age, he united with the Nicholasville Presbyterian church, in the faith of which he continued to the end of his life, and at his death he was the oldest living member of the organization. He was converted under the preaching of Rev. David Todd. He was efficient and earnest in his Christian work and was always one of the liberal and helpful members of the congregation. He was a pure, good man; long president of the Jessamine County Bible Society; he was not only active but useful in the Bible work and has left behind him no enemies and a host of friends.

Gen. Samuel Dickerson Jackman.

Gen. Samuel Dickerson Jackman was a Brigadier-General in the Confederate Army of Missouri. He was born in Nicholasville in the brick house on the left hand side of the road leading to Sulphur Well, and opposite the present house of Thos. B. Crutcher, Sept. 18, 1825. He was a courageous soldier, vigorous and active in the field, and was extremely successfuly in his raids on the Federal lines in Missouri during the war. His mother was the daughter of David Dickerson, and he served in the War of 1812. His father, Dr. John Jackman, left Jessamine county and settled in Missouri in 1831. General Jackman removed from Missouri at the close of the war, to Texas, where he died in 1893. He amassed a large fortune and died childless.

Judge Wm. H. Phillips.

It is a remarkable fact that every officeholder in Jessamine county, upon the occasion of the centennial of its capital city, was born and reared in the county. Judge Wm. H. Phillips, who is County Judge, has held that office longer than any man who ever had it. He was born in Jessamine county on the 30th of March, 1838. His education was received at the common schools, and

the early part of his life was passed on a farm. He attended Bethel Academy as a student, coming from his father's home, in Nicholasville. From the time of his earliest manhood to 1874 he was an industrious farmer, and he never sought office but was a faithful and efficient worker for his father. In that year he was nominated for County Judge. The nomination was to some ex-

18

tent unexpected by him and unsought. At that time the Democratic nominees were considered the leaders of a forlorn hope; the Republican party was organized and had able leaders, and all the county offices were held by them; but Judge Phillips was elected by a majority of fourteen votes, and the Circuit Court Clerk was chosen by the same majority. The rest of the Democratic ticket was defeated. In 1878 Judge Phillips was again elected, although opposed by the strongest man in the Republican party, and also by an independent Democrat; then his majority was 26 votes. In 1882 he was elected without opposition, and he has held the office of County Judge for 23 years. His ancestors were Huguenots, who came from the James river, and settled in Kentucky about 1790. His official career is unusual and extraordinary, and manifests the high esteem in which he is held by the people of his native county. His official acts have stood the closest scrutiny, and his numerous endorsements by the voters is a testimonial of the highest character.

Dr. Alexander K. Marshall.

Dr. Alexander K. Marshall was a member of Congress from the Ashland District in 1855. He was the third son of Dr. Louis Marshall, who was the youngest brother of Chief-Justice John Marshall. Louis Marshall lived in Woodford county, at a place called Buck Pond. There Alexander K. Marshall was born the 11th of February, 1808. He studied medicine and at the age of 25 came to Nicholasville and practiced his profession, which he did with marked success. He united with John G. Chiles in 1842, in operating a stage and mail line through the Kentucky mountains to Bean Station, Tenn., and continued in this business for more than 20 years. This, however, did not prevent him from practicing his profession.

He was a man of fine presence and of courage in the statement of his convictions. He represented Jessamine county in the Constitutional Convention of 1849, defeating George I. Brown by 80 majority. He was elected to Congress on the Know Nothing ticket, defeating James O. Harrison, a distinguished Lexington lawyer, by over 1,500 majority. He died in Fayette county in 1886.

James Willlard Mitchell.

The present County Attorney, James Willard Mitchell, was born in Nicholasville, in 1861. His father, Jas. T. Mitchell, was eldest son of Dr. Geo. W. Mitchell; his mother was the third daughter of the late Thomas Jefferson and Mary Jane Wallace Brown, who was the eldest daughter of Joseph Wallace, son of Capt John Wallace. Captain John Wallace was one of the most

distinguished of the Revolutionary soldiers who came to Jessamine. He served with General Washington and General Wayne; he was at the battles of Brandywine, Trenton, Monmouth, Long Island, and was with Washington at Valley Forge.

No man in Jessamine county commands in a higher degree the confidence of his fellow-citizens and no one is capable of arousing more enthusiasm in his party and among his friends. He has great will force, unflinching energy, and has been often compared to Gen. Joseph Wheeler, whom he is not unlike in stature and appearance.

Mr. Mitchell was elected County Attorney by a large and flattering majority. The County Attorneyship was the first position to which Mr. Mitchell was elected and he fills it with credit to himself and to his constituents. He is a man also of fine business capacity, thorough reading and preparation, great punctuality in the discharge of his official and personal business. Few men are more eloquent or effective on the stump. He understands human nature, and is destined if he chooses to follow public life, to become a leader of men.

He married Miss Annie Anderson, daughter of Capt. Samuel M. Anderson, He is thoroughly identified with the people of Jessamine, and they, in turn, feel a just pride in his success and his attainments in his profession.

Francis M. Bristow

Was born in Clark county, Ky., on the 11th of August, 1804. He lived for twenty-six years on the farm now occupied by Mrs. Mary Ann Bourne, three miles east of Nicholasville. He was well educated, studied law, and divided his time between his profession and farm. He early moved to Todd county with his father, who had settled in Jessamine county in the year 1790. In 1830-31 Mr. Bristow was elected to the Kentucky Legislature, in 1846 to the State Senate, and was a member of the State Constitutional Convention in 1849. In 1854 he was elected Representative in Congress to fill the unexpired term of Presley Ewing, and in 1859 was again elected as Representative from Kentucky to the 36th Congress.

His son, Benjamin H. Bristow, served with distinction in the Federal army, afterwards became Solicitor-General, was a candidate for President before the Republican party, was long a resident of Louisville, but moved from that city to New York, where he has achieved distinction and success in the practice of law.

Frances M. Bristow died at Elkton, Ky., January 10, 1864.

Curd Lowry, County Clerk.

Curd Lowry, the present county clerk of Jessamine county, is the third son of the late Judge Melvin T. Lowry, who was county and circuit clerk for twelve years prior to his death, in 1887. He secured the office in opposition to Robt. S. Perry, who had held it for sixteen years and his race in this respect was phenomenal.

He was born November 19, 1862, at the home of his maternal grandmother, Mrs. Harrison Daniels.

He was for two terms deputy clerk under L. D. Baldwin. In 1887 he moved to Kansas City where he remained two years and then returned to a position in the First National Bank. His great-grandfather on his mother's side was John Daniels, who settled in Fayette county in 1788 and married a sister of Col.

John Price. His paternal grandfather settled in Jessamine county long before its organization. He comes of distinguished parentage and lineage and his popularity is the result of his kindly heart and gentlemany manner.

Magistrates of Jessamine County.

In this, 1898, Jessamine county is divided into five magisterial districts. At the last November election, the gentlemen chosen to fill this responsible office were as follows:

ROBERT CLEMMONS.

Mr. Clemmons resides at Brannon on the Cincinnati Southern Railroad near Fayette county line. He is one of the leading

farmers in Jessamine county, and has been elected magistrate for several terms. He was born in Fayette county, is about fifty-five years of age, and is honest, clear-headed, and a faithful representative of the interests which his fellow-citizens entrust to his keeping.

JAMES T. BARKLEY.

He resides in Nicholasville. He was the son of Mason Barkley, who was a large farmer on the Harrodsburg Pike. He was born in 1848, and is engaged in the hardware business in Nicholasville. He is a man who is highly esteemed by his fellow-citizens.

ALLEN W. ROBINSON

Resides in the Marble creek neighborhood. He was a grandson of John Robinson. He is a man who never shrinks from doing his duty, and has made a most efficient officer.

WILSON FAIN

Lives in the Hickman neighborhood. He is a son of Larkin Fain, who represented Jessamine county in the Legislature in 1850-55. He enjoys to an unusual degree the confidence and respect of his fellow-citizens in that portion of the county in which he resides.

Col. Wm. A. Lewis.

Who commanded a regiment from Kentucky at the battle of the Raisin, in 1812, in which regiment were two companies, Gray's and Price's, from Jessamine county, was long a resident in the county. He was born in Virginia, in 1778, and died in 1835. His exposures in the War of 1812 brought on rheumatism, and the colds he contracted in the northwestern army settled in his eyes and resulted in a total loss of eyesight. He was a gallant soldier and a man respected and loved by all the people of the county. In the terrible battle of Raisin he showed splendid heroism, and a high order of courage, and had his advice been followed, the terrible tragedy of that battle would have been avoided.

Allen L. McAfee

Was long a prominent public man in Jessamine county. He died of cancer of the throat March 16, 1888. He was the second son of Col. Robert McAfee, and was born in McAfee, Mercer county, on the 15th of August, 1825. He was admitted to the bar in

Harrodsburg in 1845, and removed to Little Rock, Arkansas, where he commenced the practice of his profession. About this time the war with Mexico broke out, and he volunteered as a private in Captain Mean's company of cavalry, which was one of the companies in the regiment of Col. Ambrose Yell, who was killed at the battle of Buena Vista. In that battle Colonel McAfee bore a prominent part in the charge of Humphrey Marshall and Colonel Yell against 6,000 lancers, led by General Mineon, who attempted to take the American batteries. In the charge in which McKee, Clay and Willis were lost, Colonel McAfee saw a Mexican lancer in the act of killing a wounded soldier. He instantly shot the Mexican. He used what was in those days a celebrated gun known as the Mississippi rifle.

At the close of the Mexican war, Colonel McAfee moved to Nicholasville, and married Miss Elizabeth Shely. In 1857 he was elected a member of the Kentucky legislature. Early in 1861 Colonel McAfee was arrested as a Southern sympathizer; he was taken from his home at 12 o'clock at night on the 21st of June, and without warrant or charge was carried and lodged in prison in Lexington. A writ of habeas corpus was taken out by Frank Hunt, Esq., and W. C. P. Breckinridge, Esq., in order to get Colonel McAfee before the Federal Court, then in session at Frankfort, but the Federal officers suspended the writ of habeas corpus. On the way to Camp Chase, in Cincinnati, he escaped by walking away from the guards, passed through Central Kentucky and reached the South. He was commissioned lieutenant-colonel by James A. Seddon, Confederate Secretary of War. In 1864 he raised a battalion of 300 mounted men, and was with General Jones in Western Virginia, and helped to defeat General Averill's rail on Harrodsburg in 1864. He was severely wounded in 1862 at Big Creek Gap. He was captured in 1864, and remained in Camp Douglas until the close of the war. He was a magnificent looking man in physical appearance, and possessed a high degree of courage.

In 1866 he was elected State Senator, defeating Richard Spurr, of Fayette, by over 500 votes.

Andrew McAfee.

Andrew McAfee, who at present worthily represents his ward in the city council, is one of the younger generation of colored men, who by his conduct and character has done much to dis-

sipate the prejudice against the education of his race. He was educated in the local schools for his race, and by his energy and determination has won the confidence and trust of his constituents.

C. S. MITCHELL, Councilman.   FRANK D. SMITH, Councilman.   B. L. COOK, Councilman.
W. L. STEELE, Mayor.   J. D. HUGHES, Councilman.   ADAM ADCOCK, Councilman

Centennial Exercises, 1898.

The centennial of Nicholasville was celebrated by the citizens of the town and Jessamine county, on the 16th day of September, 1898. Both the county and the city made public subscriptions to the fund necessary for the celebration. The event created un-

B. M. ARNETT,
Chairman Executive Committee.

usual enthusiasm among the people of the county and one of the largest crowds ever seen in Central Kentucky was assembled on this occasion.

The procession, representing the industrial interests of the city and county occupied the morning; while historical and patriotic addresses took up the afternoon.

Louisville, Cincinnati, Lexington, Danville, Versailles, Shelby-
ville, and other cities and towns sent large delegations to the
celebration.

The executive committee, consisting of B. M. Arnett, chairman; W. L. Steele, J. D. Hughes, H. H. Lowry, Charles Deering,
and J. B. Stears, provided a most interesting program and conducted the exercises in the most patriotic and pleasing manner.

GEO. B. TAYLOR,
Chief Marshal Centennial Celebration.

Committees of ladies from all parts of the county united in
completing the arrangements for the great occasion. These
committees were as follows:

Hanly—Mrs. Joe Wallace, Mrs. W. J. Wilmore.

Wilmore—Mrs. John B. Chambers, Mrs. James Hawkins.

Keene—Mrs. C. E. Smith, Mrs. James Sallee.

Nealton—Mrs. Annie Davis, Mrs. E. J. Young.

Brannon—Mrs. Chas. Smith, Mrs. Len Bryant.

Logana—Mrs. Chas. Spillman.

Ambrose—Mrs. Newton Davis.

Little Hickman—Mrs. J. H. Dean.

East Hickman—Mrs. Frank Mitchell, Mrs. Henry Muir.

The following was the program for the occasion:

1798-1898.

Jessamine County and Nicholasville Centennial.

10:30 a. m.: Street parade under supervision of Chief Marshal Geo. B. Taylor, and assistants.

12 m.: Dinner on Duncan Heights.

1:30 p. m.: Music by band—"My Country, 'Tis of Thee."

Prayer by Dr. L. Beecher Todd.

Song, by quartette—"Auld Lang Syne."

Address of welcome, on behalf of Jessamine county—Judge W. H. Phillips.

Music by band—"Hail, Columbia! Happy Land."

Address of welcome, in behalf of Nicholasville—Maj. W. L. Steele.

Music by band—"Old Kentucky Home."

Address—Col. Bennett H. Young.

Song, by quartette—"Star Spangled Banner."

Address—Hon. Evan E. Settle.

Music by band—"Dixie."

INDEX.

ILLUSTRATIONS.